COLORADO'S WAR ON MILITANT UNIONISM

COLORADO'S WAR ON MILITANT UNIONISM

James H. Peabody and the Western Federation of Miners

by
George G. Suggs, Jr.
Southeast Missouri State University

Detroit
WAYNE STATE UNIVERSITY PRESS
1972

Library of Congress Cataloging in Publication Data

*Suggs, George G.   1929–
    Colorado's war on militant unionism.*

*Essay on Sources: p. 221
    1. International Union of Mine, Mill, and Smelter Workers.   2. Strikes
and lockouts—Miners—Colorado.   3. Peabody, James Hamilton, 1852–1917.
I. Title.   HD6515.M72C65   331.89'282'23309788   70–39624
ISBN 0–8143–1471–6*

To Ginny, Owen, Suzanne, Beth, and Lorrie

contents

illustrations

9. *Union posters of protest.*

10. *The main street of Telluride, Colo., about 1900.*

11. *The mountainous regions surrounding Telluride, where mines were located.*

12. *The executive board of the Western Federation of Miners in 1905.*

preface

For nearly a decade prior to the administration of Governor James H. Peabody (1903–1905) the mine owners of Colorado and the Western Federation of Miners battled each other in the mining camps, at times waging open warfare for industrial control. During the Peabody years the struggle entered a new phase when the union called a series of strikes which threatened to disrupt the vital metalliferous industry upon which the prosperity of the state rested. Peabody's term coincided with the emergence of a vigorous national employers' movement sponsored by the National Association of Manufacturers and with an increasing demand from militant labor unions for the eight-hour day and other concessions. Peabody responded readily to requests from corporate officers that he intervene in the strikes. Extremely fearful of the WFM because of its violent history, the governor ordered the National Guard into the mining camps ostensibly to preserve law and order. The troops, which were financially subsidized by the mining corporations, played a provocative role. Under the control of officers who were sympathetic to the mine owners the guard helped to break the strikes and, consequently, the power of the WFM in Colorado. Peabody believed that the WFM was a "criminal" organization and heartily approved of the results. Law and order, therefore, became synonymous with the destruction of the union.

To maintain "law and order," Peabody worked closely with the proliferating employers' organizations known as the citizens' alliances, the Colorado manifestation of the national employers' movement, whose hostility to militant unions like the WFM was phenomenal. In 1904 he formally joined the Citizens' Alliance of Denver. The meshing of his administration with such organizations placed the power of the state at the disposal of special interests which, in a climactic death-struggle with the WFM, resorted to revolutionary procedures to destroy the power of the union in Colorado and elsewhere. In this dramatic encounter the WFM confronted a hostile state, one headed by a businessman-mine owner whose values were identical with those of labor's enemies.

Despite Peabody's extraordinary role in bludgeoning the WFM historians have paid little attention to the events of his administration, except for the Cripple Creek strike. There is an obvious need for an in-depth study of the crucial Peabody years. This book seeks to fill this gap in labor history by examining the important role which Peabody played in breaking the power of the WFM in Colorado and elsewhere. That he materially affected the industrial history of the trans-Mississippi West is undeniable; that he had an important impact upon the entire American labor movement is certain.

My goal has been to relate Peabody's labor policies to the turbulent history and political program of the WFM, to the aggressive conservative forces of his era, and to the drive of the WFM for power and status and finally for its survival in the gold camps and smelting towns of Colorado. Whenever possible, I have relied upon the governor's official files to determine his motivation and role in the strikes, his relationship with corporations, and his labor policies. However, traditional sources so important in the study of the miner's union (for example, the *Miners' Magazine*) have not been ignored.

A number of people have contributed to this study. To Hal Bridges, University of California (Riverside) and Robert G. Athearn and Lee Scamehorn, University of Colorado (Boulder), I am indebted for aid and encouragement over the years. I am obligated, too, to various colleagues at Southeast Missouri State University. Conversations with Gene Nutter have helped to maintain my interest in the American labor movement. Emily Beatte read parts of the manuscript and made helpful suggestions. I owe a special debt to Harold Dugger, who read the entire manuscript. His incisive and constructive comments, generously given, contributed 'substantially to the final product. My thanks go also to the staffs of the following institutions for their assistance: the Colorado Archives and Records Service; the Western History Collection, Norlin Library, University of Colorado (Boulder); the State Historical Society of Colorado (particularly to Enid Thompson, Librarian); the Western History Department, Denver Public Library; Kent Library, Southeast Missouri State University; and the Idaho State Historical Society. The American Association for State and Local History generously supported my research with grants in the summers of 1967 and 1969, and I am grateful for its aid.

Portions of chapter one appeared in slightly different form as "Catalyst for Industrial Change; The WFM, 1893–1903," *The Colorado Magazine*, 45 (Fall 1968), 322–39. Much of chapter three first appeared in "Prelude to Industrial Warfare: The Colorado City Strike," *The Colorado Magazine*, 44 (Summer 1967), 241–62. Much of chapter six previously appeared as "Strike-breaking in Colorado: Governor James H. Peabody and the Telluride Strike, 1903–1904," *Journal of the West*, 5 (Oct. 1966), 454–76. I am indebted to the editors of these publications for permission to reprint. I also am grateful to the State Historical Society of Colorado for supplying photographs used in this book. The Idaho Historical Society and Canon City (Colo.) Museum also each supplied one photograph.

G.G.S.

1

Roots of Reaction

In the spring of 1903 the Western Federation of
Miners, then the most militant labor organization in the United
States, ended its first decade confident of its power and intent
on expanding its influence in the American labor movement. The
union then was far different from the one organized at Butte,
Montana, in May 1893 by forty delegates, representing approximately 2,000 members of fifteen unions from South Dakota,
Montana, Idaho, Utah, and Colorado, who had convened after
a disastrous strike in the Coeur d'Alene to forge an organization
for protecting the miners' interests. The number of affiliated
locals had increased to more than 180, and the membership had
climbed to 27,000. Territorially, the federation had reached out
into all but five states of the trans-Mississippi West, plus Wisconsin, Michigan, and parts of Canada.[1] However, its base of
power remained rooted in the Rocky Mountain region, particularly in states like Colorado where it had entrenched itself despite ruthless opposition from mine owners who early had recognized the WFM as a threat to property interests. There it dis-

15

played power, forcing the mine owners into making tenuous accommodations to it, although never into accepting it as a permanent voice in industrial affairs.

In Colorado the growth of the WFM had been especially marked in the decade of 1893–1903. Representatives from Aspen, Creede, Ouray, and Rico had helped to found the organization, and Colorado's miners continued to be its leaders. Despite disastrous strikes and strong opposition from mine and mill operators, who allegedly "slandered, traduced, vilified and lied about it in every imaginable way,"[2] the union spread into most of the mining camps of the state.

As early as 1896, Colorado's Bureau of Labor Statistics reported that the WFM had chartered locals in both the coal and metalliferous camps and estimated that their membership included at least 50 percent of all the miners of the state.[3] Four years later twenty-seven local unions, having a membership of 7,377 and located mostly in the hard-rock camps and smelter towns, had affiliated. There remained only seven unaffiliated miners' and millmen's unions with a membership of 1,456, and the majority of the state's hard-rock miners had joined the WFM.[4] By 1902, fifteen more local unions had been added, which increased Colorado's total, as reported by the bureau, to forty-two with a membership of 15,549, or approximately 32 percent of the union's active membership of 48,000.[5] Because the WFM had stopped organizing the coal miners, neither they nor their unions were included in these figures.

The bureau's data, which suggested an extraordinary increase in the membership of the WFM within Colorado toward the end of the decade under consideration, are not entirely consistent with statistics found in the union's own annual reports. For example, in his report to the eleventh annual convention of the WFM in 1903, the union's secretary-treasurer, William D. Haywood, enumerated the local affiliates. Included were thirty-nine from Colorado whose membership totaled only 7,361.[6] Although less than seven months separate the bureau's report of 1902 from Haywood's, they differ markedly on the number of locals and members in Colorado. Colorado's deputy labor commissioners of the era were often pro-labor, and this bias may explain the exaggerations in their biennial reports. Undoubtedly, Haywood's report more accurately reflected the numerical strength of the union in Colorado at the end of the decade.[7] Nevertheless, Haywood's report for 1903 indicated that Colorado's portion (7,361) of the WFM's membership (27,154) was a remarkably high 27 percent, and this was made more important by its strategic concentration in the state's vital metalliferous industry.

Regardless of the inconsistencies in the data, during the decade of 1893–1903 the WFM had become an important force in the industrial life of Colorado and was capable of altering the old pattern of industrial relations. Its presence meant that decisions affecting wages, hours, and working conditions could not be reached unilaterally by a mine owner and imposed upon his employees without provoking disruptive strikes. However, the more important mine owners of nearly every mining camp initially refused to recognize the altered relationship between them and their workers and refused to make negotiated settlements until forced to do so by bruising confrontations with the WFM. The history of the union's first decade in Colorado was characterized by sporadic outbreaks of violence in the hardrock camps, frequently called "labor wars," usually followed by uneasy accommodations which the mine owners grudgingly endured while maneuvering to restore their traditional dominance.

The WFM's reputation for lawlessness and violence originated in its initial encounters with the mine owners of the Cripple Creek mining district, an extremely productive gold mining area deep in the mountains southwest of Colorado Springs in what was then El Paso County. Trouble began in mid-January 1894 when some of the larger mine owners, including J. J. Hagerman, David H. Moffat, and Eben Smith, who employed nearly one-third of the miners working for wages in the district, attempted to lengthen the workday in their mines from eight to ten hours without raising the $3 a day minimum wage. As an alternative, the owners agreed to retain the eight-hour day if the minimum wage were reduced to $2.50. Local unions at Altman, Cripple Creek, Victor, and Anaconda, which had affiliated with the WFM and had earlier demanded the $3 minimum wage and the eight-hour day in all the mines, opposed the move, rejecting outright the mine owners' contention

17

that diminishing profits necessitated either the longer day or reduced wages. When the mine owners imposed the ten-hour day on February 1, a strike ensued which set the course of future walkouts in Colorado involving the WFM.[8] To renew operations, the mine owners were forced to employ strikebreakers. The WFM was unable to persuade these men to support the strike through peaceful means, so it resorted to threats and violence, intimidating the strikebreakers to such an extent that few of them dared to work for any mine owner who insisted on the longer workday. Tension increased throughout the district as parties to the dispute sparred for advantage and community support.

On March 16 near Altman a band of armed miners ambushed and captured six deputies who were enroute to protect the Victor mine of Moffat and Smith. In the exchange of blows and shots two lawmen were injured, although not seriously. An Altman judge, who was a member of the WFM, charged the deputies with carrying concealed weapons and disturbing the peace, but released them. Reacting to this episode and the subsequent riot of the miners who forced the strikebreakers from the mines, County Sheriff F. M. Bowers turned to Denver for aid. Governor Davis H. Waite promptly ordered National Guard troops into the district. But after investigating conditions there, Adjutant General T. J. Tarsney concluded that military intervention was not warranted and recommended its termination. On March 20, two days after his initial intervention, Waite pulled the troops from the district, an act that initiated seven weeks of calm in which the mine owners closed the struck mines rather than concede to union demands on hours and wages.

In a meeting in Colorado Springs in early May representatives of the striking miners and the mine owners made a last attempt to end the strike. However, their effort proved abortive when the miners rejected a final offer of $2.75 for an eight-hour day. The owners, convinced that the WFM would never accept either an extended workday or reduced wages, once again decided to force the reopening of their properties with strikebreakers who were to be protected by a privately subsidized army of deputies recruited and led by Sheriff Bowers. County authorities accepted the necessity of breaking the strike and sympathized with the mine owners' plight. They endorsed the plan and thereby enshrouded with legality the use of force to end the dispute. The striking miners were determined to prevent a renewal of operations on the terms offered by the mine owners. Fearful that the army being mustered would be used to drive them from the district, they fortified Bull Hill, which overlooked and commanded Altman, and waited as Bowers assembled his forces. By May 24 an estimated 1,200 armed men milled around in the district waiting for orders to march against the strikers who, moving from their entrenched positions on Bull Hill, had assaulted and seized the Strong mine on Battle Mountain overlooking Victor. The strikers were not content with mere possession of the property, and they dynamited the shafthouse and machinery, although three nonunion men, who fortunately escaped injury, were known to be underground. A gun battle on the morning of May 25, provoked by the aggressive maneuvering of the strikers, killed two men, wounded two, and resulted in the capture of six strikers by the deputies. Open warfare threatened to erupt in the district.

Waite stepped into this critical situation. On May 28 he went into the district, examined conditions there, and agreed to present the strikers' case to the mine owners. As a result of his negotiations in Denver with Moffat and Hagerman, two of the larger mine owners, the "Waite agreement" was reached six days later. This provided for a $3, eight-hour workday and nondiscriminatory hiring policies. The settlement did not end the dispute, because the 1,200 deputies remained and threatened further disorder. On the day of the agreement their movement toward the miners' fortification on Bull Hill forced the governor to order out all units of the National Guard to avert open warfare. After the troops arrived, the deputies, whom the sheriff no longer controlled, made other threatening moves toward Bull Hill and invaded Cripple Creek, where "they made numerous arrests of citizens and indulged in outrageous acts toward other citizens, many of whom, for no offense at all, were clubbed and kicked, dragged from the sidewalks, and forced to march between the lines of deputies."[9] Not until threatened with martial law and not until Tarsney promised to retain troops in the district for thirty days did the mine owners agree to disband their private army. After its breakup and dispersal, which began on June 11, the Waite agreement became operative and lasted for nearly a decade.[10]

In this first strike of the WFM in Colorado, violence was prevalent, but both sides bore equal responsibility for the disorder. Nevertheless, the popular image of the WFM as a ruthless, unscrupulous organization had been created in Colorado, especially among the influential mine owners and operators of Colorado Springs who, after the fusionist administrations of the Populist era, were to exercise great power in state government. The union's subsequent strikes enhanced this lawless image, for violence was always present, resulting in either a loss of life or a destruction of property.

An incident in Leadville during the summer of 1896, when Cloud City Union No. 19 struck to enforce its demands for recognition and a wage increase from balky mine owners, again illustrated the WFM's proclivity toward violence. The mine owners' attempt to resume operations with strikebreakers provoked members of the union to retaliate. They intimidated nonunion workers, purchased and distributed firearms among the strikers, and destroyed private property. A number of lives were lost in the resulting turmoil, which required the National Guard to quell. Although a special investigating committee of the Eleventh General Assembly strongly condemned both the employers and the union for the strife, their finding did not prevent the public's further identifying of the WFM with lawlessness.[11] Nor was the reputation improved by a strike in March 1899[12] by a newly formed local of the WFM at Henson near Lake City against mine owners who required their unmarried employees to live in company boarding houses. Early in the strike armed miners seized the mines and retained possession until state troops restored the properties to their owners.[13]

In 1901 a brutal strike erupted in the important Telluride mining district, located in the rugged San Juan Mountains of San Miguel County in southwestern Colorado and far from the eastern slope meccas of Denver, Colorado Springs, and Pueblo. Until 1899 the prevailing wage in the mines had been $3 for an eight-hour day. But when the Smuggler-Union mine, the leading producer in the district, was acquired by Boston capitalists, its manager, Arthur L. Collins, instituted the fathom, or contract, system which the miners claimed depressed wages, extended the working day, and increased the possibility of accidents in the mines.[14] Dissatisfaction with the system, which was generally foreign to the mining camps of Colorado, increased until on May 2, 1901, Miners' Union No. 63, WFM, struck against the Smuggler-Union over the question of how labor was to be employed in the district. Prior to the strike the powerful company generally determined the wage-hour structure in the local mines. Although the union offered to submit the dispute to the State Board of Arbitration, Collins insisted that the company had nothing to arbitrate and flatly refused.[15]

On June 17, 1901, the Smuggler-Union Company renewed operations with strikebreakers whom Collins had employed at $3 for an eight-hour day. The terms of employment were identical with those sought by the union and, if granted, would have ended the strike. Union members interpreted Collins's move as a clearcut attempt to destroy their organization, and for two weeks they tried unsuccessfully to persuade the non-union men to quit work. The dispute climaxed on July 3, 1901, when approximately 250 heavily armed strikers surrounded the Smuggler-Union properties, where the strikebreakers worked fully armed. Negotiations for work stoppage degenerated into a morning-long battle in which three men were killed and six others seriously wounded. The strikebreakers finally surrendered when promised fair treatment; however, the victorious strikers dealt harshly with their captives, forcing nearly 100 of them to leave the district on foot over the mountains.[16] This episode was to haunt the WFM because it was later used to justify a massive deportation of union members from several gold camps of Colorado.

The violence produced demands that the state intervene to restore order. Governor James B. Orman responded not by ordering in the National Guard but by sending a heavily pro-labor committee to investigate the situation. This body rejected the use of troops, advocating instead a negotiated settlement between the parties.[17] On July 6 an agreement was reached which removed union grievances against the Smuggler-Union Company. Included were provisions permitting an individual miner to accept the contract system but preventing his wage from dropping below $3 for an eight-hour day.[18] In November this minimum wage-hour standard, the heart of the settlement, was embodied in a three-year contract with all the companies of the district. Unfortunately for the peace of the area, however, the mill and surface workers were not included.

The strike left a residue of bitterness, and the mine owners and union members too regarded each other with mistrust. Telluride's *Daily Journal* aggravated the situation by its anti-union stance, which finally provoked the union to retaliate with a costly boycott. Led by Collins, who was backed by the Telluride Mining Association, district employers formed the Business Men's Association to sustain the *Journal*. Area residents rallied behind the developing factions and their involvement further undermined the precarious peace. The boycott continued for months and alienated the miners' union and its supporters from the rest of the community. Reconciliation became impossible after Collins's assassination on the night of November 19, 1902. He was killed as he was chatting at home with friends. Although local authorities promptly charged union officials with the crime, District Judge Theron Stevens quashed the indictments because of insufficient evidence.[19] But the mine owners of the district were now certain that the union would stop at nothing—even murder—to have its way, and they questioned more than ever its right to exist. Their fear and hatred eventually persuaded them that the WFM should be destroyed. Mine owners throughout the state shared this view, for Collins's murder had convinced them that the WFM was not only violent but also criminal.

Other factors made the employers of Colorado inclined to see the WFM as a dangerous organization which had to be disciplined if the status quo was not to be radically altered. Despite its violent first decade, the union's initial objectives were moderate and based upon the imperative needs of its members. It wanted wages commensurate with the dangers endured in the mines, payment in lawful money rather than company script, strictly enforced legislation to maximize health and safety in the mines, prevention of child labor, removal of company guards from areas around the mines, and preferential hiring of union men. The WFM hoped to obtain these objectives through legislation, education, and organization. It preferred arbitration and conciliation to strikes.[20] So moderate and so job conscious were its objectives that the early WFM has been described as a "typical" American labor union.[21] Moreover, on July 7, 1896, it affiliated with the American Federation of Labor, whose president was the conservative Samuel Gompers. Although the affiliation was temporary, it suggested common purpose and essential agreement between the two organizations about goals and methods to be used in labor matters.

But within a year major differences developed between Gompers and Edward Boyce, president of the miners' union, regarding basic tactics. In responding to Gompers's inquiry about rumors that he planned to pull his members out of the AFL and form a new labor organization in the West because of the weak support the AFL had given to the Leadville strike of 1896, Boyce wrote on March 16, 1897 that his grievances went beyond that complaint to a gnawing dissatisfaction with the conservatism of the AFL. Force and effective use of the ballot rather than "conservative action," he wrote, were the best methods for safeguarding labor's interests against a "vicious" political system. Boyce believed that the miners were far ahead of Eastern laborers in realizing the efficacy of active unionism; therefore, he favored a new Western labor union free from the conservative restraints of the AFL.[22] In rebuttal, Gompers refused to concede that Eastern workingmen were less sophisticated than Boyce's miners in the use of the ballot, and he rejected force as the proper means of affecting political change, pointing out that while it had altered "forms of government" in the past, force had never "attained real liberty." He candidly suggested that Boyce should resign his office and actively resist the trades union movement if he believed that it was useless.[23] Boyce responded by leading his men out of the AFL and organizing the Western Labor Union, which was dominated by the miners' union.

Boyce carried his militancy into the WFM, trying to indoctrinate its members with the necessity of political and direct action as the best means of attaining a better life. He advised delegates to the miners' annual convention of 1897 that

> every union should have a rifle club. I strongly advise you to provide every member with the latest improved rifle.

. . . I entreat you to take action on this important question, so that in two years we can hear the inspiring music of the martial tread of 25,000 armed men in the ranks of labor.[24]

Under Boyce the WFM changed a job conscious and typical American labor union to one whose proclivity toward violence was enhanced by a growing socialist and revolutionary orientation. Mesmerized by the passion of Boyce, men like Haywood, who felt the tremendous appeal of self-abnegation and sacrifice which the "labor wars" of Colorado and elsewhere demanded, dedicated themselves to a "revolutionary labor movement" whose goal was to emancipate the workingman from "wage slavery."[25] In 1901, Boyce, confident of his power, moved to commit the miners' ninth annual convention to socialism, a course which further provoked Colorado's employers.

Boyce's presidential address to the convention delegates that year was a powerful plea for altering the constitutionally expressed goals and methods of the WFM to attract those persons oppressed by corporate abuse, and to inspire its members to press on until labor received "every dollar of wealth" it produced. He thought that nothing could be gained by continuing the present policy, for, as he said:

Advise strikes as the weapon to be used by labor to obtain its rights, and you will be branded as criminals who aim to ruin the business interests of the country. Change from the policy of simple trades unionism that is fast waning, and you will be told that your action is premature, as this is not the time. Pursue the methods adopted by capitalists and you will be sent to prison for robbery or executed for murder. Demand, and your demands will be construed into threats of violence against the rights of private property calculated to scare capital. Avail yourself of your constitutional rights and propose to take political action, and you will be charged with selling out the organization to some political party. Counsel arbitration, and you will be told there is nothing to arbitrate. Be conservative, and your tameness will be construed as an appreciation of the conditions imposed upon you by trusts and syndicates. Take what action you will in the interests of labor, the trained beagles in the employ of capital from behind their loathsome fortress of disguised patriotism will howl their tirade of condemnation.[26]

Boyce saw labor's salvation in an organization powerful enough to change a system which denied the working class all but a fraction of what it produced, and he pleaded with the convention for a policy which would channel the energy of the union toward basic alterations in the prevailing society along socialist lines.

The convention gave Boyce most of what he wanted but fell short of a total commitment to the socialist cause. On June 3 the body adopted a resolution which called for divorcing the working class from the existing capitalist-dominated political parties and directed the union's executive board to aid in enlisting workers from different states in a new political movement. A supporting resolution demanded radical alterations in the status quo in the interest of justice and brotherhood. Specifically, it advised the worker to defend his rights with the ballot, but if that failed, it advocated meeting the "enemy" with his own weapons. There followed a list of suggestions for improving the lot of labor, ranging from elimination of "government by injunction" to a national land policy limiting the public domain to actual settlers. Despite the evident ardor of WFM leaders for socialism and the presence of Eugene V. Debs and Father Thomas Hagerty, a maverick Catholic priest turned socialist, the delegates refused to make a total commitment to socialism and political action. On June 6 they tabled a motion endorsing the program of the Social Democratic party and pledging the delegates to advocate its principles in their local unions.[27]

No one was more fully aware of the reluctance of the delegates than Boyce himself. In his presidential address to the tenth annual convention in 1902 he pleaded again for a commitment to a "true policy" that would abolish capitalism and free the workingman. In his opinion, there could be no permanent solution of the labor problem "except in the public ownership of the natural resources of the earth and the means of production and distribution." Although he made his personal position absolutely clear to the delegates, he did not demand that they fully endorse socialism as the official program of the WFM. Instead he told them that "the most important action which you can take at this convention is to *advise* the members of your organization to adopt the principles of socialism without equivocation, for the time has arrived when we must sever our affiliation with those political parties who have legislated us into our present state of industrial bondage."[28] Boyce confessed that he saw no point in continuing the WFM if the delegates were not prepared to follow such a course.

When the Committee on the President's Report later recommended that the convention adopt the "principles of the socialist platform," which was what Boyce clearly wanted but which went beyond his specific recommendation, the extensive debate which erupted exposed strong oposition to endorsement. Supporters of the report could obtain only a watered-down resolution of June 4 which declared "for a policy of independent political action" and which recommended the "adoption of the platform of the Socialist Party of America by the locals of the Federation in conjunction with a vigorous policy of education along the lines of political economy."[29] The delegates apparently did not feel powerful enough to adopt socialism as the WFM's official program, preferring instead to refer the matter with favorable recommendation to the locals for their consideration. Nevertheless, their action was in line with Boyce's recommendation, and it took the WFM one step beyond its position of 1901. But suggestive of the continuing reluctance to embrace socialism was the convention's decision on June 6 to table a motion inviting Debs, Hagerty, and W. H. Wise to address the convention on the "fundamental principles of scientific socialism." Furthermore, when asked if they would support the work of the convention, twenty-two of eighty voting delegates refused for various reasons: some believed that any action which seemed to endorse socialist principles was premature, others flatly rejected socialism as a program for the union, several refused because they did not want any link-up with the Socialist Party of America.[30] Nevertheless, the resolution of June 4 stamped the WFM as a socialist instrument among Colorado's employers, and some union leaders thereafter assumed that socialism had received the full endorsement of the rank and file.

In addressing the eleventh annual convention of 1903, Charles H. Moyer, Boyce's successor as president, commended the previous convention for wisely "recommending that the Western Federation of Miners adopt a policy which had for its purpose the establishing of a system under which the wage slave would be no longer known, under which the inscription on the hundreds of charters hanging in the halls of your local union might become a reality." Although Moyer attributed the sharp increase in the number of new members and locals joining the WFM to this "fearless action" taken in 1902, a conclusion supported by his executive board, he did not demand a more binding commitment to socialism but asked only that the delegates confirm their previous position. However, other delegates attempted to pull the WFM deeper into the socialist orbit and failed. On June 6 the convention rejected a recommendation of the Committee on the President's Report to amend the preamble of the constitution to include "political and independent action" as a means of abolishing capitalism and establishing socialism. And it rejected a recommendation that members of the WFM refuse nominations to political office on tickets other than that of the Socialist party. Conservative delegates prevented any action on the committee's report other than a reaffirmation of the position taken by the tenth annual convention.[31]

It is impossible to determine to what extent the membership accepted socialism as the solution to the labor problem at the end of the WFM's first decade. Concrete evidence on this point is scarce. The occasional letters from socialist members to the *Miners' Magazine*, the official voice of the union, cannot justify the conclusion that the membership backed the efforts of their leaders to place their union in the socialist camp. And the socialist slogans found on charters, union cards, and in the *Miners' Magazine* may prove only the widespread apathy and indifference of the membership rather than firm commitment. At no time was the question put to the miners in the form of a referendum before the Colorado labor troubles of 1903–1904. That the leadership of the union was socialist is beyond question; that a majority of the delegates to the annual conventions was inclined to follow Boyce, Moyer, and Haywood cannot be denied. However, that opposition within the conventions was sufficiently strong to prevent official adoption of socialism is indisputable, a fact which suggests that many delegates knew or suspected that the members they represented were not willing to accept the stance of the leadership.

Nevertheless, the great publicity given to the work of the miners' annual conventions of 1901–1903 established the WFM among Colorado's employers as a revolutionary body dissatisfied enough with the prevailing system to work for its overthrow. Already feared because of its growing power in the state's mining industry and already hated because of its willingness to use force in its strikes, the union now appeared more dangerous and threatening because of its socialist orientation. Business and industrial leaders, watching the proceedings of the miners' conventions, concluded that union officials were conspiring to make the state into a socialist mecca, a center from which the surrounding states could be subverted, and that the instrument for effecting this revolution was to be the ballot. The overwhelming endorsement by the voters in 1902 of a labor-backed constitutional amendment authorizing an eight-hour law had demonstrated the enormous potential of political action in undermining conservative interests.

As the first decade of the WFM ended, the men who controlled Colorado's economic life had ample reason to view the union with concern. Its growing strength had been a catalyst which altered power relations in the important metalliferous industry to the detriment of corporate and other conservative interests. Its willingness to resort to violence to protect the interests of its members had early provoked intransigent mining companies to reciprocate in kind, at times forcing whole communities into two hostile camps. Furthermore, the apparent capture of the WFM by militant socialists, whose revolutionary rhetoric went beyond demands for a reform of hours, wages, and working conditions to demands for a new social order, had alarmed conservative business and industrial leaders. These developments set the stage for a head-on collision between the growing aspirations of officials of the WFM and the increasing determination of their capitalist counterparts to discipline and even destroy the miners' union while there was still time. The showdown, two years of industrial warfare during the administration of James H. Peabody (1903–1905), broke the power of the WFM in Colorado and seriously damaged it elsewhere.

2

Preparation for Battle

In 1872 James H. Peabody, the man destined to check the growing power of the Western Federation of Miners, moved from Vermont to Colorado and established himself as a successful small-town businessman. He settled in Canon City, the county seat of Fremont County in the south central part of the state. An industrious and ambitious entrepreneur, he became a driving force behind the area's economic growth. He joined with other businessmen to create several important regional enterprises, such as the Canon City Water Company, the Canon City Electric Power and Light Company, the Canon City Pressed Brick Company, and the First National Bank of Canon City. Although his first love was business, Peabody was also politically active at the local level. He ran for a variety of public offices to which the people of the city and county, impressed by his drive, ability, and success, repeatedly elected him. In succession Peabody was city treasurer, city clerk, a member of the town's board of aldermen, a schoolboard director, county clerk and recorder, and mayor—offices in which he earned a reputation for integrity and business-like conduct of public affairs. Yet it was as mayor of Canon City, an office to which he was first elected in April 1901, that he demonstrated the more-than-average administrative ability which raised the possibility of statewide elective office.[1]

For nearly two years Peabody was an excellent mayor who guided the city toward accomplishments apparent more than a half century later. He led the city council in meeting the requirements of Andrew Carnegie for a grant of $13,500 to construct a public library which is still in use. He attempted to restrict the polluting of the Arkansas River, taking the initiative to have water samples analyzed, cooperating with other river towns to end the dangerous practice of running raw sewage into the stream, and initiating injunction proceedings against companies which insisted upon dumping industrial waste into the river. He encouraged the city council to assume the costs of treating smallpox cases occurring within the city limits. He pushed for new sewage lines and his bank purchased the first three $1,000 municipal bonds to get construction underway. Also, he led movements for a new city hall, a more extensive lighting and repaving of the streets, and even the curtailment of spitting on the town's sidewalks.[2]

There is little in Peabody's career in Canon City to foreshadow the vigorous stand against the WFM that he later took as governor. But as an employer residing in a county where coal mining and smelting were important industries and where the growing influence of the WFM and the United Mine Workers was increasingly exerted, he undoubtedly shared the apprehension of other employers toward militant labor unions. While Peabody was mayor, two incidents occurred which indicated that he was not prepared to act aggressively on behalf of organized labor. The first occurred when the labor unions of Canon City complained to the city council that a contractor building new sewage lines was paying substandard wages for a workday exceeding eight hours and requested that it force him to pay a $2 minimum wage for an eight-hour day on the project. Peabody refused for the council, excusing the city's inaction by the fact that, having awarded the contract, the city could not then intervene to impose wage-hour minimums.[3] The second incident oc-

1. *James H. Peabody, Governor of Colorado from 1903 to 1905. Photo courtesy of the Library, State Historical Society of Colorado.*

2. *Two major plants of the United States Reduction and Refining Company—the Standard and the Colorado—in Colorado City. Photo courtesy of the Library, State Historical Society of Colorado.*

3. *Governor Peabody surrounded by his aides-de-camp. Adjutant General Sherman M. Bell stands to Peabody's immediate left. Photo courtesy of the Canon City (Colo.) Museum.*

4. *Downtown section of Cripple Creek, Colo., about 1900. Photo courtesy of the Library, State Historical Society of Colorado.*

5. *Camp Goldfield in October 1903. Photo courtesy of the Library, State Historical Society of Colorado.*

6. *After the disastrous Independence depot explosion, riots broke out at the corner of Fourth and Victor avenues in Victor, Colo., on June 6, 1904. Photo courtesy of the Library, State Historical Society of Colorado.*

7. *Fifty union miners captured by the military on June 6, 1904 in Victor were marched down the city's main street to the "Bull Pen" of Armory Hall. Photo courtesy of the Library, State Historical Society of Colorado.*

10. *The main street of Telluride, Colo., circa 1900. Photo courtesy of the Library, State Historical Society of Colorado.*

8. *Miners gathered in front of Armory Hall in Victor after the imprisonment of fifty union miners on the top floor of the building. Photo courtesy of the Library, State Historical Society of Colorado.*

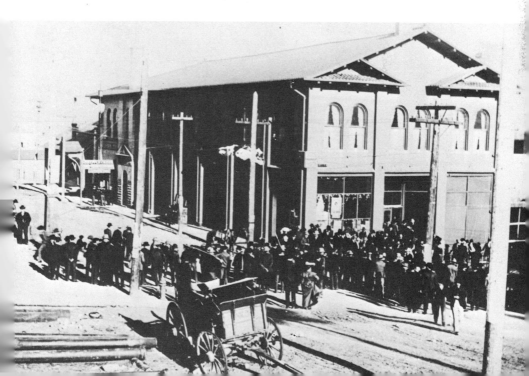

IS COLORADO IN AMERICA?

HABEAS CORPUS SUSPENDED IN COLORADO!

BULL-PENS FOR UNION MEN IN COLORADO!

SOLDIERS DEFY THE COURTS IN COLORADO!

UNION MEN EXILED FROM HOMES AND FAMILIES IN COLORADO!

CORPORATIONS CORRUPT AND CONTROL ADMINISTRATION IN COLORADO!

CITIZENS' ALLIANCE RESORTS TO MOB LAW AND VIOLENCE IN COLORADO!

UNDER THE FOLDS OF THE
AMERICAN FLAG IN
COLORADO!

EVERY WORD inscribed upon the stripes of "Old Glory" is the truth. If this flag is desecrated, the Republican Governor of Colorado is responsible for the acts that profane the emblem of liberty.

THE PICTURE represents Henry Maki, a union miner of Telluride, who was arrested for vagrancy—had money in his pocket and was being supported by his union. He was shackled to a telephone pole because he refused to work in a filthy cess-pool under the bayonets of the state militia.

WE ARE GOING TO BREAK his chains and the chains that are binding the working class of Colorado.

OUR STRUGGLE is for an eight-hour day, to establish the right to organize for mutual benefit, and to prevent discrimination against union men.

IF YOU DESIRE to assist the striking Miners, Mill and Smeltermen of the Western Federation of Miners of Colorado in this battle for industrial and political freedom, send donations to Wm. D. Haywood, Sec'y-Treasurer, Room 3, Pioneer Building, Denver, Colorado.

Charles Moyer.

PRESIDENT

Wm D Haywood

SEC'Y-TREASURER

9. *Union posters protesting acts occurring during the Peabody administration were widely circulated in the West by the WFM. Photo courtesy of the Idaho Historical Society.*

11. *The mountainous regions surrounding Telluride were the locations of the principal mines in the district. Photo courtesy of the Library, State Historical Society of Colorado, J. Fred Roberts Collection.*

12. *The executive board of the Western Federation of Miners in 1905 included President Charles Moyer and Secretary-Treasurer William D. Haywood, seated fourth and third from the left, respectively. Photo courtesy of the Library, State Historical Society of Colorado.*

curred after the election of 1902, when the voters made Peabody their governor-elect and voted overwhelmingly to amend the state constitution to allow enactment of an eight-hour law for certain hazardous occupations. At that time the local labor unions, hoping to exploit the election results, requested that the council include provisions requiring a recipient to pay a $2 minimum wage for an eight-hour day in all future franchises and contracts, as did some other towns in Colorado. But the council refused to do more than express its "wish" that in the future all successful bidders on city projects grant the wage-hour standards desired by the unions.[4] Peabody's precise role in determining the council's response is unknown, but certainly as mayor and governor-elect he was consulted on the matter, and it appears likely that the council's stand was actually his own.

In 1902 when Colorado's Republicans decided to break away from the fusionist combinations of the past decade, they searched for able candidates who could bring victory to their party. However, competent candidates alone were not enough. As party organs like the *Denver Republican* pointed out, Republican success in the forthcoming election required the support of the state's business and industrial interests. It was therefore imperative that the party's candidates have qualifications warranting that support. They should be successful businessmen who reflected the views of their associates; they should be able to conduct public affairs in a business-like manner; they should be the trusted representatives of the business community who would be sensitive to its needs and interests.[5] Peabody, who had been a loyal Republican and a businessman all his life, met these requirements. Furthermore, other assets made him politically attractive as a candidate for high office. Not only was he safely removed from the quagmire of Denver politics, but he was widely known throughout the state in Masonic and banking circles.[6] As the state convention approached, Peabody emerged as a leading contender for his party's gubernatorial nomination, despite his disclaimers to the contrary.

On September 10, Peabody set up campaign headquarters in Denver's Brown Palace Hotel, where he busied himself rallying delegate support. His successful maneuvering unleashed rumors that his nomination was but a mere formality.

This caused Denver newspapers to speculate that the powerful State Central Committee was in Peabody's camp as well as most of President Theodore Roosevelt's Colorado supporters, many wealthy and politically powerful individuals like Edward O. Wolcott, and other unidentified "influential factors." The fact that his candidacy had the backing of the party kingpins became evident on September 12 when the convention chose him by acclamation and without a contest as its nominee for governor to run against Democratic candidate E. C. Stimson, an attorney from Colorado Springs. Having obtained the nomination, Peabody set out to realize the principal expectation of the Republican party—that is, the redemption of Colorado from alleged "fusionist misrule" by restoring a conservative government which would be responsive to business and industry whose influence allegedly had been diminished in the preceding decade.[7]

In placing Peabody at the head of its ticket, the Republicans had made an excellent choice in their drive to return to power, for Peabody had an extraordinary faith in the efficacy of business principles, particularly when applied to public affairs. Although his recorded campaign statements are few, those available emphasize his belief that the state would profit from a "business" administration. After all, in Peabody's opinion, government was like

> any other great corporation and its executive officers should be asked to conduct its affairs along similar lines. The people are like stockholders in the corporation and their profit and loss is contingent largely upon the success or failure of the officers charged with the management of the affairs of the corporation.[8]

Good government, therefore, required that the state be controlled by prudent men who would act upon sound business principles. This was basic to Peabody's campaign.

Peabody's promise to operate the state on a "strictly business basis" was not a mere maneuver to obtain the support of business and industrial leaders, for he prided himself upon being a businessman with viewpoints identical to those of the business community in general. His nomination suggested that party managers had no doubts on this point. Nevertheless, his campaign statements regarding how his administration would affect the status of corporations and organized labor left something to be desired even from the viewpoint of business leaders. When asked what the proper relationship should be between corporations and the important State Board of Equalization, which the governor chaired, Peabody answered that all corporations should conform to legal requirements, that each should bear its just proportion of the state's tax burden, and that a conscientious board should enforce such a policy. In elaborating, however, he expressed satisfaction with existing statutes governing the corporations, saying the laws needed no revision if honestly and vigorously enforced.[9] Thus the corporations appeared to have nothing more to fear than strict enforcement of existing statutes if Peabody were elected, because this and other statements implied that he would not support reform legislation designed to hamper corporate interests.

Peabody's campaign itinerary took him into Victor, Cripple Creek, Denver, and other areas where union members resided in large numbers and where he could not entirely avoid questions about his attitude toward the interests of organized workingmen. Nevertheless, he made few statements on labor, certainly none that would hint of his aggressive involvement as governor in the industrial disputes that were to plague his administration. Because Peabody was recognized as the candidate of business and industry, however, his opponents sensed his vulnerability on labor matters and hoped to undermine his campaign. They circulated a report, alleged to have come from the Canon City Trades and Labor Assembly, which condemned his role as mayor in awarding the contract for the sewer line to a bidder who paid wages below the union scale and worked his men more than eight hours a day. Disregarding the assembly's denial of responsibility for the attack, many union officials used it effectively as evidence that Peabody was an enemy of organized labor. In a speech in Cripple Creek on October 14, Peabody attempted to counteract the damaging report by justifying the stand that he and the city council had taken and by expressing warm sentiments toward unionism.[10] However, labor leaders were not entirely convinced by his Cripple Creek performance.

The platforms of the Democratic and Republican parties both had endorsed a proposed constitutional amendment of 1902 authorizing the Fourteenth General Assembly to enact an eight-hour law applicable principally in the mines and ore reduction plants, a fact which removed the matter of hours legislation from the campaign as a partisan issue. But by pledging "the party and each and every candidate . . . to carrying out the principles and pledges" of the platform, the Republican state convention imposed a binding moral imperative upon Peabody and its other candidates to exercise constructive leadership in pushing for an "adequate" eight-hour law should the amendment carry.[11] Peabody answered questions concerning his attitude toward such legislation on October 23 in a rally at Victor. Unlike his Democratic opponent Stimson, who earlier had told a district audience that he would sign any eight-hour measure presented to him by the legislature, Peabody spoke evasively. The pro-labor and pro-Democratic *Victor Daily Record* reported the next day that he promised only to give any bill regulating hours his "consideration," but he would make no further commitment. And he continued to avoid comment on all labor questions except for an unsatisfactory explanation of his role as mayor in awarding the sewer line contract. The *Record*, the voice of the WFM in the Cripple Creek mining district, was not convinced that Peabody's election was in the best interests of labor, and many unionists throughout the state agreed. By November 1, thirty-four labor organizations had declared that Peabody was "unfair" to labor. They based their positions principally upon the sewer contract episode.[12]

Colorado voters went to the polls in November amidst the rumors of fraud and corruption and elected Republicans to all major offices except State Superintendent of Schools. However, neither party had the complete confidence of the voters, who gave Republicans control of the lower house of the legislature and the Democrats the upper house. Nevertheless, state administration was again in Republican hands, and their brand of redemption and restoration could begin. Party organs predicted great things for the state. Assessing the election on November 8, the *Denver Republican*, which had opposed the eight-hour amendment as a dangerous meddling with the constitution, suggested editorially that Republican victory had "tremendous consequences" for the state because it demonstrated that an "era of sanity had returned to Colorado, that investments may now safely be made here and that the day of revolutionary and idiotic legislation had passed, we hope never to return."

In his inaugural address to the Fourteenth General Assembly in January 1903, Peabody more clearly defined what Republican redemption from "fusionist misrule" meant for Colorado. Without directly referring to the eight-hour amendment which the voters had overwhelmingly approved in 1902, he obliquely voiced his opposition to hours regulation—so much desired by organized labor and so much opposed by corporate interests—when he suggested that too much "tinkering" with the laws and the constitution had already occurred. Statutes tending to "unsettle conditions or result in radical changes" ought not to be enacted by the new legislature because

> radical and far reaching legislation, fundamental changes in our laws, with resultant doubt, uncertainty, litigation and chaos, have been the affliction under which the people of this State have existed during several administrations past, until the time has arrived when the people of the State demand . . . a period of rest, so that they may familiarize themselves with the laws and adapt their interests to the existing conditions.[13]

Despite Republican promises to support an "adequate" eight-hour law if the constitutional amendment passed, the new governor was clearly not inclined to fulfill the pledge by using the powers of his office in behalf of such legislation. His attitude toward this and other innovative legislation was negative.

Peabody's comments upon the creation of the State Board of Arbitration in 1897 hinted of how he would respond to strikes. In briefly reviewing the six-year history of the board, he pointed out that, although it had successfully arbitrated six of nine strikes at a total cost of $13,000, its report of 1902 had indicated its inability to function effectively because it lacked the legal authority to compel arbitration. A constitutional amendment was required for the legislature to bestow that power. Because he opposed further "tinkering" with the constitution and

believed that the expense of the board had been "out of all proportion to the results accomplished," Peabody recommended repeal of the law creating the board and the transfer of its functions to the deputy labor commissioner. Had this advice been
followed, it would have abolished the only government machinery available for the peaceful resolution of industrial disputes.[14]

Portions of the address revealed Peabody's preoccu-
pation with the industrial turmoil that had engulfed the state
over the preceding decade. He expressed his concern over Colorado's growing reputation as an "unsafe place for the investment
of capital," which he attributed to lax law enforcement, and announced that he would use "all the power and authority" of the
governor's office to assure the protection of life and property.[15]
His solution for reducing crimes of all kinds and restoring a favorable climate for capital was simple: let the "criminal classes"
know that "conviction, sentence, and punishment are sure, speedy
and certain, without hope of pardon, reprieve, commutation of
sentence or parole, except in clearly meritorious cases."[16] His
stand had far-ranging implications, because it suggested a readi-
ness to tag as "criminal" any activities, including strikes, which
might interfere with the state's industrial development.

Peabody was also determined that his administration, unlike any of those of the previous decade, would not be
marred by public disorders, and he was prepared to use military
force if necessary to achieve that goal. He stated that domestic
tranquility would be "conserved and promoted by an efficient,
well-equipped and well-disciplined national guard" and recommended that the legislature enact a special levy to replace the
offensive and hard-to-collect military poll tax of one dollar per
capita as the method of financing the National Guard. He also
urged that the governor, upon the recommendation of the Military Board, be empowered to reorganize it to achieve the effi-
ciency of a regular army.[17] He viewed the guard as an instrument of social control which could be used effectively against
the "criminal classes" and other disturbers of the peace.

As in his campaign, Peabody called for economy in
government. He believed that members of the Fourteenth General Assembly were obligated to apply to public affairs the same

economic principles which they used to guide their own businesses. He therefore recommended that civil service rules be formulated and applied wherever possible to all departments of the government and that no one be employed whose work was not absolutely essential to the proper functioning of the state. In his opinion, it was "indefeasible" that anyone should be employed for purposes other than the needs of the state.[18]

When he entered the governor's office, Peabody assumed positions that would make the impending clash between capital and labor in Colorado extremely dangerous for the social order and the traditions upon which it rested. Although not an avowed enemy of organized labor, he obviously did not intend to tolerate the violence that had become an accepted part of labor unrest in the previous decade. His inaugural address—a powerful statement of his determination to uphold law and order, maintain property rights, and restrain further legislative and constitutional innovations opposed to conservative interests—placed his administration squarely in opposition to the labor leaders like Moyer and Haywood, who were advocating an increasingly militant and socialist course for their unions. Furthermore, Peabody assumed office at a time when employers throughout the nation were preparing, in the name of law and order and Americanism, to wage war against organized labor, especially against militant unions like the WFM. His speech revealed a strong predisposition to support this national employers' movement, a phase of which was then developing among Colorado's employers. Forces both in and outside the state were converging to make the governor's office a storm center. An outbreak of labor unrest in Colorado City forced Peabody while he was still new in his office, to decide in whose interest the power of the state was to be used—organized labor or the corporations. He acted decisively in behalf of the corporations.

3

The Die is Cast

Governor Peabody believed that the state's history of industrial warfare had diverted Eastern capital elsewhere. Convinced that this diversion was detrimental to the interests of all Coloradans, he pledged in his inaugural address to make the state safe for investments, if necessary using all the power of the state to protect lives and property and to maintain public order. His pledge was a commitment that he fully intended to keep.

Newspaper accounts of the WFM's annual conventions of 1901–1903 had pictured the union as a revolutionary body under the control of radicals who advocated a major overhaul or even overthrow of the existing social order. Like other Colorado businessmen and industrialists, Peabody viewed the union as a threat to the dominant position of his class, as well as to private property, democratic institutions, and the nation itself. He was inclined to act forcefully against the WFM or any other union which, in his opinion, disturbed the peace, threatened lives and property, or disrupted the economy in pushing for unacceptable social changes. The strike of the Mill and Smeltermen's Union No. 125, WFM, against three ore processing companies in Colorado City first revealed how forcefully he would respond to militant unionism.

The corporations, the United States Reduction and Refining Company (USRRC), the Portland Gold Mining Company, and the Telluride Reduction Company, had constructed smelting and reduction plants in Colorado City to handle ore from the Cripple Creek mining district. Of the three the USRRC, a multi-million dollar out-of-state corporation with seven plants located in Canon City, Florence, and Colorado City, was the largest and most powerful[1] Among its principal officers were such influential Coloradans as Spencer Penrose and Charles M. MacNeill, who were wealthy residents of Colorado Springs, the municipal neighbor of Colorado City. After they were unable to prevent the WFM from organizing many of the millworkers into the Mill and Smeltermen's Union in August 1902, the officials of these corporations became determined to emasculate the organization.

Within months dissension arose in the Standard mill of the USRRC. There union leaders alleged that the corporation's employment and discharge policies were discriminatory and were designed to destroy the Mill and Smeltermen's Union. The union claimed that forty-two men had been fired after becoming union members and charged that the firings denied the workers the right to organize and thus endangered the life of the organization. However, mill officials asserted that only "incompetents" had been released and that the company had been motivated solely by a desire to improve the quality of its labor force, not to deliberately attack the union.[2] Nevertheless, on February 14, 1903 a committee visited Charles MacNeill, vice-president and general manager of the USRRC, to voice the union's grievances and to propose moderate wage increases. MacNeill abruptly terminated the meeting and refused to accept a written statement outlining the union's position when he discovered that none of his employees was a member of the group. In his opinion, any proposal of nonemployees or "outsiders" was equivalent to an "ultimatum" and was an "unwarrantable" interference in company affairs. That the company's unionized employees had chosen the committee as their bargaining agent was immaterial.[3]

The memorandum which MacNeill had rejected was moderate in its demands. It requested that the minimum wage for an eight-hour day be raised from $1.80 to $2.25 and that small upward revisions be made in the wages of employees already earning more than the proposed minimum but below $3 a day. Other provisions asked that the USRRC recognize the right of the millworkers to organize and maintain a union in its mills, emphasizing that organization was essential to counteract the unfavorable attitude of the courts toward labor on matters of industrial injuries and company liability. Although there was no objection raised to the discharge of incompetent union workers, the union denounced the firing of the forty-two men for alleged incompetence when the true reason was their union membership.[4]

When MacNeill refused to negotiate, the union struck the mills of the USRRC on the evening of February 14. Seventy-six of the 212 millworkers left their jobs, but only forty of these were union members. Picket lines were quickly established. From the beginning there was close cooperation between county law enforcement personnel and company officials. Consequently, the Standard mill continued limited production under protection of deputy sheriffs appointed by W. R. Gilbert, sheriff of El Paso County. MacNeill received an appointment as deputy sheriff for the duration of the strike, and the USRRC temporarily paid the salaries of the deputies protecting its properties until the county could arrange to absorb the costs.[5]

The strike was not limited to the USRRC. Also on February 14 the union committee visited Frank G. Peck, secretary-treasurer of the Portland Gold Mining Company and Hugh W. Fullerton, general manager of the Telluride Reduction Company. Both men, unlike MacNeill, agreed to consider the statement of union grievances. Two weeks later their rejection of the recommended wage increases caused the executive board of the WFM, then meeting in Denver, to declare these companies "unfair" and to authorize strikes against them. These began on February 28.[6] By the end of the month strikes were in progress against all the mills of Colorado City, involving slightly more than 60 percent of 535 millworkers.

The situation rapidly deteriorated as mill officials refused to tolerate the union and resorted to the traditional method of fighting the WFM locals, bringing in strikebreakers. These replacements were not to be temporary employees hired solely for breaking the strike, for the USRRC employed them with the clear understanding that they had permanent jobs if their service was satisfactory. Officials of the USRRC held that the strikers had severed all relations with the company.[7] If strictly adhered to, this procedure would have left the striking workers without jobs, made their union meaningless and made reconciliation impossible.

Conditions in Colorado City were ideal for serious trouble. Picket lines and an ever-increasing number of deputies moved around outside the mills. Incidents became inevitable as the friction grew. Reports circulated about alleged assaults on the strikebreakers by members of the union and of brutal attacks on the strikers by the deputies. As tension mounted, the company officials demanded more protection for their mills and their employees until the sheriff soon had deputized more than seventy men for strike duty. Still dissatisfied, the mill owners demanded even more protection. On March 3, MacNeill insisted that threats and actual violence by the union made imperative the stationing of 250 men around the properties of the USRRC alone.[8] Gilbert received other demands for deputies from the Portland and Telluride mills, as well as from the Colorado Electric Company, which supplied power to the mills.[9] Unable to satisfy the demands for protection, he turned to Denver.

Peabody conferred with MacNeill and several associates on March 3 in Denver about the Colorado City situation. MacNeill presented Gilbert's official petition asking for the National Guard to aid in suppressing alleged mob violence and upholding the law in El Paso County. It certified that a riot prevailed in Colorado City and that groups of men were milling around and were threatening lives and property. Included as corroborating evidence were letters from MacNeill and Peck to the sheriff demanding further protection. But missing were supporting affidavits from nonunion workers said to have been the victims of assault.[10] Nevertheless, Gilbert requested that Peabody act immediately on his request for troops, although he later testified before a special investigating committee that the guard had been necessary not to suppress existing violence but only to prevent its outbreak.[11] The documents presented to the governor suggested that the sheriff had been subjected to enormous pressure from the companies to provide more protection than he could supply.

The Denver conference forced Peabody early in his administration to make a crucial decision certain to alienate either organized labor or management. Because MacNeill and his associates represented several important corporations and had the support of the chief law enforcement officer of one of the most populous counties, he could not refuse them a courteous reception. Nor was he predisposed to do so. Here was an opportunity to uphold his inaugural pledge to make Colorado an attractive place for investment by a decisive use of executive power. Although the petitioners were directly involved in the dispute, Peabody was so inclined to act favorably on their request that he neither investigated conditions in Colorado City nor conferred with union leaders on the need for troops there. To act he needed only the assurance that he had clear legal authority to intervene.

Attorney General Nathan C. Miller provided that assurance. After a brief examination of Sheriff Gilbert's petition and accompanying documents, Miller handed his opinion to the governor the same day of the conference. He advised that the conditions certified by Gilbert warranted using the guard, because it was obvious that the sheriff could not control the situation with available forces. Conditions in Colorado City, as described in the affidavits, imposed a constitutional and statutory obligation upon the governor to act in support of law and order.[12] Now confident that military intervention would bear legal scrutiny, Peabody immediately ordered Adjutant General Sherman M. Bell to mobilize the necessary units of the guard to assist Gilbert. His directive made no reference to the strike. During the evening of March 3, infantry companies from Colorado Springs stationed themselves around the Standard mill of the USRRC, and additional units were dispatched from Denver to the strike zone.

For seventeen days more than 300 soldiers patrolled corporate property and escorted nonunion employees to and from work.[13]

Peabody's decision provoked immediate oposition. Officials of Colorado City, whose sympathies were with the strikers, did not support Gilbert's request for troops.[14] When they learned that the guard had been sent, the mayor, the chief of police, and the city attorney protested, wiring the governor that a "few occasional brawls" did not justify a military occupation.[15] On March 4 a delegation presented a petition from more than 125 town residents which denied that state intervention was necessary. The signers claimed that there had been no violence other than "petty quarrels" which had been easily controlled by local police officers. Furthermore, no one expected imminent "riots," for the striking millworkers were among the "best citizens and old residents of El Paso County" who believed in law and order. The signers of the petition asked that the troops be withdrawn.[16]

The governor's action also provoked a quick response from Charles Moyer, president of the WFM. Moyer publicly condemned Peabody for intervening without a "personal investigation of conditions" and for failing to hear labor's side of the controversy. Moyer believed that Peabody had thrown the "armed machinery" of the state into the strike on behalf of the corporations without sufficient justification. State intervention altered the entire character of the dispute.[17] Despite the protests, however, the troops remained.

Among the governor's supporters were some of the most powerful, influential men in the state. In the five months after his order of March 3, Peabody answered approximately forty-five letters praising his action in Colorado City and less than a half dozen criticizing it. His letters to J. A. Kebler, president of the Colorado Fuel and Iron Company, and M. D. Thatcher, president of the First National Bank of Pueblo, who had written to commend his intervention, indicated that he was immensely pleased by their support.[18] Kebler and Thatcher were representative of the hundreds of businessmen who rallied behind the administration and who were then flocking into employers' organizations such as the citizens' alliance.

The strike of the millworkers threatened to involve the Cripple Creek district, the richest mining area of the state, and all the power of the WFM. As early as February 17, Moyer had said in an interview with the *Rocky Mountain News* that the Cripple Creek miners would strike if necessary to block shipments of ore to the struck mills of Colorado City. On the day of Peabody's order union officials in the district asked the mine owners to halt their shipments to these mills. On March 5, when the Cripple Creek District Mine Owners' Association rejected the request, the WFM in a power play threatened to pull its members from the mines whose owners failed to comply. The presence of troops in Colorado City also encouraged a broadening of the strike because, in addition to complicating the issues, the state intervention forced the miners' union to become more actively involved if the millworkers were to succeed. Restricting the dispute to Colorado City seemed to depend on Peabody's willingness to intervene further and effect a settlement satisfactory to all parties. But the governor planned no further personal involvement, despite the gathering storm that threatened to engulf Colorado's entire metalliferous industry. On March 7 the *Rocky Mountain News* quoted him as saying:

> I have done my full duty. I have taken steps for the preservation of life and property, and for the enforcement of the law. That is all I was asked to do. Taking a hand in the settlement of the strike is out of my jurisdiction. . . . I do not propose to have anything to do with the differences which prevail between the mill owners and their men, and will take no part in any negotiation which they may have as to wages or anything else. [p. 1]

Yet the formal machinery for preventing the spread of the strike was limited. Under existing statutes Colorado's Board of Arbitration was powerless to force arbitration, and it could not intervene unless requested to do so by one or more parties in the dispute.[19] It was partly because of this inability that Peabody had recommended the abolition of the board in his inauguration address. Therefore, he refused to encourage the board's intervention in the Colorado City strike without a formal request either from the striking millworkers or the companies.

Although Peabody's stand was legally correct, his sending of troops had made this "do-nothing-further" position untenable. Democratic newspapers, particularly the *Rocky Moun-*

tain News, severely criticized the administration for its failure to seek a settlement.[20] Furthermore, a strike by the Cripple Creek miners was imminent. And though tabled without consideration, a petition of March 6 to the house from hundreds of El Paso County residents protesting the use of troops had increased the pressure.[21] MacNeill's rigid position also helped to speed Peabody's further involvement. On March 6 when the *Denver Post* pointedly asked whether he would "submit to arbitration," Mac-Neill flatly refused, wiring that there was "no trouble between our company and mill workers employed by us. Our employees are now and have been perfectly satisfied with wages and treatment. Wages paid by us more and hours less than ore reducing plants with whom we compete. Our employees don't ask to arbitrate." In contrast, officials of the WFM, although they did not actually ask the Board of Arbitration to intervene, indicated in their statements to the press a willingness to arbitrate.

Responding to the growing pressure, Peabody wired MacNeill on March 7 that a Cripple Creek strike was avoidable if he would "only agree not to discriminate against union men." Would he publish such a statement or consent to arbitration by the Board of Arbitration? If not, a strike of the Cripple Creek miners was inevitable and the results would be "deplorable."[22] Upon receipt of the telegram, MacNeill and Peck rushed to Denver where they spent most of the next day conferring with the governor. Before adjourning, they asked that he have the WFM present a formal statement of its terms, and they in turn left position papers with him.

Not yielding at all, MacNeill restated the position of the USRRC on the events of the past month. He argued that any concession to the miners' union meant further trouble, for in the past the union had interpreted compromise as weakness and this fact encouraged the growth of "intolerable" conditions in milling and mining.[23] Peck's statement was substantially the same, but he was more precise on the subject of arbitration. Because his employees were satisfied, there was no one with "whom the company could arbitrate, for the company had no dealings whatsoever with any person who manifests or expresses any dissatisfaction with the present condition of affairs."[24] Fullerton of the Telluride mill did not attend the conference, but the next day he mailed a letter to the governor stating his views. He insisted upon his right to employ the best men available, regardless of whether or not they belonged to the union. He would not, however, tolerate any anarchistic tendencies among his employees, nor any discussion of labor, political, or religious matters which interfered with mill operations.[25]

On March 8, William D. Haywood, secretary-treasurer of the WFM, complied with Peabody's request and submitted a statement of the union's terms for ending the strike. These included the eight-hour day for the millworkers, a reinstatement of the men discharged for their union membership, an end to discrimination against union members, a recognition of the right of employees to organize and affiliate with the WFM, an acceptance of the wage proposals of February 14, and arbitration of the strike by a board selected by all parties.[26] The next day the governor relayed the terms to MacNeill, Peck, and Fullerton in identical letters.[27]

Meanwhile, pressures for a rapid settlement continued to build up. Apparently unaware of the Denver conference, both houses of the General Assembly concurred in a resolution of March 9 which declared it the "duty" of the WFM and the companies to submit statements of their differences either to the governor, the Board of Arbitration, or to another acceptable arbitrator so that a settlement could be reached.[28] Mass meetings of citizens in Cripple Creek and Victor also called for a delay of the threatened miners' strike so that arbitration might be arranged. The WFM agreed to the delay.[29] Also, labor leaders indicated to the press that they were willing to arbitrate their differences with the companies, making it appear that only corporate officials blocked an immediate, peaceful settlement of the strike.

Peabody became more active on March 11 and went to Colorado City for a personal investigation, conferring with Moyer enroute. He talked with employees of the Standard mill, municipal officials, officers of the Mill and Smeltermen's Union, and company officials, but he refused to confer with the striking millworkers. At the Standard mill he had a stenographic report made of his interviews with employees who expressed satisfaction with their jobs. He did not visit the other struck mills. Nevertheless, nearly 100 of the Portland millworkers later forwarded a statement indicating they had no grievances. Not to be outdone, however, striking union members of the Telluride mill sent a statement expressing their dissatisfaction with both wages and working conditions.[30] Although Peabody concluded from his personal survey of conditions in Colorado City that the atmosphere of fear prevailing there justified the further retention of troops, he did not blame the Mill and Smeltermen's Union for this state of affairs. He placed responsibility instead upon other unnamed parties.[31] His investigation convinced him of the need for further involvement.

Despite the governor's personal investigation, demands for arbitration of the dispute increased. On March 12 a joint resolution of the General Assembly requested that the Board of Arbitration investigate the strike, find out why the National Guard had been sent, and offer its services to settle the issues.[32] That same day Peabody wrote letters to company officials and to Moyer requesting that they confer with him in Denver on March 14. His investigation, he wrote, had convinced him that he needed more information. He emphasized that the meeting he was proposing was solely for his enlightenment and that attendance would not represent any waiver of demands or concessions by the parties concerned.[33] All parties agreed to confer. Peabody had earlier asked his attorney general what authority a governor possessed under the Arbitration Act of 1897 to compel employers and their employees to arbitrate industrial disputes. Miller advised that compulsory arbitration was illegal.[34] Peabody apparently dropped whatever plans he may have had to force arbitration, and he prepared for the worst. Upon Adjutant General Bell's recommendation, he inquired of Secretary of War Elihu Root whether an "allotment of Krag guns" was available to Colorado, because a "serious strike was imminent."[35]

The Denver conference, consisting of all parties and their attorneys, representatives of the General Assembly, the adjutant general, the attorney general, and the governor, was more successful than had been expected. Officials of the Portland and Telluride companies, breaking an earlier agreement with MacNeill to stand firm, came to terms with the WFM. Their agreements incorporated the substance of the union's terms of

March 9: an eight-hour day, a guarantee of no discrimination against union men, a reinstatement of all striking workers within twenty days, and a promise to confer with a union committee on wages. (By March 23 the Portland and Telluride mills were completely unionized.)[36] MacNeill reacted to this development by withdrawing from the conference, but at the governor's request he returned the next day for further discussion. Negotiations broke down when he refused to discharge his strikebreakers to reinstate the striking millworkers and to discuss wages and union recognition. He had been prepared to concede the eight-hour day, already in effect in his mills except in a few departments, and to promise not to discriminate in the future against union men. But these concessions were not enough for Moyer and Haywood, and the strike continued.[37]

Peabody's success in partially ending the strike proved awkward for his administration. Troops remained in Colorado City, and their presence tended to validate charges that they served corporate rather than public interest. Yet the strike continued against the USRRC, the company most responsible for military intervention. Complicating matters was a civil suit instigated by the WFM on March 14 in El Paso County against officers of the National Guard and Sheriff Gilbert, alleging unlawful violations of civil liberties and illegal seizure of property. The case threatened to force a public examination of the governor's policies, for the union charged that intervention had been unnecessary and that it had occurred at the request of the USRRC to break the strike. Peabody again responded to the pressure. When negotiations collapsed between MacNeill and the WFM, he reached an agreement with union officials regarding the troops. He promised to withdraw the guard, and they agreed to drop the suit against his officers.[38] Minor disturbances and alarmist letters from Brigadier General John Chase, his field commander, and Gilbert, neither of whom wanted the soldiers deactivated, delayed the withdrawal until March 19.

Before that date, however, another crisis developed. After MacNeill's refusal to accept the terms of the WFM at the Denver conference, Moyer had gone directly to the Cripple Creek district to confer with District Union No. 1, which consisted of thirteen representatives of nine local unions. Among these were delegates of the Mill and Smeltermen's Union of Colorado City. On March 16 the District Union requested that all mine owners halt their ore shipments to the Colorado City and Florence mills of the USRRC. If they failed to comply, the miners would strike. It was now clear that the WFM intended to back up the demands of the millworkers against the USRRC by pulling out nearly 1,750 miners, 80 percent of whom were union men. Possibly fourteen mines would be closed.[39]

District businessmen, already alarmed because the week-long moratorium granted by the WFM on March 8 had expired, were thoroughly frightened by the possibility of another shutdown. Hoping to avert economic disaster for the district, Nelson Franklin, mayor of Victor and president and general manager of the Eagle Ore Sampling company, went to Colorado Springs with several associates on March 17 to plead with Mac-Neill to arbitrate. MacNeill declined because, in his opinion, there was nothing to arbitrate with his satisfied employees. However, he was willing to accept another investigation of conditions in the Standard mill to determine if there were any unknown grievances among his workers. If so, he would accept an arbitration board appointed by the governor or by the chief justice of the Colorado Supreme Court. Such a procedure obviously ignored the strikers. As for them, MacNeill agreed to their reemployment when vacancies occurred in his mills, but he had no intentions of discharging the strikebreakers to return striking millworkers to their jobs. Moyer naturally rejected a scheme based on the assumption that the striking millworkers had severed all relationship with the company and were entitled to no special consideration. MacNeill in turn rejected Franklin's proposal, endorsed by Moyer, for a three-man arbitration board—consisting of one member selected by the WFM, one appointed by MacNeill or Peabody, and the third chosen by the other two appointees—which would be empowered to settle all the issues.[40] Despite their efforts, the businessmen of Victor failed. However, because some mine owners discontinued their shipments as requested, the strike order of March 17 involved less than 800 men working in mines obligated by contract to continue shipments to the USRRC.

MacNeill's stubbornness was responsible for spreading the strike. But the absence of negotiable differences with the mine owners and the apparent injustice of striking against them when they were contractually obligated to ship ore or suffer heavy financial penalties aroused public indignation against the WFM. Opponents of labor quickly concluded that union leaders had arbitrarily called a "sympathetic strike," a conclusion that Moyer did not accept.[41]

Nevertheless, an enlarged strike now confronted the governor. In a surprise move on March 19, he issued a proclamation creating an Advisory Board to investigate the causes of the strikes, the demands of the union, and the reasons for the USRRC's stand. In addition to personal enlightenment, Peabody hoped the investigation would convince the public that his administration was doing everything possible for both the "benefit of labor and the protection of capital."[42] The members of the board were William F. Slocum, president of Colorado College; Judge Charles D. Hayt, former member of the state Supreme Court; Republican Representative Frank Frewen of Teller County; and the Reverend Thomas A. Uzzell and Father Joseph P. Carrigan, Denver ministers who were interested in labor problems. Slocum immediately asked to be relieved of the assignment, and Peabody did not appoint a replacement. In followup letters to members of the board, to MacNeill, and to Moyer, the governor indicated that he had acted upon the advice of business and labor leaders.[43]

Under the chairmanship of Judge Hayt the board on March 21 began its work in Denver, hearing first the testimony of Moyer, who blamed the strike upon the discriminatory policies of the USRRC in discharging men from the Standard mill solely because of their membership in a local of the WFM.[44] In responding to interrogation by W. K. Babbit, attorney for the USRRC, Moyer criticized state intervention and described the damaging effect which it had had upon the strike of the millworkers. He claimed that the troops had not only helped the company secure strikebreakers but that they had dispersed union pickets and made it impossible to "induce the men peacefully to discontinue work in the mills."[45] Because of the way the National

Guard had been used, according to Moyer, it had made the crucial difference between success and failure of the Mill and Smeltermen's Union to remedy conditions in the mills of the USRRC.

Speaking for the USRRC, Babbitt stated that the strike had originated in the efforts of the WFM to dictate company policy. He complained that union members had intimidated, threatened, and assaulted nonunion workers until they feared for their lives, homes, and families. The company did not regard the striking millworkers as employees. Their deserted positions had been taken by contented nonunion replacements who had been promised permanent employment. For the strikers to return to work, they would have to submit applications, which would be processed along with others without discrimination when vacancies occurred. But there would be no immediate reinstatement. As for arbitration, Babbitt insisted that there was nothing to arbitrate, for the men then employed "were contented and anxious to remain in the employ of the company."[46]

The testimony of J. D. Hawkins, general superintendent of the USRRC, generally verified Moyer's contention that the Colorado City strike resulted from the discharge of men because they dared to join the union. Hawkins admitted that he had released some individuals because they were "agitators," and he acknowledged that an employee's membership in the Mill and Smeltermen's Union was incompatible with company interests.[47] However, in later testimony, which revealed extraordinarily inept communication between key management officials, MacNeill denied that prior to newspaper stories of the strike he had had any personal knowledge of Hawkins's dismissal of workers as "agitators" or as union members.[48]

On March 28, MacNeill presented proposals to the board for a settlement of the strike. The company would grant the eight-hour day to all employees except those working in the sampling department of the mills; it would not discriminate against union employees; it would reemploy the men on strike within sixty days; and it would meet with its employees or their representatives at any time. There was nothing in these proposals to suggest a softening of MacNeill's former position. They rested on the premise that the striking millworkers were not employees of the company. All the proposals had been previously offered and rejected. But Moyer, who wanted recognition of the WFM, pushed MacNeill on the matter of meeting with representatives of the workers. Under questioning, MacNeill explained that he would meet with any committee representing the workers, but only if all its members were employees. He agreed to receive a committee composed of union men, provided it represented the majority of his employees and consisted of employees only. However, he would not immediately recognize a union committee, even if composed of employees, because the majority of his workers were then content with their situation. MacNeill pointedly refused Moyer's demand that he recognize the Mill and Smelter-men's Union and its committees, whether or not composed of employees.[49] Recognition of the WFM was unobtainable.

The principal obstacle to settlement, therefore, was the status of the striking millworkers. The WFM pushed for their immediate reinstatement to their old jobs; the company refused because it would have to discharge their replacements. At the board's request Mayor Franklin of Victor stepped in with a solution. Representing the businessmen of the Cripple Creek mining district, he offered to find a job for any striker whom the USRRC could not rehire within sixty days. Moyer rejected the offer, pointing out that some of his men owned homes and other property in Colorado City and the district was more than forty miles away. Franklin then suggested that MacNeill discharge the strike-breakers whom he had offered the same guarantee of employment. MacNeill refused. Moyer countered with a compromise proposal that the company release only the unmarried men employed as replacements, arguing that they were freer to move from Colorado City to the district. But MacNeill rejected this as contrary to promises made to the men.[50]

It was Moyer's concessions that finally led to a temporary settlement. He waived a demand for wage increases, a demand that union committees submit all employee grievances to the company, and a demand that any agreement then reached between the parties be formalized in writing. (MacNeill had rejected all written agreements because these would be tantamount to recognition of the WFM.) He acquiesced to MacNeill's absolute refusal to rehire fourteen former union employees considered to be "obnoxious" or "agitators" by the company, and he accepted MacNeill's oral promise to reinstate all the strikers within sixty days and faster if circumstances permitted.[51] Franklin recognized that Moyer's concessions had made a settlement possible, for on March 31 he praised him before the board, saying: "To thank you is not sufficient payment. You have averted what would have been probably the worse calamity that ever befell the state in your action today."[52]

Moyer, who had made concessions reluctantly, was none too pleased with the settlement. It provided the striking millworkers with little except reinstatement to their old jobs and, as MacNeill's testimony indicated, it was subject to various interpretations. Moyer distrusted MacNeill, and his distrust lingered, despite repeated assurances from members of the board that MacNeill was completely trustworthy. Moreover, the agreement was unfair to officials of the Portland and Telluride mills who at the Denver conference of March 14 had granted the union liberal concessions which now placed these mills at a competitive disadvantage with the USRRC. The Portland and Telluride officials might now insist upon reopening negotiations. Nevertheless, Moyer was willing that MacNeill have until May 18, the date when the union's executive board met prior to the annual convention of 1903, to justify the Advisory Board's faith in his integrity. Moyer expected the strikers to be reinstated in the old positions by then.[53] He thought that this could be done without discharging any of the strikebreakers simply by shifting mill personnel within the company's two mills in Colorado City, for the Colorado mill, which had been closed, was scheduled to reopen soon. But if MacNeill failed to fulfill his promises on reinstatement, the WFM's annual convention would be poised to force compliance. Thus within twelve days, Peabody's Advisory Board had found a formula for ending the strike; however, the settlement rested on an ambiguous, unwritten agreement protecting the interests of the USRRC.

Disagreements soon occurred over the interpretation and the meaning of the terms "reinstate" and "reemploy," which had been used interchangeably by both parties during the negotiations. Union leaders insisted that the agreement provided for reinstatement of the striking millworkers to the exact positions held prior to the walkout, but company officials claimed that it meant nothing more than rehiring the men as any jobs became available. Throughout April and early May the controversy persisted, preventing a complete restoration of industrial harmony in Colorado City. MacNeill further complicated the problem when he refused to consider a wage increase like that granted by the Portland and Telluride mills on May 1. Conditions were precarious when the Advisory Board convened on May 23 to determine whether or not MacNeill had fulfilled his promise.

John Murphy, an attorney for the WFM, focused upon the failure of the USRRC to reinstate the strikers to their former positions, and he questioned MacNeill's integrity.[54] This was a tactical error, for members of the Advisory Board had previously expressed great confidence in MacNeill's character and were inclined to dismiss such allegations. Moreover, Babbitt, the company's attorney, quickly exploited the blunder, saying that although peace was desirable, it could not be had at the price of surrendering "MacNeill's integrity before the people of Colorado."[55] The opening testimony of the two attorneys created an early dilemma for the board, because whatever its decision, a renewal of the strike seemed certain.

In support of the company's position, Hawkins presented a written statement in which he claimed that the USRRC had acted in good faith in offering to reemploy sixty of the seventy strikers and that all the men, except those specifically excluded by the agreement, would have been offered jobs had there been sufficient ore to resume operations in the company's Colorado mill. He emphasized that forty-seven of the sixty refused to return to work because the positions offered were not the identical ones held on February 14. Satisfactory replacements filled the original jobs, and the company had refused to discharge them. Hawkins denied that any promise had been made to reinstate the strikers in their exact pre-strike positions.[56]

Charles R. Burr, an official of the Mill and Smeltermen's Union, submitted a statement on May 26 explaining why his men refused to return to work. Some of them understood that reinstatement of their old jobs was basic to the agreement, but the men had been offered other positions. Others refused because the company offered jobs formerly held by fellow strikers who had unsuccessfully applied for reinstatement. A few rejected their former jobs because the hours had been extended from eight to ten. Others refused because their new positions would have paid less than the old.[57] And several men had refused to accept jobs paying higher wages than their old positions because they thought that the company's procedures were designed to create dissension within the union.[58]

The second round of testimony by union and mill officials showed that the failure to record the agreement of March 31 in writing, especially in regard to definition of terms, was a serious mistake. Two issues confronted the Advisory Board. First, did MacNeill promise to reemploy the strikers to fill whatever vacancies occurred in the mills, or did he promise to reinstate them to their old positions? Second, did MacNeill discriminate against union men by offering jobs which he manipulated to assure their refusal, or did he act in good faith and try to choose the best men available for the vacancies that occurred? In reporting to Peabody, members of the Advisory Board opted in favor of MacNeill. They concluded that he had only promised to reemploy the striking millworkers as vacancies occurred and that he had made "all possible efforts to reemploy the striking mill men" in conformity with that promise. Furthermore, he had "faithfully carried out" his pledge not to discriminate against union men when employing new personnel.[59] Their conclusions had the effect of placing responsibility for the continuing unrest in Colorado City upon union leaders.

Although the report of the Advisory Board absolved MacNeill of responsibility for the labor trouble in the mills of the USRRC, the evidence suggests that he was not entirely blameless. It is true that he had consistently refused to discharge the strikebreakers to rehire the striking millworkers and that his interpretation of the agreement of March 31 conformed with his prior stand on this point. But reinstatement as interpreted and voiced in the union complaint might have been reconciled with the continued employment of the strikebreakers had MacNeill been more conciliatory. On May 23, Murphy stated to the Advisory Board that the major complaint of the WFM was the failure of the USRRC to reinstate union men to their old jobs when vacancies in the mill made it possible to do so. He suggested that the company was deliberately preventing the strikers from reassuming their former positions even when these were vacant. MacNeill could thus have removed a major grievance with a very minor concession, but he did not make it. Nor should his refusal to commit the agreement of March 31 to writing be overlooked. He rejected this procedure because it was equivalent to recognizing the WFM as the negotiating agent of the striking millworkers, whose relationship with the USRRC, from his standpoint, had been severed. In contrast, Moyer was anxious that the agreement be written, a procedure that might have averted the squabble over definitions. Furthermore, it was Moyer's concessions that had made even possible an oral agreement. MacNeill's unbending attitude had much to do with the breakdown of the agreement, for he was not prepared to make any substantive concession whatsoever in the interest of industrial peace in Colorado City.

The precarious truce ended on July 3 when the Mill and Smeltermen's Union resumed its strike against the USRRC. Ironically, pressure upon the union from MacNeill's former colleagues, Peck and Fullerton, was instrumental in forcing the renewal. These men had raised wages in their mills with the understanding that the USRRC would follow suit, and they now threatened a reduction to the old wage level unless MacNeill's company met their higher scale. The renewed strike, therefore, was called not only to bring about reinstatement as interpreted by the union but to force wages up in the mills of the USRRC to maintain wage increases in the Portland and Telluride mills.

The WFM's unresolved difficulties with the USRRC remained a festering sore which threatened at any time to reinvolve the important Cripple Creek district. This was unfortunate, because already other strikes of the miners' union were underway elsewhere in Colorado, adding new dimensions to the industrial unrest. Furthermore, the failure of the Advisory Board to reach a permanent settlement and its final report relieving officials of the USRRC of responsibility for the lingering problem in Colorado City had a major impact upon the thinking of Peabody. Although rash in ordering troops into the strike zone, he had eventually bowed to public pressure and withdrawn the National Guard, and he had then attempted to settle the strike by

other-than-military means. His failure in Colorado City apparently convinced him that, despite the conciliatory posture of
Moyer, persuasions were futile when dealing with the WFM.
During the spring and summer of 1903 the governor fell under
the influence of the state's employers, who were flocking into an
emerging employers' movement in an organization called the
citizens' alliance, a body specifically created to discipline militant labor unions like the WFM. Thus, for the industrial history
of Colorado and the West, the Colorado City strike was an important turning point because it helped to place the resources of
the Peabody administration at the disposal of forces destined to
break the miners' union in the name of law and order. Thereafter the fusion of corporate and government power was rapid,
accelerated by the increasing labor troubles throughout the state
and the alleged threat to the prevailing society posed by the
WFM with its socialist leaders.

4

Link Up: Peabody and the Employers' Movement

The Peabody administration coincided with the rapid growth of a national employers' movement which was to exert a powerful influence on industrial relations and public affairs throughout the nation. Nowhere was the movement more pronounced than in Colorado, where employers, fearfully reacting to the increasing power, the militancy, and the radical tendencies of unions like the Western Federation of Miners, enthusiastically joined the drive to discipline labor. Employers were prepared to support any means of reestablishing their unquestioned control over business and industrial matters. Consequently, they did not hesitate to use Peabody, who was politically in their debt and likely to use the power of the state in their behalf. In time, the governor joined their campaign against militant labor unions, particularly against the WFM. An important step in this alliance was his connection with the citizens' alliance organizations.

At the time of Peabody's inauguration there were only a few employers' associations in the nation which were working effectively against union labor. The groups, linked only by their consuming hostility toward organized labor, were located principally in Ohio, Illinois, Missouri, and Wisconsin. There they fought the unions to a standstill in open shop campaigns that emphasized the employer's right to manage his business without interference from labor. These organizations were not content with destroying militant unionism, and, in the words of two historians, ambitiously tried to erase the "organized labor pattern from the consciousness of the average American citizen" by the adroit use of propaganda which placed "organized labor on a moral defensive." [1] They skillfully cloaked their public releases in the rhetoric of American individualism, and they convincingly portrayed union members and leaders as tyrants who oppressed the community and victimized the employer. Their propaganda proved successful in rallying local communities to support crusades against specific unions. Perceptive employers, watching these effective experiments in union control, decided that organized labor could be checked if they organized and marshalled public opinion behind their cause. What was obviously needed was a nationwide anti-union effort, one which would both curtail labor's growth and reduce its power in the economy. That kind of effort, however, required a type of leadership, organization, and commitment absent prior to 1903, when Peabody assumed office.

In April 1903 a powerful and dynamic leader for the incipient employers' movement came to prominence as David M. Parry delivered his presidential address to the annual convention of the National Association of Manufacturers. His speech was a diatribe against organized labor, and it played upon the growing hostility of many delegates toward militant unions like the WFM. Describing union practices as "un-American," Parry asserted that trade unionism and socialism differed only in method—the former relying on force and the latter on the ballot to forge a social order which denied "individual and property rights." He claimed that the efforts of unions to obtain wage-hour legislation, participate in industrial decisions, and acquire a larger share of the products of industry for the workingman interfered in the natural laws which governed the nation's economy. He argued that union's goals ultimately would lead to "despotism, tyranny, and slavery" and the "ruin of civilization." "Freedom," "justice," and "progress," he insisted, lay in maintaining the old system of unfettered economic freedom. Parry also charged that unions recruited members by intimidation; that union members were "men of muscles rather than men of intelligence"—mere puppets who depended upon the "brains of others for guidance"; that the AFL was a breeder of "boycotters, picketers, and socialists"; that conciliation was a "myth" and arbitration was a "failure" as a means of settling industrial disputes; that unions denied individual workers the "right" to sell their labor as they saw fit and bullied unyielding employers into accepting unreasonable terms; and that union leaders preached "hatred of wealth and ability." In his opinion, organized labor knew but "one law, and that is the law of physical force—the law of the Huns and the Vandals, the law of the savage." It did not rely on "reason and justice, but on strikes, boycotts, and coercion. It is in all essential features a mob power, knowing no master except its own will, and is continually condemning or defying the constituted authorities." Such a threat to public safety and individual freedom had to be contained, he argued.[2]

To control the menace, Parry recommended that the NAM assume responsibility for organizing employers and manufacturers' associations into a great national anti-union federation. The convention, with only minor opposition, created a nine-man committee, headed by Parry, and empowered it to mobilize the nation's employers. It then issued a statement of principles regarding industrial relations. Although embellished with the rhetoric of reasonableness and fair play, the statement emphasized the employers' right to operate without interference from unions and became the public rationale of the employers' movement.[3]

Parry lost no time in opening the campaign. In an April meeting with representatives of various employers' associations he helped to formulate plans for intensifying the "open shop" crusade already underway, organizing additional groups, and combining them into a powerful national organization.[4] Among those present at the conference in Chicago was James C. Craig, president of the recently formed Citizens' Alliance of Denver, who was to play a vital role in mustering opposition to the WFM in Colorado during Peabody's administration. Through the presence of Craig, who represented the organized employers of the state's largest city, Colorado's embryonic alliance movement was linked to Parry's nationwide anti-union effort at its inception. The combination was mutually beneficial, for each contributed materially to the success of the other.

Herbert George, editor of *George's Weekly* (Denver), the voice of Colorado's local alliances, was the principal founder of the Denver alliance and a major force in establishing similar groups elsewhere. But it was Craig who led and directed the statewide fight of the organized employers against union labor.[5] He successfully extended the Denver organization's influence far beyond the city limits into the distant mining camps and industrial towns. What began as a local response to the annual springtime disruption of Denver business by strikes over wages, hours, the hiring of union labor, and the use of union labels escalated under Craig into a statewide drive to protect all employers against alleged coercive measures of the unions.[6] Within three weeks after its creation on April 9, the Citizens' Alliance of Denver had enrolled nearly 3,000 individual and corporate members, had found a war chest of nearly $20,000, had adopted a constitution, and had obtained the support of the highly influential *Denver Republican*. However, the alliance met immediate resistance from the unions and from labor organs like the *Colorado Chronicle*, which recognized it as a genuine threat to organized labor.[7]

The constitution of the alliance contained clear ideological links to the statement of principles issued by the NAM's annual convention of 1903. Both sought to encourage business stability by discouraging boycotts, strikes, lockouts, etc., by promoting friendly employer-employee relations; both wanted the recognition of the right of the workingman to work without interference and union membership; and both considered it a truism that an employer had the right of absolute control over the management of his business.[8] However, just as Parry's presidential address more accurately revealed the intent of the national employers' movement than the NAM's statement of principles, Craig's letter of May 13 to T. E. McKenna, managing editor of the *Rocky Mountain News*, more accurately revealed the objectives of the alliance. He wrote that the employers of Denver had organized to uphold certain "elementary truths": first, the freedom of the worker to quit a job and that of the employer to fire an employee for whatever reason at any time in the absence of a contract, thus making the two equal; second, a worker's automatic loss of any claim to a job when he struck or when his employer locked him out; third, the right of a workingman to organize into unions which, nevertheless, had no right to interfere in an employer's business, especially in filling vacancies, intimidating nonunion labor, and coercive picketing; fourth, the use of violence in labor disputes by either party was "indefensible, un-American, criminal and lawless" and ought to be condemned.[9] Craig's elementary truths upheld the exclusive right of an employer to determine business and industrial matters without reference to the unions, thereby rendering them ineffective as means of improving the lot of the workingman.

Although the initial constitution of the alliance did not specifically bar organized workingmen from membership, it imposed requirements which reflected a strong anti-union bias and drew few workers as affiliates. After promising to abide by the constitution and bylaws and pledging never to reveal what was said or done either by the organization or any of its members, an applicant had to affirm that he was not a member of any union which used boycotts or illegal coercion and to agree "to discountenance all strikes and schemes of persecution resorted to by organized labor." Also, no one could be enrolled without the endorsement of at least two members.[10] Membership was thus restricted to those persons in fundamental agreement with the necessity of constraining organized labor. The absence of a clause specifically prohibiting union members from joining did not diminish its anti-union character and objectives. The organization's clandestine character should not be overlooked. Enshrouding in deep secrecy all the inner workings of the body raised the possibility that the group might take extralegal action against all organized labor. Significantly, other alliances in Colorado patterned their constitutions after that of the Denver alliance.

Led by Craig, the alliance experienced early success in its bouts with the unions of Denver, and it gained quick prestige among employers throughout the state. Its formula for success was first revealed when nearly 160 of the 200 employees of the Hurlbut Grocery Company, a corporate member of the alliance, struck on May 9. Craig exploited the situation to test the power of the alliance by using threats of an employer boycott against the company and prevented an amicable settlement of the dispute.[11] Other strikes involving various trades then erupted. Although they threatened to paralyze the city, the strikes enlarged the opportunity for a showdown with the unions which Craig craved. He assumed in the name of the alliance the sole responsibility for dealing with the striking unions. It was Craig who represented the struck employers before the Denver Fire and Police Board, which had worked for an early settlement of the disputes. It was Craig who insisted that the alliance was the sole bargaining agent of the city's employers and that the unions must recognize this fact. It was Craig who rejected an offer of the State Board of Arbitration to negotiate a settlement of the strikes until the unions agreed to deal with the alliance. His adamant insistence upon negotiations between organized bodies so thoroughly blocked progress toward settlement that on May 15 about 8,000 workers of twenty-one trades were on strike against various businesses of Denver.

Union leaders were determined not to deal with the alliance because to them it was a "strikebreaking and labor union destroying organization" and initially rejected Craig's demands that they recognize his association. But when the conservative Typographical Union created a "Peace Commission" of six businessmen to help end the strike, the unions and the alliance, responding to increasing public pressure for a settlement, utilized its services to reach an agreement on May 21. The settlement provided for an arbitration board composed of an equal number of struck employers and union representatives whose decision on the issues would be final. However, the board never reached a settlement because a few days after the agreement was made, union leaders charged that the city's employers were violating their interim pledge to reinstate without prejudice their employees who had struck. As a result, the employers freed the unions to pursue their traditional methods in settling the disputes. Craig denied that any promise of reinstatement had been made and insisted that the agreement of May 21 meant only that each workingman was free to sell his labor to whomever he pleased and that each employer was free to hire whomever he pleased.

By coincidence, the dispute over reinstatement occurred simultaneously with that raging between the WFM and the USRRC over a similar issue at Colorado City. In both cases, labor failed to uphold its position. The duel between the unions and the alliance in Denver ended in a clear victory for the latter, for the momentum of the earlier strikes dissipated and could not be recovered in the face of increasing resistance from the alliance. A powerful employers' association which stopped the unions of Denver in their tracks and forced them to extend de facto recognition to it as the sole representative of the city's employers had emerged out of the struggle. The alliance's victory had the added significance of damaging the prestige throughout the state of Moyer and Haywood. They had failed to force the USRRC to raise wages and to reinstate its striking millworkers, and, rumor had it, they also led the unsuccessful struggle for the unions of Denver.[12] Craig had demonstrated to the businessmen of Colorado that when they were properly organized, they were more than a match for the unions, perhaps even the WFM.

As if to emphasize that point, Craig deliberately intervened in a strike called by the Denver Mill and Smeltermen's Union, No. 93, WFM, against the American Smelting and Refining Company (ASRC), the so-called "smelter trust," whose Globe and Grant mills were located in Denver. The failure of Peabody and the Fourteenth General Assembly to pass an eight-hour law, although authorized to do so by a constitutional amendment of 1902, led to the conclusion by several locals of the WFM that the only way to obtain the eight-hour day was through direct action against their employers. They resorted to strikes to obtain by force what apparently could not be obtained through constitutional and legislative processes. When Franklin Guiterman, general manager of the ASRC, refused to concede the eight-hour day in the company's Denver mills because of adverse economic conditions, members of the millworkers' union met with Moyer and Haywood on the night of July 3 and voted to strike immediately.[13] After the meeting union members went into the mills, forced the working employees out—beating and kicking those

71

who resisted—and ruined a number of furnaces by outing the fires.

In an interview on July 4, Moyer placed responsibility for the strike on Peabody and the assembly for their failure to heed the mandate of the people and enact an eight-hour law. Labor, having failed to acquire the shorter day through established political procedures, now had no alternative but to strike.[14] However, Guiterman denied that the eight-hour question was the central issue in the strike. What was really involved was whether corporations like the ASRC were to be dominated and dictated to by labor unions like the WFM, he said. From his standpoint, the eight-hour question was irrelevant and had been raised only to hide the union's drive to control the mining and milling industry in Colorado.[15] Guiterman's conception of the strike found ready acceptance among the conservative elements of Denver who, like the *Denver Republican* of July 7, threw their support behind the company because they believed that the dispute had been caused by a "cabal" of labor agitators who were interested only in creating trouble.

Craig swung the alliance behind the ASRC, not a surprising move because James B. Grant, an official of the company, was an influential member of the organization. Craig formally offered two kinds of aid to company officials: first, legal assistance in prosecuting any striking worker who broke the law and, second, help in rounding up strikebreakers. Other assistance was later extended. In an obvious play for public support, resolutions condemning the union for using force and destroying property poured forth from alliance headquarters, along with pledges to protect the company and anyone willing to work when production was resumed.[16] Craig and Guiterman together conferred with city officials about extra policemen to protect the mills if they reopened, with the result that Denver officials assumed the cost of preserving order around the mills.[17] This joining of corporate, municipal, and alliance power against the union virtually assured its defeat. Gradually the strike of the millworkers became overshadowed by the more dramatic clashes between capital and labor which erupted elsewhere in Colorado in the summer and early fall of 1903.

Denver's employers, fully supported by the alliance and municipal authorities, successfully resumed operations in the face of the strikes without state intervention. Although Peabody had remained aloof from the city's labor troubles, he was nevertheless implicated in the strike against the ASRC because of his stand on the controversial eight-hour question. The Fourteenth General Assembly had adjourned without enacting an eight-hour law. Divided political control of the assembly, political maneuvering and bickering, corporate propaganda, lobbying, and possibly outright bribery all combined to defeat the measure. Responsibility rested with both parties. Peabody, whose party controlled the lower house, demonstrated a singular lack of interest in eight-hour legislation. He had conspicuously failed to mention the eight-hour amendment or to recommend the passage of legislation regulating hours of labor in his inaugural address. Furthermore, during the legislative squabbling over the question, he refused to commit himself either for or against the bills introduced by the various factions. That his party had pledged its candidates to support an "adequate" eight-hour law made little difference to Peabody, and his failure to exert positive leadership undoubtedly influenced Republican members of the assembly. Peabody thus bore substantial responsibility for the assembly's inability to come up with a bill satisfactory to all parties, although he later tried to deny responsibility when the WFM exploited the failure to justify widespread strikes throughout the state.[18]

As early as April 7, one day after the assembly adjourned, the *Denver Post* had advocated a special session to reconsider eight-hour legislation, arguing that this was a wholesome alternative to direct action by labor. Similar advice came from other sources, but the governor ignored it. However, when the Colorado Supreme Court declared null and void a general appropriations act after its legality had been challenged by Senator T. M. Patterson, owner of the *Rocky Mountain News*, Peabody had no choice but to call an extra session of the legislature to obtain vital operating funds. But in his call of July 6 he refused to include the eight-hour matter and limited the legislature to acting on general appropriations. At the time the WFM was strik-

ing for the eight-hour day against the ASRC and the mine owners of Idaho Springs, and its millworkers were threatening strikes
in Pueblo and Leadville. On July 3 the union had renewed its
strike against the USRRC in Colorado City, possibly timing the
renewal to exert pressure upon the governor to place the eight-
hour question on the agenda of the extra session. But most significant was the WFM's appeal of July 11 for an eight-hour fund.
It was obvious that the union was preparing to force the issue,
taking from the employers what could not be obtained through
the legislative process. It was equally obvious that the employers were determined to resist.

Despite these predictions of industrial turmoil, Peabody resisted new demands for a supplementary call to allow
the eight-hour matter to be reconsidered. Writing to John C.
Osgood, chairman of the board of the Colorado Fuel and Iron
Company, whose opposition had helped to block the passage of
a bill to regulate hours during the regular session, Peabody
claimed that his stand at Colorado City and his resistance to a
supplementary call were but attempts to do his "duty, and to
preserve the commercial and industrial enterprises of Colorado
from assault and annihilation." He indicated that he would stand
fast in protecting the individual and corporate enterprises which
the state depended on.[19]

Not even a joint resolution of the special session
asking for a supplementary call altered his stand.[20] Four days before their adjournment Peabody informed legislative leaders that
before he would issue such a call, they must agree on an acceptable eight-hour bill and sign a statement that they would support it. Their inability to hammer out a compromise measure
allowed Peabody to announce on July 25 that he would not issue
the call. Logic seemed to support his position. Why should the
taxpayers finance a useless debate? His correspondence suggests,
however, that he had maneuvered the assembly into providing a
much-wanted escape from personal involvement in the eight-
hour question. In a letter of July 24 to M. D. Thatcher, president
of the First National Bank of Pueblo, he wrote:

> I have at no time seriously considered the calling of an
> extra session of our legislature for the purpose of con-
> sidering an Eight-Hour Law, and the present legislature,

74

convened in extra session, is expending much time and large sums of public money in consideration of and passing resolutions bearing upon this subject, which have no manner of weight or influence, and upon which question they have not been asked to either legislate or express an opinion.[21]

It appears likely that Peabody would have vetoed any eight-hour measure resulting from a supplementary call, even if the leaders had reached an agreement.

 The governor's rejection of the supplementary call placed him in line with all those interests which had opposed the passage of eight-hour legislation, including leading corporations and employers' associations like the Colorado Fuel and Iron Company, the ASRC, the Victor Fuel Company, and the Citizens' Alliance of Denver. His refusal to be bound by the mandate of the people and his party and the Republican platform of 1902 was a major cause of the strikes which beset his administration and of his growing identification with the alliance movement. The enactment of an eight-hour law would have removed a major grievance of the millworkers and the miners, possibly precluding the strikes against the ASRC and that of Idaho Springs Miners' Union, No. 136, WFM, against the mine owners of Clear Creek County. It was the latter which further exposed the predisposition of the governor to side with the employers and led to his first official contact with Craig of the Denver alliance.

 The miners' union of Idaho Springs, having failed to obtain the shorter workday through legislative enactment, demanded in April that the mine owners accept the eight-hour day as the standard for the district. When the owners rejected this demand, the union struck on May 1 and shut down mining operations on the properties of six companies. Although the owners of three concerns soon conceded the shorter day, the others remained adamantly opposed. When the Sun and Moon mine resumed production with strikebreakers, trouble erupted. On the night of July 28 an explosion shattered the powerhouse of the mine, but none of the nineteen men working in the immediate area were injured. Deputies found Phillip Fire, a WFM member who had been mortally wounded in the blast, on a hillside nearby and hastily concluded that the striking miners were responsible for what had happened. That night and the next morning local officials arrested prominent union members.

The incident at the Sun and Moon mine provoked a quick response from the Citizens' Protective League, an employers' association whose membership included, according to the *Denver Post* of July 30, the "best citizens" of Idaho Springs. For several months prior to the explosion, the league had infiltrated the union with spies who reported that union leaders and "agitators" were inflaming the rank and file with "incendiary" talk in support of the strike for an eight-hour day.[22] It had also established contact with the Denver alliance. On September 10 the *Colorado Springs Gazette* reported that the night before the destruction of the powerhouse Craig had been in Idaho Springs consulting with officials of the league. Just as Craig had assumed command of anti-union forces in the Denver strikes, officials of the league took charge in Idaho Springs and, for all practical purposes, displaced the local authorities. This was the first takeover of civil government by an employers' association which occurred during the Peabody administration. The league was responsible for what happened to the union members who were swept up in the dragnet following the blast.

Determined to exploit the surge of anti-union sentiment generated by the Sun and Moon outrage, officials of the league decided that the most effective way to stop the thrust for an eight-hour day was to drive union leaders from the district. However, despite their control of the community, the league hesitated to use this drastic measure without public endorsement. On the night of July 29, after a day of angry threats to dynamite the jail and its prisoners, nearly 500 citizens, including the majority of the town's businessmen, convened at the call of the league to plan a course of action. City officials openly participated in the proceedings. Prominent residents like Lafayette Hanchette, president of the First National Bank, whipped up the emotions of the crowd with inflammatory speeches which condemned the WFM, blamed its local officials for the powerhouse episode, and demanded that the men arrested and jailed for the crime be driven out of town. Moderates who counseled against mob action and urged that the guilt of the prisoners be determined by due process were ignored. At the end of the meeting the crowd left for the jail. There the leaders obtained custody of fourteen of the twenty-three prisoners—all union men—whom they ran out of town with strict warnings that they never return to Clear Creek County.[23] Within two days the other nine had also been banished.

The league, whose motto was "They Who Furnish the Capital Should Conduct the Business. Law and Order First—Politics, Creeds and Unions Afterwards," stepped up its campaign against the union on July 30 with a statement defending the humaneness of the expulsions and expressing a strong determination never to submit to the dictates of "imported union agitators." League officials also took steps to counter possible retaliation from the union: they directed law enforcement, held secret strategy sessions, ordered the arrest and interrogation of suspects whom they held incommunicado, watched incoming trains, and warned union sympathizers to leave town.[24]

Reaction throughout the state to this brazen, illegal exercise of power was predictable. Impartial newspapers like the *Denver Post* and pro-labor organs like the *Rocky Mountain News* soundly condemned the league, but anti-union papers like the *Denver Republican*, holding that responsible citizens were justified in using force to protect their industries from disruption by irresponsible labor agitators, exonerated the league and blamed the union for the trouble at Idaho Springs.[25] Employers' organizations naturally rallied behind the league. Craig encouraged all "good" and "law-abiding" citizens to withdraw their support from newspapers like the *Rocky Mountain News*, which had a pro-labor editorial policy.[26] Moreover, on August 3 the Denver alliance passed resolutions which charged that there was an "inner circle" within the WFM that encouraged violence and destruction of property, and it defended the action of the league in terms of "expediency," "self-preservation," "necessity," "law and order," and a "higher law," rhetoric which often appeared in later alliance propaganda in defense of extreme measures used against the WFM.[27] Wherever the employers had organized, they demonstrated vociferous support for their colleagues in Idaho Springs who had solved their labor troubles by force.

The success of the league in thwarting the drive of the WFM for an eight-hour day gave employers a decisive weapon—banishment from a community of those labor leaders who called strikes when their demands had been rejected. However, the expulsion could not be permanent unless it was sanctioned by government authority, as had been the case in Idaho Springs where civil officials allowed the league to usurp the power of their offices. But how would Peabody and the courts respond if the banished miners appealed to them? Further use of expulsion to break strikes clearly depended upon the attitudes of the governor and the courts.

Peabody became directly involved when a five-man committee representing the banished miners wrote him on July 31 to request that he intervene in the interest of justice. They charged that although the expelled miners were innocent of any crime, the league, "aided and abetted by civil authorities," had arrested, imprisoned, and banished them "without warrant or due process of law."[28] The appeal embarrassed the governor. He had refused to receive the committee, and he told reporters that he had not been asked to intervene, although his private secretary had indicated otherwise.[29] Another source also pressured the governer in this instance. Craig, hoping to prevent Peabody's intervention, wired that the Denver alliance hoped that he would "recognize the gravity of the situation that caused such action ⌊banishment of the miners] and concur with us in the view that their [members' of the League] conduct was necessary and justifiable for safety and self-defense."[30]

When he had ordered troops to Colorado City, Peabody had displayed a strong tendency to uphold the law at all cost. He had repeatedly justified his military intervention there as necessary to prevent an expected outbreak of violence. In Idaho Springs violence was not an expectation but a reality, and the breakdown of law and order was apparent. How he reacted to the petition, therefore, was an important indication of his attitude on the impending clash between labor and capital in Colorado and of his proclivity to use the power of the state in the struggle. His response acquired an even greater significance when the league issued a statement that the banished men had been "conducted out of town for good" and that their appeals to the governor and other authorities were futile.[31] The message was clear: force had been used to expel them and, if necessary, it would be employed to keep them out. If Peabody intervened in behalf of ·the miners, even in the name of "justice" or "law and order," he would alienate his strongest supporters. He elected not to act.

In the governor's opinion, the plight of the petitioners was a matter for the courts to rule on, and any action on his part would be an unconstitutional exercise of judicial powers. Furthermore, the legal prerequisites necessary to order out the guard on behalf of the miners (that is, the exhaustion of all avenues of civil relief and the acknowledged inability of local authorities to preserve order and their formal request for state aid) had not been satisfied. Consequently, he claimed to have "no right, power, or authority" under the constitution to intervene in behalf of the banished miners.[32] Peabody's position was legally correct. Under the conditions existing in Idaho Springs there was no way to satisfy the legal requirements for military intervention unless union members overthrew the local government and replaced it with one sympathetic to their cause. What influence Craig's telegram and the bellicose announcements of the league had in shaping the governor's stand cannot be determined, but his inaction was tantamount to support of the league. Organized labor, especially the WFM, had further cause to view the governor's course with apprehension and to question his commitment to law and order.

Failing to obtain protection from the governor, the banished miners turned to the courts. District Judge Frank W. Owers, a Populist whose anger had been aroused by the expulsions, granted an injunction ordering the league not to interfere with the miners' return to Idaho Springs.[33] Eight of the men then returned, only to be arrested and charged with the destruction of the powerhouse. However, when they were tried, all were acquitted. The union countered by having Owers issue bench warrants leading to the arrest of 129 men who were charged with "rioting and making threats and assaults." But the district attorney, who had cooperated with the league, chose not to prosecute because of insufficient evidence and the enormous cost to the county if each man insisted on a separate trial.[34] The litigation brought little relief. Like the strike of the millworkers of Denver, that of the miners failed to obtain the eight-hour day and was therefore a shattering defeat for the WFM. The WFM's power was broken in Clear Creek County because the mine owners now refused to hire its members. Once again an association of local employers, with the aid of government, had taken the measure of the WFM.

As the state's labor troubles proliferated, Peabody's relationship with the alliance movement strengthened. Employers in the mining and industrial towns, impressed by the defeat of the WFM in Denver and Idaho Springs, called on Craig for assistance in organizing to resist the accelerating campaign for the eight-hour day which the union had launched in July. With the approval of the Denver alliance and with the support of newspapers like the *Denver Republican*, Craig and George eagerly organized similar organizations, doing for Colorado what Parry of the NAM was doing for the nation. The governor, whose troubles with the WFM were increasing, recognized the potential of these associations for forcing local unions into line, and in September he asked Craig "to induce the businessmen of Canon City to form a Citizens' Alliance" similar to that in Denver. In a letter of September 24, Craig recommended to Peabody that he "quietly prepare a list . . . of a dozen or so good, strong businessmen" who were sympathetic to the movement. Craig promised to confer with them on how best to proceed.[35] Within two days Peabody had submitted the names. Unable to visit Canon City immediately because of a previous commitment in Chicago, Craig forwarded "complete data relating to the formation of a Citizens' Alliance" to W. T. Bridwell, a leading businessman of Canon City, and asked that he contact the others named by the governor.[36] By November 26 an alliance organization with a membership estimated at 400 to 500 operated in Peabody's hometown.[37] In February 1904 the governor finally joined the alliance.

During the strikes and the fight over eight-hour legislation other evidence accumulated which suggested that an understanding regarding labor problems had been reached between the governor and employers. In his inaugural address, Peabody had stated that "an efficient, well-equipped and well disciplined national guard" was an effective means of preserving "domestic tranquillity" and had recommended various steps to upgrade the military arm of the state.[38] Because he used the guard so frequently in connection with labor strife, his military appointments, particularly those given to labor's opponents, are most significant.

To the office of adjutant general, a post of extensive power under the National Guard Act (1897), Peabody appointed Sherman M. Bell. Who recommended Bell is a mystery, for the governor's appointment files contain nothing to identify his supporters.[39] Several factors may have influenced the choice. Bell had served under Theodore Roosevelt in Cuba, where his conduct under fire had inspired Roosevelt to scribble a note of praise on the back of Bell's discharge papers. Roosevelt may have personally engineered the appointment, not only as a favor to Bell but to other supporters as well, for rumors circulated that he had exerted his influence on behalf of certain "interests" in Colorado.[40] Certainly Peabody was obligated to Roosevelt, whose supporters had backed him for the gubernatorial nomination. Moreover, when he was appointed, Bell was a mine manager for the Smith-Moffat interests in Independence, a thriving gold camp in the Cripple Creek mining district with a history marked by sporadic outbreaks of violence in labor troubles. Through the years Bell had been strongly anti-labor.[41] His appointment undoubtedly had the endorsement of every mine owner in the state. As manager Bell's annual salary was $5,000; as adjutant general, it would be $1,800. If he remained in office for two years, he stood to lose $6,400. This fact caused the *Colorado Chronicle*, a strong pro-labor organ, to charge on February 25 that Bell had been appointed at the demand of the mine owners, who had agreed to pay him the difference in salary. The *Chronicle* further alleged that the appointment was part of a plot against organized labor, especially the WFM, whereby strikes and violence would be provoked and blamed upon the WFM to justify using the guard to crush the union.

In the absence of concrete evidence, whether or not Peabody was involved with the mine owners in a plot against the WFM must remain conjecture. However, his ready use of the guard against the union and his rejection of its use in behalf of union members was a notable characteristic of his administration. The appointment of Bell, an arrogant megalomaniac who thought that all labor problems involving the WFM were susceptible to a military solution, helped to stamp Peabody as definitely anti-labor among the state's workingmen.[42] If Bell's close identification with the mine owners of Cripple Creek and his well known hostility to unionism lent creditability to the charges levied by the *Colorado Chronicle*, certainly his extensive use of the guard against the WFM, authorized by Peabody, added further substantiation. In any case, Bell provided a vital link between Peabody and the mine owners of the state, who in 1902 had begun to beef up their associations for the purpose of stopping the WFM.

Peabody's appointment of John Q. MacDonald as secretary of the State Military Board on October 6 undoubtedly influenced his labor policy. Ordinarily this post was inconsequential, because the secretary was not an official member of the board and simply recorded the proceedings. However, MacDonald was the manager of the Union smelter at Florence, one of seven mills owned by the United States Reduction and Refining Company. The WFM had renewed its strike against the USRRC in July after the collapse of the agreement put together by Peabody's Advisory Board. MacDonald's position was unique. He remained as manager of the mill while serving as military secretary. He was in a position to inform his employers, and through them every employers' association in the state, of every item of business handled by the board. Letters of transmittal accompanying his reports to Peabody bore the letterhead of the USRRC.[43] MacDonald seems to have been the choice of Bell, whose troops were then occupying the Cripple Creek district to break a strike which the WFM had called to support the millworkers of Colorado City against the USRRC.

The National Guard Act (1897) permitted the governor to appoint two or more aides-de-camp, each with the rank of colonel, to his military staff. Under normal circumstances these positions were honorary and important only for their social value. But the appointment on May 5 of Spencer Penrose, treasurer of the USRRC, as an aide-de-camp revealed more than the governor's desire to honor an old friend, award an outstanding citizen, or add one of Colorado's most prominent citizens to his staff. At the time of the appointment the millworkers' union of Colorado City was charging that the USRRC had violated the agreement reached by the Advisory Board. On July 27, Peabody appointed

Charles M. MacNeill, vice-president and general manager of the USRRC, to his staff. At the time the millworkers had renewed their strike, and the strike of the miners of the Cripple Creek district was in the offing. Others closely associated with the company received appointments. These included Sheriff Gilbert of El Paso County, who had been instrumental in obtaining troops for MacNeill, and D. C. Jackling, a metallurgist at the USRRC's plant in Canon City who was to make millions for his employers in Utah copper.[44] Throughout his term Peabody enjoyed a close relationship with Penrose and MacNeill, whom he called his "two Colorado Springs Colonels" and thought of as "jolly good fellows."[45]

Peabody's military appointments clearly exposed his sympathies and identified him with the enemies of the WFM. Certainly he must have realized the implications of appointing men known to be hostile to organized labor and officials of a company which the guard had recently served. There were other appointments which were also closely connected with corporations, but none so blatantly revealed the governor's desire to protect business interests than those of Bell, MacDonald, Penrose, MacNeill, Gilbert, and Jackling. When the great strikes erupted in Cripple Creek, and Telluride, the employers of Colorado knew that help was available in Denver if it was requested.

5

The "Labor Wars" at Cripple Creek

During his first eight months as governor Peabody had convinced organized labor that it should expect nothing from him but indifference. He had revealed that when requested to do so he would use the power of the state in behalf of employers beset by strikes and that he would not intervene in behalf of militant unionists, even if necessary to safeguard their civil rights against mob action. On July 3 when the millworkers of Colorado City renewed their strike against the United States Reduction and Refining Company, organized labor in Colorado realized that the state government was anything but an impartial force.

Unlike the strikes against the American Smelting and Refining Company and the mining companies of Idaho Springs, the millworkers' strike did not stem from the eight-hour day question but rather from unresolved differences over reinstatement and the USRRC's refusal to raise its minimum wage to that prevailing in the mills of its Colorado City competitors. Nevertheless, after the WFM had suffered defeats in eight-hour strikes in Denver and Idaho Springs and after it had launched a formal drive in July for the eight-hour day, the success of the millworkers became imperative if the union's prestige in Colorado was to be maintained. It is unlikely, as one historian has maintained, that union officials subsequently involved the Cripple Creek miners merely to show by a "spectacular display" of power their unhappiness at failing to obtain eight-hour legislation.[1] Such a conclusion ignores the strike of the miners in March in support of the millworkers as well as the industrial character of the WFM. It also ignores the resolution, adopted by the annual convention of 1903 and subsequently embodied in a constitutional amendment, which empowered the executive board "to call out every member of the Federation when they see fit in the interest of the Federation" without the vote of the locals as was formerly required.[2] This action, which was taken while the convention debated whether to call out the Cripple Creek miners a second time and before the eight-hour strikes of July had occurred, suggested that the WFM had no intention of deserting the millworkers and that its officials were even then maneuvering to focus the total power of the union on the USRRC. Furthermore, the Cripple Creek miners had recognized that another effort might be necessary on behalf of the millworkers. They had authorized District Union No. 1, composed of thirteen representatives from the district's eight locals and the millmen's union of Colorado City, to call a strike when necessary without reference to the locals. Thus, it seems likely that the WFM would have again used the miners against the USRRC to force a settlement, even when the eight-hour question was not at issue.

After attempting but failing to negotiate a settlement with Charles MacNeill, manager of the USRRC, District Union No. 1, fully backed by the WFM's executive board, issued a strike order effective August 10. The order pulled out more than 3,500 miners from properties supplying ore to the mills of the USRRC and to other "unfair" companies. Although the men obeyed the order, many of them seriously questioned the wisdom of a second strike in support of the millworkers. How many would have opposed the move had a vote been taken in the locals is an open question, but some estimates run as high as 90 percent. Striking a second time over issues outside the district sparked little enthusiasm among the rank and file, a fact which the mine owners fully exploited.[3]

The strike was hazardous for all interests for several reasons. In the fall of 1903 the district, the recognized center of Colorado's gold-mining industry, was booming and prosperous. The prosperity depended solely upon uninterrupted mining, because there were no other significant industries there. The economy was thus extremely vulnerable to the machinations of the WFM, which had enrolled a large majority of the wage-earning miners, at times using threats and violence to do so. The WFM had failed in completely organizing the district and, for example, the great Portland mine operated on the "open shop" principle, employing both union and nonunion labor. Nevertheless, because most of the miners were members of the WFM, its power to disrupt the local economy was enormous. A prolonged strike could be catastrophic to the approximately 50,000 residents of the district. Moreover, for nearly a decade the WFM had been deeply involved in the political structure of the district, thereby acquiring influence and power it lacked in other mining camps in the state. Its members filled numerous municipal and county offices, particularly those responsible for law enforcement.[4] The power of the union at the time of the strike was sufficient to make Cripple Creek a major stronghold.

The mining companies, however, were not powerless. Many local officials, such as mayors, district judges, and county commissioners, were neither members of the WFM nor under its control. For months the Cripple Creek Mine Owners' Association (CCMOA) had been informally preparing for possible trouble with the union. And looming ominously in the background was the emerging employers' movement, which Craig and his Denver associates carried to every town and camp where strikes occurred. Other factors offset the power of the WFM. The district was rich in gold reserves, but the extraction of this wealth required enormous investment of capital for the expensive development work and machinery. Corporations, many of them foreign, had entered the district to exploit its resources. Their presence immensely complicated the strike by increasing the possibility that Peabody, who had placed top priority on protect-

ing capital investments, would intervene in their behalf if requested to do so.

Ominous, too, was the controversial character of the
strike. Since the Waite agreement of 1894, the miners had been
paid a minimum wage of $3 for an eight-hour day and, as evi-
denced by their general reluctance to strike a second time, were
apparently content with their situation. Consequently, opponents
of the strike concluded that it was ill-advised, even reprehensible,
because there were no issues to settle and nothing to negotiate
between the mine owners and their men. The objective of the
strike was to stop shipments to the mills of the USRRC and other
allegedly "unfair" mills where strikes were in progress. From the
start, the mine owners, who were contractually obligated to continue shipments to these mills and stood to lose heavily if they
stopped, labeled the strike "sympathetic" and charged that they
were being unscrupulously used in a power play of the union.[5]
Charles Moyer, WFM president, rejected this interpretation of
the strike. From his standpoint, the physical separation and occu-
pational differences between the miners and the millworkers were
of little significance. All were part of the same industrial union
in which the welfare of one was the concern of all. He intended
to use the full power of the WFM to force the USRRC and other
companies to be "fair" to their employees or to stop doing business in Colorado. Moyer expected the mine owners of the Cripple
Creek district to cooperate with him in this endeavor so that the
strike might be ended quickly.[6]

For the mine owners to join the WFM in bringing
the "unfair" companies to heel, however, would be both expensive and publicly humiliating. Such cooperation would, in effect,
transfer control of the mines to the union. Convinced that officials of the WFM had determined either to control or wreck the
economic life of the district, the mine owners concluded that the
time had come to resist. On August 13 the CCMOA found a new
unity developing in the crisis and issued a statement deploring
the strike as an "outrage against both the employers and the employed" and condemning the union for its "arbitrary and unjustifiable" action. On the grounds that there was nothing to negotiate
or adjust, the group announced that as "fast as new men can be

secured, our mining operations will be resumed under former conditions, preference being given to former employees, and all men applying for work will be protected to the last degree."[7] After nearly a decade the stage was set for a massive confrontation between the WFM and the mine owners, who considered it absurd to throttle the district's principal industry over matters not directly related to the gold camp.

It became evident that the contest would be long and arduous as each side maneuvered for advantage in the early weeks of the strike. Protected by a high fence and armed guards and with the support of the CCMOA, the El Paso mine resumed operations on August 18 with a work force that included a dozen defecting union miners.[8] Other mines were scheduled to follow. But within a week James F. Burns, the maverick president of the Portland Gold Mining Company, and union officials reached a settlement that sent nearly 500 men back to work in the Portland mine, whose ores were processed in the company's mill at Colorado City. As a competitor of the USRRC, Burns had no difficulty in agreeing not to ship ores to its "unfair mills." In return, union officials agreed that the Portland would remain an "open shop" mine with the same wage-hour structure.[9] Even so, the settlement was crucial for the WFM because it broke the solidarity of the mine owners, shut off a potential source of ores to the struck mills, and returned to work several hundred union members on whom special assessments could be levied.

The struggle assumed new dimensions when the merchants of the district announced that for the duration of the strike they would sell only for cash, a decision which left many striking miners who had already paid them their end-of-July bills with no cash or credit. To meet the needs of its members the WFM opened cooperative stores in Cripple Creek, Victor, Altman, and Goldfield which competed with the established merchants for the shrinking business of the district. Confronted with financial ruin, the merchants, whom Haywood soon branded as an "aggregation of nincompoops" more dangerous than the mine owners and their strikebreakers, rushed to organize.[10] On August 27 they established the Cripple Creek District Citizens' Alliance (CCDCA), with the aid of Craig. Within a week approximately 500 businessmen and others, aware of the success which their counterparts in Denver and Idaho Springs had had in reducing the power of the union, flocked into the organization to counteract the threat which the WFM posed to the business community.[11]

By the end of August the possibility of a compromise settlement had all but vanished. Businessmen and mine owners concluded that the central issue of the strike had become who or what interests should control the district, and they steadily marshalled their resources and prepared to break the miners' union rather than accept its dictates and surrender their control. The CCMOA and the CCDCA, with the same objectives and a substantially common membership, began coordinating their efforts and functioning as one, although retaining their separate organizational identities. The district was tense, all parties were prepared for the worst, and anxiety increased the outbreaks of strike-related "incidents."

Fire destroyed the shafthouse of the Sunset Eclipse mine on the night of August 29 and rumors quickly spread throughout the district that union arsonists were responsible. Other incidents occurred three days later. Outside the Golden Cycle mine a picket brandishing a gun stopped a carpenter who had come to construct a fence around the mine, but the picket was arrested. When an undersheriff, a WFM member, released the man on a technicality, opponents of the union expressed concern over the state of law enforcement. That afternoon John T. Hawkins, a justice of the peace from Anaconda, was assaulted in Altman. Some immediately blamed the assault on the union because Hawkins had earlier freed a mine guard who had been charged with carrying a concealed weapon. The same evening five masked men kidnapped Thomas M. Stewart, an elderly carpenter employed at the Golden Cycle, who was beaten, shot, and left for dead. Stewart miraculously survived. When he told that his abductors had called him a "scab," numerous residents concluded that the brutal assault had been the work of the WFM. Also, on the morning of September 2 guards at the El Paso mine exchanged shots with several unidentified men who were seen prowling around the property.[12]

Fearful that the incidents signaled a campaign of terror to prevent a resumption of mining, the mine owners demanded that County Sheriff H. M. Robertson appoint additional deputies whom the owners would select and pay. They also asked him to petition Governor Peabody for troops, certifying that he could not control conditions in Teller County. Robertson, with the approval of the county commissioners, met the first demand but rejected the second. His stand caused the officers of the CCMOA and the CCDCA to turn to Denver, where they expected that the need for military intervention would be more readily recognized. In a telegram of September 2 to the governor they recited the recent developments and blamed the WFM for the troubles of the district. They described Robertson as "incapable of handling the situation" and asked for troops to preserve order, protect property, and prevent a "reign of terror." F. D. French, mayor of Victor and manager of an ore sampler, supported their petition with several followup telegrams which demanded that troops be sent immediately to restrain an allegedly armed body of men who were threatening lives and property.[13] Ironically, within a month after his refusal to intervene in behalf of the banished miners of Idaho Springs, Peabody again had to decide whether to intervene in a labor dispute involving the WFM, this time to aid powerful business and mining interests which were determined to break the union.

Despite his strong inclination to honor the request, Peabody hesitated. His attorney general, Nathan Miller, unconvinced that conditions warranted intervention, withheld his support until an investigation had been held. After all, Robertson had refused to endorse the request of the CCMOA and the CCDCA and had claimed that military force was not needed. Moreover, there were no state funds available for a military operation of the magnitude that would be necessary. A means of sustaining large numbers of troops in the field had to be found before they could be committed to the gold camp. Furthermore, in a letter of September 3, Moyer, who hoped to prevent intervention, reminded Peabody that earlier he had been bamboozled into sending troops into Colorado City by men who wanted to use the state to crush labor, a mistake that he ought not to repeat.

Moyer insisted that the striking miners were peaceful and would submit to arrest if formally charged with a crime. Quoting Section 4, Article V of the state constitution, he advised that the constitutional conditions which would authorize intervention (that is, a failure of local officials to enforce the law or an invasion or insurrection) did not prevail in the district.[14] But unimpressed with Moyer's letter and Robertson's opposition, Peabody moved rapidly to clear the way for state intervention.

On September 3 the governor appointed Miller, Brigadier General John Chase, and Lieutenant Tom E. McClelland of the National Guard to investigate conditions in the district. The latter two were questionable choices if an impartial investigation were intended, because they had already recommended intervention and would be directly involved if troops were sent. Nor was the investigative procedure of the trio any less suspect. They arrived in Victor at 9:05 p.m. on September 3 and conferred with leading businessmen and mine owners. These included Mayor French and former Mayor Nelson Franklin, who feared they would be assassinated, charging that members of the strike committee were criminals, and recommended that none of the striking miners be called on to testify. All the witnesses agreed that troops were necessary. Around midnight the investigators went to Cripple Creek where they heard the views of Sheriff Robertson, Mayor W. L. Shockey, businessmen, and mine owners. Robertson, who admitted to being an inactive member of the WFM, was the only witness to oppose military intervention. He claimed that he could control the district, unless mining was resumed with strikebreakers. As to future violence, he stated that if it erupted, it would be at the "instigation of the mine owners, and not the miners." Furthermore, he was convinced that not more than 10 percent of the strikers would return to work if troops were sent, because they were determined to stay out of the mines until the issues were settled. Shockey and others refuted the sheriff's testimony. They contended that unless troops were sent, private citizens would be forced to police the district since local peace officers were under union control. In their opinion, 80 to 90 percent of the striking miners would return to work if troops were sent to expel the lawless element and to protect the men who wanted to work. Like their counterparts in Victor, they urged utmost secrecy in the investigation, allegedly to protect citizens who had testified from union retaliation.[15]

The failure of the governor's representatives to invite union testimony converted the investigation into a meaningless sham, a maneuver apparently contrived to shore up a decision which had already been made. Except for Robertson and Shockey, all the witnesses were members of the CCMOA and the CCDCA. Clearly, there had been no honest effort made to gather factual data for an unbiased decision on the need for troops, a fact which partially substantiated the union's earlier charges of collusion between Peabody and anti-labor interests. Having gone through the motions of an investigation in the dead of night, the investigators left for Denver at 4 a.m., September 4. Upon reaching Colorado Springs, they wired the governor that after a "careful inquiry among representative citizens and property owners," they had concluded that a "reign of terror" prevailed in the district which threatened lives and property. The situation was critical and required prompt action by the state. They paused at Palmer Lake and sent a second telegram, certain to impress upon Peabody the need for immediate action, which asserted that more than 800 miners had left the district because of the mining shutdown.[16]

Meanwhile, Peabody had worked to remove the major obstacle to intervention, a lack of funds. He conferred in Denver with E. A. Colburn and W. H. Bainbridge, the president and treasurer of the CCMOA, respectively, and explained that the state could not finance the military occupation of the district. Consequently, unless the mine owners agreed beforehand to underwrite the expenses of the men in the field, there would be no intervention. Wanting to renew mining protected by the military arm of the state, Colburn and Bainbridge accepted this necessary obligation. It was agreed that Adjutant General Sherman Bell, acting through the Military Board, would issue certificates of indebtedness, payable in four years at 4 percent interest, to pay his men and purchase supplies. The CCMOA would provide the money necessary to cash the certificates when presented and hold them until the General Assembly appropriated funds to retire the debt.[17] A. E. Carlton, president of the First National Bank of Cripple Creek and a prominent mine owner, was later chosen to handle the cashing of the certificates in the district.[18] This arrangement was eventually exposed, and it reflected Peabody's extraordinary commitment to property interests. It resulted in caustic criticism, not all of which came from labor.[19] Even the most naive observers saw that the agreement made the National Guard an instrument for serving special interests. Nevertheless, Nathan Miller later upheld its legality.[20]

Having set the stage for intervention, Peabody moved forcefully. In doing so he ignored the prerequisites for intervening that he had set in early September when rejecting the plea from the miners chased from Idaho Springs. On September 4, 1903, he ordered units of the National Guard into the district, supposedly to execute the laws, prevent a "threatened insurrection," maintain public order, and protect lives and property. The next day hundreds of soldiers, who had been previously alerted, poured into the district and quickly set up military outposts and an elaborate system of communication. At the end of September nearly 1,000 uniformed men were guarding the principal mines and patrolling the public roads.[21] Opponents of the WFM, exploiting to the hilt the earlier "incidents," had maneuvered to their support the only force capable of breaking the strike. What now confronted the union was the combined power of the CCMOA, the CCDCA, and the guard, an especially dangerous coalition because resistance to the mine owners could now be interpreted as insurrection and rebellion against the state.

A number of factors prompted Peabody's intervention in the Cripple Creek mining district. Among these were his background and training, his commitment to propertied interests, his gradual involvement in the alliance movement, and his alienation from organized labor. Furthermore, in explaining his Cripple Creek decision to his supporters, he expressed views that were essentially those of David M. Parry, Charles M. MacNeill, James C. Craig, and the mine owners. Like them, he believed that the workingman's problems could best be solved by hard work and loyalty to his employer rather than by senseless boycotts and strikes; like them, he was opposed to militant unions such as the WFM, which he blamed for the industrial unrest and turmoil that had rocked Colorado for a decade; like them, he had concluded that the leadership of militant unions was lawless and that their methods and goals were un-American. In his opinion, the strike of the WFM in the Cripple Creek district was unjust and reflected neither the wishes nor the needs of the miners. Consequently, he felt compelled to use the power of the state in protecting lives and property and upholding the right of every man to work unmolested. As far as he was concerned, union membership neither endowed the workingman with special privileges nor made him less amenable to the law than his nonunion counterpart.[22] The governor undoubtedly considered that the presence of the guard in a strikebreaking role might provoke disorder and violence and compel the state to become an increasingly active agent in the designs of the petitioners. Nevertheless, he aggressively intervened.

It soon became evident that the civil authorities and large numbers of people in the district deplored the governor's intervention. The county commissioners unanimously condemned the action, charging that the troops were unnecessary and that the investigation of September 3 had been a farce.[23] Victor's city council claimed that Mayor French had deliberately misrepresented conditions and the wishes of his constituents to the governor when he independently asked for troops.[24] Moreover, Sheriff Robertson contended publicly that Peabody had exceeded his authority in sending troops.[25] On September 5, hundreds of residents gathered in Victor to protest the presence of the guard. Their resolutions lambasted the governor's action as "unwarranted by the facts and as anarchistic in its inception, spirit, and consequences." A mass meeting in Cripple Creek resulted in similar resolutions attacking Peabody.[26]

As expected, the CCMOA and the CCDCA, the principal beneficiaries of the governor's action, rushed to Peabody's support. So did other employers' associations throughout the state, like the Denver Alliance.[27] Anticipating large-scale violence when mining resumed with nonunion labor, these groups approved of Peabody's decision to prevent it. However, a peaceful reopening of the mines was not the sole objective of the mine owners in asking for assistance. They had concluded that permanent industrial peace in the district was impossible as long as the WFM maintained a foothold there. In a statement of September 8, the

CCMOA blamed the disruption of mining on a "few irresponsible agitators" whose character and methods were "inimical to the rights and obligations" of all, and it pledged to continue the fight against the WFM until its "pernicious influence" had been "swept from the district." Thereafter, anyone wanting employment in the mines would have to quit the union.[28] With this statement, the CCMOA declared war upon the WFM.

In his order of September 4, Peabody had not required that Bell cooperate with or remain subordinate to local officials, who had loudly denied that troops were necessary to maintain law and order. On the contrary, he had unwisely ordered Bell to assume functions which were the legal responsibility of Robertson and other elected officials whom he believed were controlled by the WFM because they had refused to give in to the CCMOA and the CCDCA. Consequently, a strong possibility of conflict between civil and military authorities existed at the start of the occupation. Furthermore, Bell increased the chances of a major crisis. His history of anti-unionism, his controversial performance at Colorado City, his close relationship with the mine owners, his volatile personality, and his unfailing tendency to seek military solutions to nonmilitary problems all made it inevitable that he would interpret the governor's orders as authorization to use the guard not merely to uphold law and order but "to do up this damned anarchistic federation."[29] His intention of crushing the miners' union quickly became evident, and this fact further substantiated labor's charge that he had been appointed adjutant general with that purpose in mind.

Using force and intimidation to shut off debate about the advisability of the state's intervention, Brigadier General John Chase, Bell's field commander, systematically imprisoned without formal charges union officials and others who openly questioned the need for troops. Included among those jailed were a justice of the peace, the chairman of the Board of County Commissioners, and a member of the WFM who had criticized the guard and advised the strikers not to return to the mines.[30] So frequently were individuals placed in the military stockade or "bull pen" at Goldfield for reasons of "military necessity" and for "talking too much" in support of the strike that the *Cripple Creek Times* of September 15 advised its readers not to comment on the strike situation. Not even the newspapers escaped harassment. When the *Victor Daily Record*, a strong voice of the WFM, erroneously charged that one of the soldiers was an ex-convict, its staff was imprisoned before an intended retraction could be published. Not until Peabody personally intervened were the men released and formally charged with criminal libel. Publisher George E. Kyner later charged that the *Record's* position on the strike and its publication of union notices had provoked the arrests.[31]

This crude display of power raised important constitutional questions regarding the role of the military when occupying areas where civil authority was fully operative. Angry local officials refused to surrender their jurisdiction over civil affairs and resisted Bell's attempt to govern under the rationale of "military necessity."[32] Their effort to uphold the supremacy of civil authority and procedures produced several confrontations with the guard.

In a letter of September 14 to the governor, Deputy District Attorney J. C. Cole complained about the refusal of Bell's officers to transfer custody of Charles Kennison, president of a WFM local, to Robertson so that the prisoner might appear at a preliminary hearing on a charge of criminal assault.[33] Later Cole criticized their refusal to allow Robertson to arrest a Lt. Hartung on a similar charge filed by a strikebreaker, who charged that the officer had attempted to shoot him for fleeing a group of workers being escorted to the mines. Cole complained that the guard's officers' defiant rejection of "legal process, such as warrants and capiases in the hands of the proper officers [was] an uncalled for obstruction and violation of the law of our state" and reflected their belief that they were a "law unto themselves, and did not propose to be amenable to the civil authorities or recognize criminal process." He revealed that the officers had failed to contact the district attorney's office regarding any of the local citizens imprisoned in the Goldfield stockade.[34] Uncertain how to respond to these extraordinary procedures and to growing popular demands that strong counter-measures be taken, the county commissioners retained Senator Thomas M. Patterson and C. S.

Thomas, a former governor, to advise them and Robertson "relative to the rights and duties of the civil authorities."[35]

That the civil authorities desperately needed advice became more evident when on September 14 District Judge W. P. Seeds granted writs of habeas corpus to four union men held in the military stockade, forcing the military authorities to reveal just how far they would go in the name of "military necessity." On September 18, the returnable date of the writs, S. D. Crump, counsel for Bell and Chase, advised the court that under the authority derived from Peabody's order of September 4, his clients were holding the petitioners while formal charges were being prepared. When counsel for the prisoners moved to cancel the return, Seeds set the morning of September 21 for hearing arguments on the motion. At that time he permitted Crump to file an amended return, but he demanded that the four men be present when the hearing began on the motion to quash. That afternoon approximately ninety cavalrymen entered Cripple Creek and surrounded the court. Escorted by a company of infantrymen armed with rifles and fixed bayonets, the prisoners entered the courtroom with fourteen of their escorts. The next day, however, the officers again ignored a direct order of the court to produce the men. But on September 23 soldiers again surrounded the court and took sniper positions on top the National Hotel directly across the street to control the principal avenues. Others set up a Gatling gun, positioning it to command the immediate area. After these extraordinary preparations had been taken, the prisoners, escorted by a detail of thirty-four armed men, entered the court. Their stay was short.

Angered by the presence of armed soldiers in the court, Eugene Engley, a former state attorney general and one of two attorneys representing the petitioners, refused to proceed and left the courtroom. Before departing with his associate, however, he remarked to Seeds:

> The court may say that it is not intimidated, but the fact remains . . . that the forces of intimidation are present. The constitutional guarantee that courts shall be open and free and untrammeled for public business of a legal character has been invaded and overthrown. It is no longer

under the constitution, a constitutional court; on the contrary, it is an armed camp. This court is surrounded by soldiery. The court and I and all other citizens present are now facing glimmering bayonets.[36]

In rebuttal, Crump contended that Peabody possessed the constitutional authority to order troops anywhere in the state and to declare martial law whether the civil authorities had requested such action or not. To preserve law and order the governor had used that authority to declare a "qualified state of martial law" in the district. In holding the four men, Bell and Chase were merely implementing the governor's order of September 4; therefore, their action was both legal and constitutional. Crump questioned the power of the court under the circumstances to issue writs of habeas corpus for the relief of the men.[37] After Crump's remarks, Seeds adjourned the court.

On the next day when the court convened, troops again surrounded the courthouse. Undaunted, Seeds ruled in favor of the petitioners, holding that the habeas corpus provisions in the state constitution made their release mandatory.[38] Although he conceded that Bell and Chase possessed the power of arrest when ordered out by the governor during an emergency, Seeds ruled that their prisoners must be surrendered immediately to the civil authorities because under the state constitution the military must always remain subordinate to civil authority.[39] Condemning the military display outside as "offensive to the court," Seeds ordered the prisoners released. However, Chase stubbornly refused to obey the mandate until Peabody personally ordered him to do so.

The antics of the military in the district created an uproar throughout the state. Although Republican organs like the *Denver Republican* and the *Colorado Springs Gazette* fully backed Peabody's intervention in the district, they remained discreetly silent regarding the tactics employed by the guard. But even they took the position that court orders should be obeyed. Democratic newspapers strongly condemned the military's arbitrary use of power, particularly around the court. In extensive editorials on September 24 and October 4 the *Rocky Mountain News* condemned both the intervention and the methods used by Bell. Senator Patterson, who owned the *News*, personally wrote the editorial of October 4. Although he deplored the strike, he deplored even more the use of the guard to destroy the WFM, an action he claimed was tantamount to "prostituting that great arm of the state's defense to a revolutionary and criminal purpose." In his opinion, troops had been unnecessary, and their provocative role was the natural result of the method chosen to underwrite their operation within the district. The pro-labor *Victor Daily Record* and the *Denver Times* joined the *News* in denouncing Bell's methods as reprehensible. Such criticisms, combined with a general public clamor over events in the district, produced a mild dissension within the administration regarding the proper role of the guard.

As early as September 16, Attorney General Miller opposed the tactics of Bell and Chase which, in his opinion, effectively suspended the writ of habeas corpus and established a condition of martial law. Not even the President of the United States, he believed, could exercise such power unless confronted with a rebellion or an invasion.[40] Miller's views apparently influenced Peabody. After receiving Cole's letter of September 20, the governor instructed Bell that troops had been sent into the Cripple Creek district because local authorities had failed "to enforce law and order" and uphold judicial functions. In refusing to surrender custody of a man charged with a crime to legally constituted authority so that a hearing might be held, the military had contributed to the lawlessness it had been sent to suppress. He emphasized that there had been "no declaration of military law . . . and there would be none, if the civil courts, under the protection of the military authorities, perform their duties." Only obedience to court orders could determine this. If the courts failed to uphold the law, then more drastic steps could be taken. In the meantime, however, Bell should obey their mandates, surrendering custody of his prisoners to civil officers and following regular civil proccesses.[41] Despite this clarification of the order of September 4, Bell's officers continued to arrest and hold unionists without filing formal charges. The courts countered with writs of habeas corpus which the officers obeyed, at least through November. However, prisoners released by the writs usually enjoyed a short-lived freedom, for they were immediately rearrested if the officers thought their detention was necessary.

Conditions in the district now clearly favored the mine owners, and they sent their agents scouring the country for strikebreakers to work the mines protected by troops. Renewal of operations began on the larger properties. By October 10 the CCMOA claimed that of 2,900 men at work, only 1,200 were union men employed at the Portland mine and other "fair" properties. The remainder, strikebreakers and miners who had quit the WFM, worked for members of the association. Significant progress, therefore, had been made toward breaking the strike—so much progress that throughout October and November, Peabody withdrew approximately 50 percent of the troops. The CCMOA continued to remind the public that its basic objective was to destroy the WFM in the district. On October 5, Clarence C. Hamlin, secretary of the association, declared that either the union or the CCMOA had to go, and eleven days later he stated flatly that his associates would never again employ members of the WFM.[42] Before the end of October the CCMOA ordered its members to include a clause in their new leases providing for automatic cancellation if a member of the WFM were employed on the property.[43]

General Bell fully supported this policy. He made no secret of his intention to drive out the "unlawful population and professional agitators," whom he estimated at 10 percent of the district population, until only those willing to work, the "good people," remained.[44] Having weathered the public criticism of September and now pleased with the resumption of mining, the governor evidenced an increasing willingness to support Bell's drive to wreck the WFM. In a letter of October 3 he praised the general for the "cool manner" in which he had conducted the campaign. Perhaps, Peabody suggested, Bell would soon convince the WFM that strikes like that in the Cripple Creek district would not be tolerated either in Colorado or elsewhere.[45] With success so apparent, Peabody was clearly less concerned than formerly about the controversial character of the campaign. His optimism was unwarranted, for the worst was yet to come.

During the nights of November 14 and 16, unknown persons unsuccessfully attempted to wreck passenger trains on the Florence and Cripple Creek line near Anaconda by removing spikes and bolts from the rails. Railroad detectives twice averted disaster when they discovered the damaged track in time to warn approaching trains. Based on information provided by D. C. Scott, a detective for the Midland Terminal Railroad Company, and K. C. Sterling, a detective for the CCMOA, civil authorities charged H. H. McKinney with attempted murder in connection with the railroad incident after he and Thomas Foster, an activist in the strike, had been arrested by the military. In December, Scott wrangled a written confession from McKinney which implicated Sherman Parker, president of District Union No. 1, W. F. Davis, president of the Altman union, and Foster. They all were charged with conspiracy to commit murder. But in a second written confession to Frank J. Hangs, an attorney for the WFM, McKinney repudiated the first, claiming that he had made it after Scott had promised a pardon, $1,000, and transportation from the district. Furthermore, he stated that Scott and Sterling were only protecting themselves when they induced him to make the first confession. A letter to his wife, which Hangs obtained, gave credence to this second confession, although McKinney later repudiated it, too.

Because of its connection with the strike, the case created a sensation. In an extraordinary trial marked by charges and countercharges, it became evident that the CCMOA, possibly in connivance with state officials, was attempting to send Parker, Davis, and Foster to prison. The court soon dismissed the charge against Davis for lack of evidence, and a jury composed of nonresidents of the district eventually returned a verdict of not guilty for the others.[46] Afterwards, District Attorney Henry Trowbridge dropped the charges against McKinney, who had testified that at the request of Parker he had tried to wreck two trains carrying hundreds of people, including members of the WFM, for a payment of $500. Although he was later arrested for perjury, McKinney was released on bond provided by representatives of the CCMOA.

Evidence introduced at the trial suggested at least mild conspiracy between officials within the Peabody administration and the CCMOA in constructing the case against the union members. First, there was McKinney's contention that he had been promised a pardon if convicted. Other evidence suggests that a promise of executive leniency had been extended to others in return for assistance in the case. In forwarding to Peabody a petition for pardon from James Hudgins, J. L. Beaman, sheriff of Pueblo County, pointed out in a cover letter that Hudgins had been of "great service to Mr. Scott . . . in his 'train wrecking case,'" information that had not been incorporated in the petition for fear that it might become public knowledge. Beaman asked Peabody *"not to place* this letter on file *with the petition."*[47] The governor immediately forwarded Hudgin's pardon. How extensive the collusion was is impossible to determine from the available evidence, but the train-wrecking episode played a significant role in the subsequent events in Cripple Creek.

On November 21, Charles H. McCormick and Melvin Beck, superintendent and shift-boss at the Vindicator mine, respectively, were killed by an explosion at the 600-foot level while riding a cage through the main shaft. Although the mine, particularly the entrance to its shaft, was heavily guarded by soldiers who had been ordered to keep out all unauthorized personnel, the CCMOA immediately blamed the WFM for the tragedy. The union answered that the men had been killed while trying to set off a blast that they had intended to blame upon the striking miners to prevent the further withdrawal of troops from the district. Several investigations—one by Robertson who was assisted by company employees, another by a coroner's jury composed of union and nonunion miners, and a third by the state commissioner of mines—could not determine precisely what had happened or who was responsible. Nevertheless, military authorities arrested fifteen men, mostly union members, and charged them with having knowledge of the explosion. The district attorney, however, eventually did not prosecute the cases, because, even after offers of large rewards from the CCMOA, the CCDCA, and the Board of County Commissioners, evidence sufficient to warrant further prosecution never materialized.[48]

The explosion at the Vindicator and the attempts at train wrecking, which opponents in the strike blamed on each other, renewed tension throughout the district. Rumors spread that a vigilante group, the Committee of 40, consisting of known "killers" and the "best" citizens, had been formed to uphold law and order. To counter this group, according to rumor, a Committee of Safety had been organized among the striking miners

102

who feared that the Committee of 40 intended to commit acts of violence and blame them on the WFM to justify the union's destruction.[49] Such rumors increased the apprehension. Furthermore, the military now stepped up its harassment, arresting individuals who vocally supported the strike and even children who chided the soldiers on the streets.[50] Each party to the strike was convinced more than ever that the other would resort to murder to control the district.

Despite the presence of nearly 500 troops, members of the CCMOA and the CCDCA experienced a gnawing anxiety about conditions. Although they were convinced that the strike was broken, the incidents of November revealed that they could not establish total control as long as the courts seemingly provided a sanctuary for the men arrested by the military. More than a "qualified state of martial law" was obviously necessary if the WFM was to be destroyed. State officials had reached similar conclusions. In interviews on December 3 the governor and his attorney general claimed that the courts had nullified the state's efforts to pacify the district by releasing prisoners upon obtaining custody from the military. In effect, the courts had aided and abetted the lawless element (that is, the WFM) with the result that anarchy prevailed, making a "fair trial" impossible until conditions returned to normal. The next day, Judge Seeds strongly denied their contention and pointed out that prisoners surrendered by the military were never released under habeas corpus proceedings unless the evidence failed to justify their detention. As for the others, they were always remanded to the sheriff who then fixed bail commensurate with the alleged crime as the records would show.[51] Nevertheless, the administration, the CCMOA, and the CCDCA now moved to circumvent the district courts. The time had arrived for the drastic action which Peabody had promised Bell, when and if Peabody felt that the courts failed to uphold the law.

On December 4, after conferring with officers of the CCMOA and the CCDCA, Peabody proclaimed that Teller County was in a "state of insurrection and rebellion." To justify this move, he cited the train-wrecking attempts and the Vindicator explosion, the apparent failure of local authorities to check widespread lawlessness and protect lives and property, and the existence of organizations controlled by "desperate men."[52] He freely admitted that he was maneuvering to neutralize the courts, using an Idaho Supreme Court decision of 1899 (*In re Boyle*) as legal grounds. Somehow the safeguards of due process had to be sidestepped so that the military might act forcefully against the WFM, yet do so with the aura of legality.

Although Peabody and Miller publicly denied that the proclamation had imposed martial law on the county, Bell interpreted it otherwise. In his opinion, total control had passed into the hands of military authorities who were now free to "arrest all Socialists" and even "Presbyterians" unobstructed by the courts. In an extraordinary, rambling statement of December 5, Bell elaborated his views on martial law, treason, spying, military necessity, assassination, and insurrection, apparently for the public's enlightenment, and suggested that his will alone prevailed in Teller County. He wrote:

> The county of Teller, in consequence of the occupation of the militia, is subject to the supreme military authority and control when necessity requires and occasion demands, and it becomes necessary to suspend, in part or its entirety, by the occupying military authority, of the criminal and civil law and of the domestic administration and government in the occupied place or territory, and in the substitution of military rule and force for the same, as well as in the dictation of general laws, as far as military necessity requires this suspension, substitution or dictation.[53]

Peabody and Miller treated the announcement lightly, but Bell began to act as if martial law had been declared.[54]

On December 5, Colonel Edward Verdeckberg, Bell's new field commander, issued a local proclamation announcing that until further notice the county was under military control. All citizens were ordered to surrender their "arms, equipments and munitions of war," stop assisting organizations controlled by "desperate men," avoid street assemblies, and go about their normal pursuits. According to Verdeckberg's edit:

> No publication either by newspaper, pamphlet or handbill reflecting in any way upon the United States and the State of Colorado, or its officers, or tending in any way to influence the public mind against the government of the United States and the State of Colorado, will be permitted;

and all articles of news or editorial comments or correspondence, making comments upon the action or actions of the military forces of the State of Colorado, or the organizations above referred to, will not be tolerated.[55]

Censorship had already been imposed on the night of December 4 when Major H. A. Naylor warned George Kyner, publisher of the *Victor Daily Record*, that any future publication of critical editorials and official statements of the WFM would lead to the paper's suppression. The major ordered Kyner not to print an editorial he had prepared for the next edition which condemned the state's intervention as tyrannical, malicious, and politically inspired.[56] Thus, military censorship stilled a powerful voice of the WFM and denied its officers the means of directing the rank and file by releases to the press.

A stepped-up campaign of harassment against the WFM and its supporters followed. County residents obediently surrendered their firearms, most of which were returned when registered. When they became convinced that the colonel intended to disarm only the supporters of the strike, union officials advised members to keep and hide their weapons, claiming that their constitutional right to bear arms could not be abridged. Provoked at this attempt to thwart their disarming of the striking miners, military authorities resorted to arbitrary raids to find the hidden guns, a procedure which resulted in numerous incidents. For example, an attempt to seize the weapons of John M. Glover, an attorney and former congressman from Missouri who publicly refused to obey Verdeckberg's order, produced a spectacular and much publicized gun battle in which Glover was wounded before surrendering.[57]

"Agitators" who kept the strike alive were singled out for special harassment. On December 10 soldiers arrested A. G. Paul, secretary of the Cripple Creek Miners' Union, No. 40; on December 13, D. C. Copley, a member of the WFM's executive board; on December 19, James A. Baker, another member of the executive board; on December 23, M. E. White, a member of the executive board of the WFM-controlled American Labor Union. After their arrests, principally for harassment, punishment ranged from imprisonment to banishment. For example, Baker, who was setting up a union store in Goldfield, was ordered from the district after Verdeckberg had informed him that another grocery store was not needed.[58] With each arrest the strategy of the military became clearer: divorce the rank and file from the allegedly "desperate men" who controlled the unions. Peabody stood behind these dictatorial procedures, going so far as to suspend the writ of habeas corpus in the case of one prisoner, Victor Poole.

On December 30, Verdeckberg broadened his assault on the WFM with a proclamation on vagrancy, a term so broadly defined as to include the striking miners whom he hoped to coerce back into the mines or out of the district. Such a procedure had been used with minor success at Telluride. Vagrants were given one week to find gainful employment, but after January 7, 1904 they were to be arrested and dealt with according to law.[59] To counter this move, Moyer and Haywood advised the locals of court decisions which held that striking members of labor organizations were not vagrants under the law; therefore, the strikers should keep their union cards, stay in the district, and, if forced out, return immediately. Furthermore, on January 7, Seeds issued an injunction, a useless gesture under the circumstances, forbidding the guard to expel any member of the WFM for vagrancy.[60] But unexpectedly, Verdeckberg scuttled the vagrancy policy and took steps to reduce the role of the military in the district.

This change in policy did not reflect a softening attitude toward the WFM. Peabody believed that most Coloradans supported his tough policy toward "dynamiters, night assassins and violators of the law." He thought most citizens favored strong action against the WFM so that the people would not "surrender the industrial and commercial interests of this State to a lawless, ignorant class of people, and thereby have a government for labor unions, instead of a government 'by and for the people.'" Peabody backed his military commanders in full. In his opinion, "heroic" if unorthodox tactics had been necessary because, "when dealing with a cancer, nothing short of such measures will produce either relief or a permanent cure." Like the mine owners, he was totally convinced that the WFM was the "most powerful and unprincipled and unforgiving labor organization on the face of the earth" and under the control of criminals. In early 1904 the governor's attitude toward organized labor as revealed in his correspondence had hardened rather than softened.[61]

Nor was there a change in the position of the CCMOA and the CCDCA, which, in their zeal to destroy the WFM, were making a sham of the principles they claimed to support. At a meeting of the CCDCA on December 15, its officers distributed a list of businesses which had rejected membership in the organization and advised that these firms be in effect, boycotted.[62] The CCMOA was less subtle about its objectives and methods—all of which made suspect the governor's private and public statements regarding boycotts, coercion, and the right of workers to organize. On December 10 the association ordered the Dorcas Mining and Milling Company of Florence to discharge all its employees who would not quit the WFM if it were to receive unrestricted shipments of ore from members of the association. Confronted with the prospect of heavy losses, the manager obeyed the dictate. The similarity between the CCMOA's use of the Dorcas Company, located approximately forty miles from the district, to strike at the union and the WFM's use of the Cripple Creek mine owners to coerce the United States Reduction and Refining Company is obvious. Steps were also taken to convert the CCMOA into a permanent instrument to assure the supremacy of the mine owners and to root out the remnants of the WFM. Funds for this purpose were solicited on December 26. Furthermore, on March 19, 1904, the CCMOA established a "central bureau" to pass upon all applications for jobs in the mines of its members. The bureau's "card system" required applicants to disclaim any connection with the WFM as a condition for employment.[63] It blacklisted members of the WFM, abridged their right to organize, and made a mockery of the "open shop" principle which employers' associations across the nation professed to uphold.

What forced a reduction in the role of the military, therefore, was not a change of objectives, but other considerations. Although the system of financing the campaign had placed the substance of military policy into the hands of the mine owners, it had also saddled them with the burden of underwriting the cost. Thousands of dollars had been tied up in cashing the state's certificates of indebtedness, and there was no guarantee that subsequent legislatures would appropriate funds to redeem them. Furthermore, pressure to restore civil control was developing outside the state. On December 11, Senator Patterson introduced a resolution into the U. S. Senate calling for an investigation into conditions in Colorado. This was followed in January and February 1904 by statements from the CCMOA and the WFM, which were introduced in the Senate. The possibility of federal intervention, perhaps in behalf of the striking miners, threatened to expose nationally all the facets of the governor's policy.[64] Moreover, the CCMOA was now confident that the strike was broken and that the mine owners could control the situation.

On January 7, the date set for implementing the vagrancy policy, there were 265 troops in the district; however, officials of the CCMOA, who were concerned about the growing financial burden they had assumed, conferred with Peabody in Denver shortly before that date and urged that he reduce the number of soldiers by 100. In a letter of January 6, the governor passed on their wishes to Verdeckberg, who reduced his command within a week to 170.[65] This diminished force was inadequate to sustain the vigorous harassment policy which had begun with the proclamation of insurrection and rebellion. On January 8, Verdeckberg informed union leaders that he would not arrest any striking miner as long as he obeyed the law.

Although the military continued to make scattered arrests and expulsions, conditions in the district remained comparatively calm throughout January. Except for an accident at the Independence mine which killed fifteen men, little of consequence occurred.[66] Military control thus became less and less realistic, so much so that on February 2 the governor ordered the remaining troops to "act in support of, and in subordination to, the legally constituted civil authorities" of Teller County.[67] For the first time since intervention, the military had been placed in definite subordination to local officials. Minor conflicts still occurred, but none comparable to those of September.

The CCMOA continued to urge a reduction in the number of men stationed in the gold camp. In a letter of March 12, A. E. Carlton, president of the Cripple Creek First National

Bank, principal owner of the Findley mine, and financial agent of the CCMOA, informed Peabody that the burden of maintaining the troops had become too much for his organization. He suggested that the number be further reduced to two officers and twenty-five enlisted men. In response, Peabody wrote that he would "be glad to reduce all along the line in keeping with your wishes, whose interests, with those of your associates, are what I am attempting to protect and save from assault or destruction." He regretted that troops were still needed to control the "lawless" element; however, he promised that they would be available as long as necessary.[68] Finally, on April 11, at the request of the mine owners and the local authorities, the governor withdrew the remaining troops, ending the first phase of state intervention in the district's affairs.

Peabody's correspondence indicates that he was reluctant to withdraw the troops, because although the mine owners had successfully resumed operations, the WFM officially maintained the strike. Peabody, who had now become a member of the Denver Citizens' Alliance, was increasingly irritated by the refusal of Moyer and Haywood to concede defeat. He began to interpret the strike as a struggle between advocates of law and order and labor leaders who advocated "the fallacies and unrealities of the socialistic doctrine." He was convinced that he, the mine owners, and the alliances had been "fighting the socialistic, anarchistic and violent element of the property-destroying minority of certain unions" and, in doing so, they had been protecting life, liberty, and property. What prevailed in the Cripple Creek and other mining camps where strikes were in progress was an open "rebellion by imported anarchists, labor agitators and walking delegates, who [were] still attempting to over-throw the laws of this state and supplant in their place the rules and regulations of the Western Federation of Miners." It was to crush the "rebellion" of such rabble-rousers, he wired the NAM's annual convention of 1904, that he had intervened in the strikes of the WFM and the United Mine Workers.[69] However, few unbiased observers accepted Peabody's explanation prior to June 6.

Early that morning a devastating explosion wrecked the Independence station on the Florence and Cripple Creek railroad, killing thirteen and seriously wounding six of the twenty-seven nonunion men from the Findley and Deadwood mines who waited for the 2:15 a.m. train. Other miners, hurrying from the Shurtloff mine to catch the train, reached the depot moments later to view with horror the mutilated bodies of dying men. So violent was the blast that clean-up crews found it necessary to use buckets and pails for the carnage. Robertson hurried to the scene and began an immediate investigation. Meanwhile, Bell activated local units of the guard, placing Major H. A. Naylor in temporary command.[70]

The murders threw the district into an uproar. At sunrise hundreds of armed and angry residents thronged the downtown streets, their number unnecessarily increased when all the mines and mills except the Portland were shut down, releasing scores of nonunion workers to swell the mobs. Because the victims had been nonunion miners, alarming rumors spread which blamed the WFM for the tragedy. Repeated and exaggerated, they set off charges and countercharges which threatened to provoke additional violence. On the question of union responsibility, the district rapidly split into two hostile factions: one which readily assumed the WFM's guilt and another which just as readily assumed its innocence. Each viewed the other apprehensively, creating a volatile situation.

Moving to exploit the crisis, the leaders of the CCMOA and the CCDCA gathered in Victor's Military Club to plan a course of action. Since they were convinced that the local authorities backed the WFM, they decided that a purge was imperative if the union was to be eliminated. They began with Robertson, whom they forced to resign by threatening to hang him if he refused. His resignation was accepted by the county commissioners who were sitting at Victor in emergency session. To replace Robertson, the commissioners quickly appointed Edward Bell, a member of the CCMOA and the CCDCA whom the *Denver Republican* of June 7 called a "non-union sympathizer, in short a strikebreaker," whose $10,000 bond had already been arranged among several influential mine owners. Bell's first act was to dismiss Robertson's undersheriff and to appoint L. F. Parsons, secretary of the CCDCA, to the post.[71] Within days the CCMOA and the CCDCA forced the resignation of more than thirty officials suspected of having union sympathies and replaced them with enemies of the WFM.[72] This revolutionary overthrow of duly constituted authority placed local government under the control of men who were determined to annihilate the union.

Not content with their seizure of political power, enemies of the WFM worked to mobilize the mobs for more direct blows at the union. Against the advice of the county commissioners, they forged ahead with an announced public meeting to be held on the afternoon of June 6 in a vacant lot across the street from the union hall in Victor. Clarence Hamlin, secretary of the CCMOA, before a crowd of several thousand intemperately urged that nonunion miners purge the district of union influence. When a member of the WFM objected, a fight began, which led to indiscriminate firing which killed two and wounded five others. As the throng scattered, members of the WFM fled to their hall. A short while later, Sheriff Bell, who believed that the initial shot had been fired from a second story window of the building, ordered the men out. Fearing the mob, they refused. Another shooting battle erupted, this time between members of Company L, who surrounded the hall, and the men inside. It ended with the surrender of forty unionists, four of whom were wounded. Afterwards, members of the alliance entered the hall, seized union records, and wrecked the interior, including a substantial library.[73] Similar incidents occurred in other towns throughout the district. Directed by prominent members of the local alliances, mobs turned their fury against union halls and stores, looting and destroying records and merchandise. By midnight of June 6, every union store and hall in Teller County had been wrecked.[74]

On June 7, spurred on by a morning editorial of the *Cripple Creek Times* which blamed the WFM for the "cold blooded murder" at Independence depot, officials of the CCMOA and the CCDCA convened and added a new dimension to their union-wrecking campaign, a seven-man examining committee to select unionists for deportation from among the prisoners captured in Sheriff Bell's raids throughout the district. What determined a man's fate was his stand on union membership. A refusal to quit the WFM and accept a mine owners' recommendation card meant banishment. Before nightfall, Bell, on orders from the committee, had deported twenty-five men.[75] Ignoring due process, opponents of the union forged ahead, apparently confident of aid from Denver should their tactics spark a massive revolt.

Although out of state attending the St. Louis Exposition of 1904 when the new crisis arose, Peabody had been informed of developments by his adjutant and attorney generals and reacted swiftly when formally petitioned for help on June 7. Acting Governor Warren A. Haggott immediately declared Teller County again in a state of "insurrection and rebellion"; General Bell promptly ordered additional troops into the district and left Denver to assume personal command. Buttressed by a recent Colorado Supreme Court decision which empowered the governor to use extraordinary means in subduing "insurrection and rebellion," the general, upon arriving in the district, approved the expulsion procedure and converted the examining committee into a "military commission" to judge the guilt or innocence of Sheriff Bell's growing list of prisoners.[76] In effect, General Bell placed the guard at the disposal of special interests for the purpose of exterminating the miners' union.

By the end of July, the commission had questioned 1,569 men. Of these it recommended that 238 be banished. Military personnel carried out the expulsions, shipping the prisoners by train to Denver and points close to the Kansas and New Mexico state lines. It also recommended that charges be filed against forty-two persons and that 1,289 be released. Although official statements indicated that only "agitators, ore thieves, keepers of fences for stolen ores, habitues of bawdyhouses, saloon bums, and vagrants" had been banished, the criterion of expulsion was a worker's attitude toward the WFM.[77] To stay in the district he had to renounce his affiliation with or sympathy for the union.[78] Long residence, property ownership, and family considerations meant nothing if a prisoner refused to reject the union.

The fact that the campaign against the WFM violated wholesale the civil rights of its members did not trouble the enemies of the union, particularly General Bell, himself a former mine manager from Independence. His concern for the rights of the banished men was at best minimal. In his opinion, the WFM was a criminal and socialistic organization which had waged war on society. Its destruction, therefore, was essential for the peace and happiness of district residents, whose general welfare transcended the rights of an individual as guaranteed by the federal and state constitutions.[79] Consequently, he enthusiastically supported the drive of his former mining associates to break the WFM, making his military objective identical with theirs.

General Bell took extraordinary measures to maximize military harassment of the union. All who refused to conform to the new order became victims of his wrath. Independent-minded mine managers like James F. Burns, president of the Portland mine which had come to terms with the WFM early in the strike, discovered that operating on the "open shop" principle did not protect them from the hostility of their anti-union associates who professed to work in behalf of the principle. As early as December 5, for example, the ultra-conservative magazine *Polly Pry* charged that James Burns, because he refused to discharge a large number of WFM members who worked in the Portland, was an associate of an "unknown circle of bomb-throwing, train-wrecking, infernal-machine-sending, cut-throats and assassins" and suggested that something ought to be done to him. Although he operated the Portland on principles endorsed by Peabody and every employers' association in the country, this was ignored because he dared to employ members of the WFM. On June 10, General Bell closed the mine to "prevent union men from contributing to lawless strikes." Other open shop mines were similarly closed, and they did not reopen until their owners accepted the CCMOA's card system blacklisting members of the WFM.[80] Ironically, the general was prepared to assault property rights to preserve them and to undermine basic principles of Peabody's labor policy to uphold them.

General Bell subjected members of the union to additional pressures. On June 14, Colonel Verdeckberg issued an order requiring that all aid to the families of the banished miners be dispensed by the military authorities. According to the colonel, he intended to restrict such assistance to that absolutely necessary. He wanted to impress upon its recipients that it was temporary and would be extended only until they could join a deported relative. In no case would he allow the families of the banished miners to remain, supported by the WFM, for a long period of time.[81]

More subtle attacks on the WFM followed. On June 9 the *Victor Daily Record*, a heretofore powerful voice of labor, called upon union leaders to end the strike, pointing out that the expulsions, broken families, and property losses were all for a hopeless cause. That night eight armed men smashed the *Record's* equipment with sledge hammers. Although printers identified two of the mob as members of the local alliances, enemies of the WFM blamed the destruction upon unionists who resented the editorial. Before resuming regular publication, George Kyner, publisher of the *Record*, underwent a radical change on the labor question. He soon blossomed out as a major critic of the WFM, especially its leaders, and an open supporter of men whom he had recently condemned. What caused this conversion is not precisely known; however, Peabody's decision to order the Military Board to pay $4,206 to Kyner for his losses undoubtedly influenced his change of policy. On November 10 the board issued a certificate of indebtedness for that amount, payable to Kyner.[82] The switchover silenced labor's strongest voice in the district and strengthened the supporters of the new order.

Working in conjunction with the military, the CCMOA and the CCDCA exploited to the full their new power and the continuing crisis. Upon the recommendation of Secretary Hamlin of the CCMOA and T. P. Airheart, president of the CCDCA, the Board of County Commissioners, still intact but now submissive, employed S. D. Crump, an attorney for the CCMOA and the Peabody administration, to prepare cases against individuals charged with crimes growing out of the labor troubles. Crump's fee was $10,000, payable at $2,000 per month. Influential mine owners served as suretors for the attorney's $10,000 bond, just as they had done for Sheriff Bell.[83] With their man as special prosecutor, the opponents of the WFM were in a position to use the county's legal machinery to their own advantage.

Even so, the campaign of extralegal harassment did not subside, for violence against union members and sympathizers was common. Scores were driven from the district. Moreover,

businessmen, some of whom had been blacklisted in December
for refusing to join the alliance movement, were again asked to
discriminate against those connected with the WFM, the American Labor Union, and the local Trades Assembly. This time few
refused. Formal statements of the CCMOA and the CCDCA emphasized that "agitators," "walking delegates," or their unions
would not be tolerated.[84] Never again, the *Cripple Creek Times*
of June 22 editorialized, would a member of the WFM "earn
another dollar in the mines of the district," and the legal efforts
of the WFM to force the return of the banished miners was a
waste of time because "These men can not come back."

What happened in the Cripple Creek district produced a state and national uproar which, nevertheless, had little
if any effect upon events there.[85] Toward the end of July, the
CCMOA and the CCDCA, confident that the WFM had been
uprooted and that their control was absolute, allowed Sheriff
Bell to ask for an end to state intervention. On July 27, Peabody
withdrew the troops, a move which placed responsibility for
order upon the shoulders of district employers. In doing so, he
asked that the WFM end its strike and submit all the issues to
the voters in the forthcoming election, but he was quick to point
out that, in his opinion, the Teller County campaign had been
"conducted honorably, justly, conscientiously, and humanely."[86]
He was more than satisfied with its outcome.

The withdrawal of troops produced a new out-
break of violence, instigating what *The New York Times* of August 11 called a "reign of terror." Although union sympathizers
were terrorized, their tormentors were rarely caught and punished. Committees openly intimidated bondsmen who furnished
bail for the men who had been charged with crimes connected
with the labor troubles. Mobs took prisoners from deputies and
abused them with impunity; the manager of the union store in
Victor, who had returned under a promise of protection from
the sheriff to settle the affairs of the business, was abducted and
beaten; a Methodist minister at Victor who criticized Peabody,
the CCMOA, and the CCDCA was threatened with violence.
Moreover, on August 20 a mob of 500, led by prominent mine
owners and businessmen, ransacked the union store at Cripple
Creek only four days after it had been reopened by the Inter-

state Mercantile Company, an out-of-state corporation controlled by the WFM. Undersheriff L. F. Parsons, whose office was directly across the street, made no effort to protect either the store or its personnel. That night mobs banished the clerks as well as Eugene Engley, a former attorney general under Governor Waite, J. C. Cole, a former deputy district attorney until deposed in June, Frank Hangs, an attorney representing the WFM, and others, some of whom were savagely beaten and robbed.[87]

After this fresh outbreak of violence, Peabody remained aloof and refused to intervene on behalf of the victims because he had received no "official" notice that state assistance was needed in the "settlement of local differences." His response, like that to similar outbursts of lawlessness from "law and order" groups at Idaho Springs and Telluride, was to evade involvement with legalistic excuses. Although he had earlier stretched both the state and federal constitutions to their limits in protecting propertied interests, he now refused to act unless Sheriff Bell officially requested state intervention. But Bell, who charged that stories of violence had been exaggerated and who asserted that he was "perfectly competent to handle the situation," refused to make the request, even after the governor had offered to place troops at his disposal.[88]

Peabody was undoubtedly relieved at the sheriff's stand. Already his intervention in the district had cost the taxpayers $402,855.14, and his sending in troops again would increase this amount.[89] Moreover, the new disturbances were directed at the union, as they had been during June and July when the guard had occupied the district. At that time the military had joined the campaign to suppress what Peabody had called a "hydra-headed monster, anarchy, assassination, murder, dynamiter [which had] attempted to control the industrial and commercial prosperity of Colorado under the cloak of organized labor."[90] Unless the interests of his supporters in Teller County were again threatened by the WFM, there appeared no immediate need for intervention, despite the public clamor to the contrary. Besides, with the November election only weeks away, such a move was politically unwise, for it might jeopardize Peabody's bid for reelection and his party's control of the state. Moreover, a Republican victory in Teller County was imperative to establish the legitimacy of the new order, and intervening contrary to the wishes of the CCMOA and the CCDCA might undermine their drive for popular approval of their drastic course.

With the local press and all municipal and county offices controlled by opponents of the WFM and with hundreds of union sympathizers banished or intimidated into silence, a popular endorsement of the new regime in the election seemed inevitable. Amidst continuing violence, county voters went to the polls and, with a few minor exceptions, elected the entire Republican ticket, including prominent members of the CCMOA and the CCDCA who had assumed office after their predecessors had been forced to resign.[91] In doing so, the county electorate legitimized the seizure of power by the district employers' associations and apparently endorsed Peabody's course of action in the gold camp.

After the Independence depot explosion and the decision of the Colorado Supreme Court in *In Re Moyer* Peabody never doubted that the tactics employed against the WFM had been both legal and proper. The results of the election in Teller County were therefore gratifying and confirmed his belief that his course there had been the one the people really wanted. However, even before the dramatic episodes of the summer, a strike of the WFM at Telluride had exposed just how far Peabody had been prepared to go in breaking the WFM. His intervention in Cripple Creek had not been an isolated phenomenon.

6

Strikebreaking in the San Juans

In the fall of 1903, Telluride, located deep in the San Juan Mountains of southwestern Colorado, was the center of a thriving gold district with a history of labor violence. The strike of 1901 over the fathom system had been settled by a three-year contract between Miners' Union No. 63, WFM, and the Telluride Mining Association (TMA) which had established a $3 a day minimum wage and an eight-hour day as the wage-hour standard for all but the mill and surface workers. But the violence surrounding the strike left labor relations so embittered that a restoration of mutual confidence between the mine owners and their workers was nearly impossible. The continued anti-union stance of the Telluride *Daily Journal*, the union's retaliatory boycott, the formation of a Business Men's Association to sustain the *Journal*, and the assassination of Arthur Collins, a mine manager, shortly after Peabody's election in 1902 exacerbated conditions in the district. Consequently, like their counterparts elsewhere in the state, the mine owners and their supporters, distressed by the violent history, the militancy, and the growing socialist orientation of the WFM, concluded that the time had come to break the union. Their chance came in the late summer of 1903.

In part, the renewal of trouble in Telluride was but a wave of the general labor unrest then sweeping Colorado. Outraged by labor's failure to obtain an eight-hour law which Coloradans had overwhelmingly endorsed in the election of 1902, officials of the WFM had resorted to strikes, hoping to gain by direct action what political action had failed to deliver. On July 11 they formally launched a campaign for an eight-hour day for all the membership throughout the state. Inevitably, Miners' Union No. 63 became involved in this drive. Although most of its members already enjoyed an eight-hour day under the contract of 1901, the millworkers had been excluded. The union's effort to obtain the shorter workday for its millmen sparked a new struggle in the gold camp.

At its annual meeting in early August 1903 the San Juan District Union passed a resolution demanding an eight-hour day by September 1 for all millworkers within its jurisdiction. However, the TMA promptly rejected the demand, pointing out that it contained no provision for a simultaneous reduction in wages and that some of the millworkers were under contract to work a ten to twelve-hour day, in some cases for another year. But when the union agreed to exclude the men under contract and to accept a 13 percent reduction in wages for the remainder as long as wages did not drop below a $3 minimum, the TMA responded by organizing the San Juan District Mine Owners' Association, whose membership included all the mine and mill operators in Ouray, San Juan, and San Miguel counties. All were determined to resist the eight-hour drive of the WFM. On August 29, Charles A. Chase, secretary of the new tri-county organization and a member of the TMA, informed the union that because of the poor quality of ore then being mined around Telluride, its modified demand would not be granted. Chase's statement left the union no choice, therefore, but to strike if a shorter day was to be gained for its millworkers.[1]

At the start of the strike on September 1, approximately 100 millmen walked off their jobs, forcing six mills to close. Immediately, the Liberty Bell, Tomboy, and Nellie mines, which shipped ore to the mills, closed because their ore bins were full. The shutdown threw nearly 400 miners out of work. There followed a sympathetic strike by the Telluride Federal Labor Union, composed of cooks and waiters working in the company boarding houses, which forced the Smuggler-Union and Alta mines to close, putting additional miners out of work. Within a week, an estimated 700 men left Telluride in search of work because they anticipated a long struggle. Despite the union's attempt to restrict its effort to the millworkers, the entire district had become involved. Economic stagnation settled over the area as the union and the mine owners maneuvered for a showdown.[2]

At this point, the sole issue was an eight-hour day for the millworkers. However, an attempt by the management of the Tomboy Gold Mining Company to resume operations with nonunion labor added a new dimension to the strike, for it allowed Guy Miller, president of Miners' Union No. 63, to charge that the company was discriminating against union members in its hiring and firing procedures. Consequently, a strike was ordered against the Tomboy mine. Miller leveled similar charges against the Liberty Gold Mining Company when it refused to employ a striking Tomboy miner for development work because of his union membership.[3] No longer was the eight-hour day for the millmen the critical issue. Now in question was the right of the miners to organize without fear of reprisals from their employers. Survival of the union had become the crucial issue. Union officials realized that the refusal of the Tomboy and Liberty mines to employ members of the WFM reflected the position of the powerful TMA and the newly formed San Juan District Mine Operators' Association. If successful, that policy meant death to the local union.

In spite of the hardening attitudes, some hope for a peaceful settlement remained. In early October representatives of the WFM and the two employers' associations met in Denver with Assistant Attorney General I. B. Melville, Peabody's personal representative. They reached an informal agreement, subject to ratification by the mining companies and the local union, calling for an eight-hour day and a $3 a day minimum wage for all employees in the Telluride mines and mills. However, according to Bill Haywood, the settlement collapsed when the Telluride

Business Men's Association sabotaged the agreement.[4] The result was a continuation of the strike and sporadic altercations between unionists and strikebreakers which had tragic consequences. Substantial responsibility rests, therefore, upon the organized businessmen of Telluride, who insisted on extending their vendetta against the WFM.

Early in October the businessmen converted their association into the Telluride Citizens' Alliance (TCA), becoming a part of the national employers' movement. On October 27 it became a charter member of the State Citizens' Alliance of Colorado, the first statewide federation of alliances, whose primary objective was the destruction of the WFM and other militant unions in Colorado.[5] This goal had the full support of Telluride's businessmen, who became intensely hostile toward the local miners' union after the murder of Collins, manager of the Smuggler-Union properties, in November 1902, an act for which they blamed the union. However, crushing an affiliate of the WFM required more power than the TCA, the TMA, and the San Juan District Operators' Association possessed. Furthermore, memories of the labor war of 1901 were strong. Some means had to be found to break the union with a minimum of force. The leaders of the employers' associations turned to Denver.

On October 14 representatives of the associations and County Sheriff J. C. Rutan conferred with Peabody about their plans to resume full operations with nonunion labor. Because they expected trouble from the miners' union similar to that of 1901, they asked that the governor send troops to prevent the anticipated violence. Peabody, who had already honored similar requests from employers in other parts of the state, listened sympathetically. He finally promised to intervene militarily in the Telluride district prior to November 1. However, before doing so, he required a formal petition for troops from the leaders of the TCA and the TMA, plus county and city officials. Upon receiving it, he promised to send his own investigators. Peabody wanted "written evidence" on file to support the intervention that he had pledged.[6]

W. E. Wheeler, chairman of the alliance and the president of the First National Bank of Telluride, acted swiftly to compile the "evidence." Within a week the governor received

121

a formal petition requesting 300 members of the National Guard to prevent a threatened outbreak of violence which the civil authorities certified that they could not control. Five officers of the alliance, nine city and county officials, and seven managers and superintendents of mining, milling, and power companies endorsed the petition. Military force, they wrote in an enclosure in their petition, was essential to protect property, the right to work, and the right of everyone in San Miguel County to "life, liberty and the pursuit of happiness." On October 24, Peabody informed Wheeler that his personal investigators would soon arrive and asked that they be given "explicit information" regarding conditions there. To make the assessment he chose C. E. Hagar, secretary of the State Board of Pardons, and G. E. Randolph, a former Union colonel in the Civil War. Their reports were based principally upon interviews with persons who favored intervention or who had signed the petition, and they substantiated the need for state involvement. In their opinion, the governor had to order out the guard if mining and milling were to resume without violence.[7] Although he now had "written evidence" for the record, Peabody hesitated.

He had heard that Republican Congressman H. M. Hogg of the Second Congressional District (which included Telluride) considered state intervention unnecessary. To extend the protection desired by the employers and then have the congressman publicly deny its necessity would be humiliating. Peabody asked Wheeler to contact Hogg and, if the rumor of his opposition were true, persuade him that Colorado's development and the peaceful resumption of industry in his district depended upon the cooperative efforts of all public officers. The rumor of Hogg's oposition proved false, for he fully supported state intervention.[8]

Still the governor failed to act. Late in October threats of an impending coal strike came from the northern and southern coal fields. Troops might be needed there. How could a large corporation like the Colorado Fuel and Iron Company, for example, be ignored if it requested aid in controlling hundreds of striking miners? Furthermore, a large portion of the National Guard had been in the Cripple Creek district since early September. Despite demands from the TCA and the TMA that he fulfill his promise to intervene, Peabody refused until the intentions of the coal miners had been clarified.[9]

Meanwhile, he collected additional evidence to justify intervention when it became possible. Wheeler resubmitted the initial petition with further statements urging the need for troops. On Melville's request, union officials forwarded a report which strongly denied the need for state action. S. D. Crump, a prominent Cripple Creek lawyer whom Peabody sent to Telluride, reported an immediate need for intervention. And Charles A. Chase sent statistical data detailing the losses suffered by the district from the strike to support the mine owners' contention that quick intervention was imperative.[10]

Rutan also submitted an affidavit declaring it "sheer folly" for him to assume responsibility for protecting the lives and property of the mine owners if they resumed operations against the wishes of the miners' union. He suggested a remedy: banish the obstreperous leaders and members of the union from the county, a method already employed with the tacit approval of the governor at Idaho Springs. "Two hundred to two hundred and fifty well drilled, armed and equipped members of the National Guard" patrolling the mining district, he wrote, would force out most of the "lawless element" within ninety days. Rutan believed that competent and law-abiding miners would work if protected.[11] Peabody referred this and other statements to Nathan Miller, the attorney general, for an advisory opinion, which, if favorable, would also become part of the "written evidence" to support intervention.

Nevertheless, the governor continued to delay intervening in Telluride. The coal miners did strike, thereby increasing the possibility that the requests for troops would exceed the available supply. Moreover, the state lacked funds to underwrite a military expedition of the scope required. Consequently, on November 16, Peabody turned to Washington. He pleaded that the "dangerous" industrial situation in Colorado and the growing demands for troops necessitated federal assistance and asked President Theodore Roosevelt for army regulars to protect life and property in the mining camps. Roosevelt refused, although his response encouraged Peabody to believe that aid would be forthcoming if conditions further deteriorated. However, a second request of November 18 failed to convince the President of the necessity for federal military intervention. He refused to act unless conditions escalated into "an insurrection against the government of the State" which would permit federal action in conformity with Section 5297, Title LXIX, United States *Revised Codes*.[12] Roosevelt would go no further than to send Major General John C. Bates to investigate the labor troubles. Within a week Bates visited the state and, after a hurried examination, concluded that federal troops were unnecessary "unless Peabody had to intervene in the coal fields." Nevertheless, Bates investigation convinced Peabody that should he again ask Roosevelt for aid, the request would be "promptly" honored.[13]

Meanwhile, officials of the TCA and the TMA continued to press for state intervention with or without federal aid. Although conditions in the district were peaceful, the mine owners were anxious to resume operations with nonunion labor, and they expected this to provoke violence from the striking miners. On November 17 a delegation from the TMA conferred with the governor, pressing him to act. The next day several businessmen, including Charles F. Painter, publisher of the Telluride *Daily Journal*, conveyed a telegram to Peabody from officials of the TMA, TCA, and the county which threatened to close the mines for the winter if troops were not immediately sent. In a telegram of November 19 the TCA again demanded soldiers to protect lives and property so that mining might resume.[14] If the mines were to reopen in 1903, Peabody could no longer delay intervention, despite Roosevelt's rejection of his requests for assistance.

On November 18, Miller, who had examined the "evidence" on Telluride, advised the governor that Section 3, Article VII of the National Guard Act (1897) authorized him "to send troops when a tumult, a riot or mob" was threatened, and that the affidavits in Peabody's possession showed the "absolute necessity of calling out the troops if mining and other business" were to resume, except on "terms dictated by the Western Federation of Miners." Moreover, he recommended that the "greatest publicity" be given to the documents, except the letter of November 4 from Congressman Hogg. Peabody, now convinced that intervening in Telluride was legally defensible and that there would be no immediate demands from the coal operators for assistance, issued an executive order on November 20 sending troops into San Miguel County allegedly to assist Rutan in "the enforcement of the constitution and laws of this State, and in maintaining peace and good order." His decision activated six companies of infantry, two troops of cavalry, and other detachments of the guard, altogether more than 400 men.[15]

Because the state treasury was empty, certificates of indebtedness were issued to finance the campaign, the same procedure used to underwrite the military operations then underway in Cripple Creek. Until these were sold, the soldiers in Telluride could not be paid. It seems probable that Wheeler, president of the First National Bank of Telluride as well as chairman of the TCA, in cooperation with the TMA, agreed to purchase enough certificates to pay the men while they were in the field. Miller of the miners' local later charged that Peabody had required the TMA and the TCA to "put up $155,000 in colateral securities" to guarantee the payment of the troops before issuing his order of November 20. The governor had made a similar demand upon the Cripple Creek Mine Owners' Association before ordering soldiers into Cripple Creek. Although there was no other way to finance the expeditions, the practical effect was to convert the military forces entering the mining camps into paid agents of the interests demanding intervention.[16]

On November 24, Major Zeph T. Hill arrived in Telluride with his command and, following the recommendations of Rutan, deployed his forces throughout the district in such a manner as to protect the mines, mills, and power facilities from an anticipated union assault. To control the movement of traffic on trails leading to and from the mines he set up an elaborate pass system in collaboration with the mill and mine owners. From the start Hill worked closely with local property owners, whom he described in letters to Peabody as the "best people" who saw in the presence of the troops the "dawn of a better day" for the district.[17] Such people, of course, cooperated fully with him.

The various interests responsible for intervention found it difficult to do enough for the soldiers to make their stay as comfortable and inexpensive as possible. Major H. M. Randolph, assistant commissary general, arranged with the managers of every major company in the district—the Smuggler-Union, the Liberty Bell, the Telluride Light and Power, the Ella, the San Miguel Consolidated, the Tomboy, the Butterfly-Terrible, and the Contention—to provide free goods and services ranging from electricity to sleeping quarters and meals. Such aid reduced the expenses of keeping the troops in the field. Never did these services become financial obligations of the state to be paid in the future. Significantly, each manager who reached an agreement with Randolph had endorsed the original petition for troops. Peabody gave his full support to this close working relationship with the beneficiaries of intervention and approved Randolph's agreements with the companies as "most satisfactory."[18]

Unconvinced that control alone would assure a peaceful resumption of mining and milling with nonunion labor, Peabody became further involved in the strikes. In a letter of November 23, written while Hill was enroute to Telluride, he recommended to his commander that he examine carefully Section 1362 of *Mills' Annotated Statutes*, which concerned the arrest and punishment of vagrants, and that he arrange with the local authorities to arrest on a vagrancy charge any loiterer who had no visible means of support. At the discretion of the judge anyone so arrested might choose a fine, imprisonment, or a permanent exile from the county. Peabody believed that this procedure would force "very much of the lawless, good-for-nothing, intimidating class of citizens [union leaders]" out of the district and reduce Hill's problem of maintaining peace and order.[19] His proposal launched a campaign of legal harassment designed to drive the more vociferous striking miners either back into the mines on company terms or out of the district.

Upon receipt of the governor's proposal Hill conferred with Rutan, who strongly supported Peabody's recommended use of Section 1362. After all, as early as November 13, Rutan had suggested to the governor that the expulsions of hardcore leaders and members of the local union, which military intervention would make possible, would effectively break the strike. The sheriff now proposed to Hill that all unemployed men, especially those using the union's soup kitchen, be arrested as vagrants, and he asked that Hill provide soldiers to aid in the arrests. In Rutan's opinion, it was desireable to expel the more obnoxious "vagrants" rather than allow them to return to the mines or to pay fines.[20] On November 30, Rutan, aided by military personnel, arrested thirty-eight union members on vagrancy charges. However, the police judge before whom the men were arraigned discharged twenty of the prisoners. The others, who received fines ranging from twenty-five to thirty-five dollars which were suspended for two days, received instructions to report back at the end of the suspension to pay their fines, leave town, or work off the penalties. When at the end of two days they failed to return as required, the judge ordered their rearrest and sentenced them to work off their fines in the public works.

The legal harassment of the striking miners brought a quick response from officials of the WFM in Denver. Haywood wired officers of the local union to advise their men to remain in Telluride should they be charged with vagrancy, promising that whoever violated the miners' civil rights guaranteed by the U. S. Constitution would be prosecuted. He also informed Roosevelt, Senator H. M. Teller, and Senator T. M. Patterson of the situation and asked that they initiate a federal investigation. The President, who had recently refused to intervene in behalf of Peabody and who had just received Major-General Bates's report, refused, saying that he had "neither the power nor the right" to act as requested. Moreover, a controversial resolution introduced by Patterson on December 11 which called upon the Senate Judiciary Committee to investigate Peabody's extraordinary conduct in the strikes failed to provoke an enquiry.[21]

Meanwhile, lawyers of the WFM initiated habeas corpus proceedings to force a hearing for union members incarcerated on the charge of vagrancy. Their efforts proved futile, for on December 7, County Judge J. M. Wardlaw sustained a motion to set aside the proceedings. Nevertheless, the litigation raised the possibility of legal action against Hill, who had now concluded that martial law was the most effective way to remove troublemakers from the district. But Peabody did not want a clash between the military and the courts in Telluride. The arrogant display of power in September by General Bell in Cripple Creek had produced bitter criticism of Peabody's administration there. The governor did not want a similar incident in San Miguel County. He therefore ordered Hill to obey any writ of habeas corpus issued by the local courts without unnecessary military display. If the courts released persons whom the major considered dangerous to the community, however, Hill was to rearrest them and await instructions from Denver. If necessary, the governor promised to declare San Miguel County in a state of insurrection and rebellion as he had done in Teller County on December 4.[22]

The strike was now at a critical phase. Peabody had hoped that the presence of troops would produce a wholesale desertion from union ranks and a resumption of mining and milling in the district. This had not happened. Union members remained on strike, forcing the mine owners to comb the country for nonunion personnel to work their properties. Replacements for the strikers began arriving as the tempo of legal harassment picked up. There were, for example, eight-four strikebreakers arriving on December 8 and forty others six days later. With the arrival of strikebreakers the Tomboy mine reopened, soon followed by others. Joining together, the mine owners adopted for the entire district a uniform wage-hour schedule, which ignored the demand of the union for an eight-hour day for the millworkers. The influx of strikebreakers and the reopening of major mines clearly threatened to destroy the miners' union. If violence was to occur, it seemed likely to occur at this point.

Hill, who had the governor's promise to place the district under military rule at his request, remained confident that he could control the situation even if violence erupted. Contrary to his expectations, however, conditions remained quiet and did not warrant a further extension of military authority. Hill therefore explored other means of helping the mine owners.

He became concerned about the inflammatory talk among some of the strikers and their sympathizers. For example, a certain Hetrick, who operated a small store containing a post office which had become a favorite gathering place for some of the striking miners, had allegedly threatened both strikebreakers and members of the guard. Hill believed that Hetrick's incendiary talk among a "lot of ignorant Italians and other foreigners" could provoke "a great deal of trouble" from the strikers. Under the circumstances, Hetrick and other "agitators" were dangerous because they could set off outbreaks of violence. However, Hill was uncertain of his authority to restrain their provocative talk. He asked Peabody to consult a "competent legal authority" to determine whether persons engaging in inflammatory speech might not be arrested and tried for "sedition or as a traitor." The governor referred the question to Miller, who blocked such action as unconstitutional under Section 107, Article II, of the state constitution. Miller suggested instead that Hill fully enforce the vagrancy and misdemeanor laws (Section 1305, *Mills' Annotated Statutes*), which allowed fines up to fifty dollars and imprisonment up to ninety days.[23]

Hill tried a different tack. He suggested to the governor that "a couple of Pinkerton men" be sent down to "mingle with the striking element." Valuable information might be obtained for use against the striking miners. Although Peabody agreed that the agents would be useful, he thought that the TMA ought to assume the expense, just as the Cripple Creek Mine Owners' Association was doing in the Cripple Creek district where agents were employed for similar purposes. Through E. C. Howe, the county attorney, Hill contacted the executive committee of the TMA only to learn that it had already employed an agent who was on the scene and that the mine owners wanted the matter kept strictly secret.[24]

As Christmas aproached, the strikers were in dire straits. If they persuaded others not to work, they were "agitators"; if they refused to work on company terms, they were "vagrants"; if they consulted with one another, they were "conspirators" who bred mischief and misdemeanors; if they objected to the treatment by their employers, they could exercise their right to find other employment. Their displacement by strikebreakers had made them "outsiders." But most damaging of all was the renewal of mining in face of the strike. Even Peabody considered their situation hopeless, for he now believed that the "dangerous influence" of the WFM in Telluride had been "crushed" or "completely subjected to law." On December 18, he informed Hill that, in his opinion, the time had come to reduce the number of soldiers in the district. However, he pointedly insisted that the "mine owners and the citizens' alliance" had to concur in any

129

decision to reduce the number of troops on active duty; otherwise there would be no reduction of the forces under Hill's command.[25]

Hill and the mine owners disagreed with the governor's assessment of the situation, for they believed more rather than less pressure ought to be exerted on the union. Hill responded by recommending that all San Miguel County, plus the land extending for two miles on either side of the railroads running to Ridgeway (about forty-five miles) and Montrose (about seventy-five miles), be made a military district. He wanted military control over the lines so that his patrols could block the return of banished vagrants to Telluride without setting off a conflict with civil authorities outside San Miguel County. The major's proposal was part of a broader scheme being concocted to harass and drive out more of the strikers. Howe, who also represented the TMA and the TCA, conferred in Denver with Peabody about another scheme of legal harassment that he had contrived. He suggested that Section 3165 of *Mills' Annotated Statutes* be fully enforced. This provision imposed fines up to $250 and six months in jail for persons convicted of conspiring to seize a mine by force or intimidation. Peabody endorsed Howe's plan, but he withheld immediate approval of Hill's proposal.[26]

On December 22, Sheriff Rutan arrested eighteen strikers under Section 3165 and charged them with intimidating nonunion men working in the mines. He sent eleven of his prisoners to Montrose for confinement, alleging that the Telluride jail was inadequate. Rutan then asked Hill to place military guards at the railroad stations nearest the county line to block the return of any deported or objectionable person. Hill complied. On December 27 he stationed a detail at Placerville. No one could enter San Miguel County by rail without the approval of a county deputy sheriff assigned to the station. Afterward Rutan dropped charges against his prisoners in Montrose and ordered their release, but he knew that they could not reenter Telluride by train.[27] Even so, numerous strikers remained in the district, and their presence kept alive vivid memories of 1901 among members of the TMA and the TCA. What would happen when the troops left the county? Would there be another labor war? The mine owners and their sympathizers thought so, and so did Hill.

Hill and Rutan now exerted pressure on Peabody to declare martial law so that they might institute a final solution. In a letter of December 28 the major complained that all efforts had failed to drive the "disturbers and law breakers" from the district. The men simply kept returning. Proclaiming martial law was the most effective way to remove the troublemakers until the troops withdrew, hopefully by February 1, 1904. Hill believed that a military banishment of undesirables would be permanent; Rutan concurred. In their opinion, the campaign of legal harassment had failed, and martial law was the only answer. Years later Hill conceded that the district was quiet and that the mills and mines were operating when he recommended martial law. Contrary to his expectations, the renewal of operations had not produced the anticipated violence from the union. He even admitted that the alleged troublemakers had operated within the letter of the law. Nevertheless, the threatening presence of the strikers compelled the authorities to act under the "more flexible rule of military necessity." The danger of an armed uprising like that around the Smuggler-Union in 1901 had to be eliminated.[28] That could be done only by the permanent removal of the striking miners who adamantly refused to work on company terms.

Unlike the circumstances surrounding the imposition of military rule upon Teller County on December 4, there had been no dramatic mine explosion or train-wrecking in the Telluride district to get the public ready for a similar step there. Conditions were relatively calm. Consequently, there was no concrete justification for extending the military's jurisdiction, only the intangible fears of Hill and Rutan that unusual violence like that of 1901 would erupt once the troops had departed and that it was necessary to authorize action beyond the restrictive orders of the courts to prevent it. For more than a week Peabody mulled over their request and then acted. On January 3, 1904, he proclaimed that conditions in San Miguel County bordered on "absolute insurrection and rebellion." A lawless band of men, he announced, had committed crimes, violated the laws, threatened lives and property, and imposed a reign of terror which civil and military officials with "limited power" could not control. The

governor ordered Hill to use whatever means he judged suitable
to restore peace and to enforce the laws. Hill now had extensive
authority to act against union members whom he considered potential troublemakers, authority which he intended to exploit to
the full in "cleaning out" San Miguel County so thoroughly that
when the troops left, the civil authorities would be in "absolute
control."[29] He immediately went to work eliminating all threats
by a wholesale banishment of union members.

After posting and reading the governor's proclamation on the main streets of Telluride, Hill ordered a detachment
of soldiers to accompany Rutan to the union hospital where a
meeting of the strikers was in progress. There Rutan arrested
eighteen union members whom Hill blamed for past disturbances
in the district. Civil authorities also arrested thirteen others elsewhere. Among those seized were Eugene Engley, a former attorney general of Colorado who represented the WFM in the district, J. C. Williams, vice-president of the WFM who had taken
charge of the strike, and Guy Miller, president of the local miners' union. More drastic action was still ahead. On January 4,
Hill deported his prisoners to Ridgeway, forty-five miles away,
and ordered them not to return. He imposed censorship on all
press reports leaving Telluride over the telegraph and telephone
lines; he ordered a nine p.m. curfew; he commanded that all firearms be brought to military headquarters, registered, and surrendered, unless the owners could convince him that they were
"good law-abiding citizens"; he restricted freedom of assembly.
Hill interpreted Peabody's proclamation and subsequent orders
of January 3 to mean that martial law had been established in
San Miguel County.[30]

In Denver, however, Miller questioned whether
martial law had been imposed. On January 4 he cautioned Peabody that his proclamation had described conditions in San
Miguel County as only "bordering" on insurrection and rebellion.
Any attempt, therefore, to suspend the writ of habeas corpus
would be illegal under the state constitution. The governor immediately informed Hill that his order did not contemplate any
arrest which would necessitate a writ issued by the local courts.
Hill could follow two courses of action against undesirable persons: he could deport the ones he arrested, or he could turn

132

them over to the civil authorities after filing charges. But the governor emphasized that Hill had "complete control" over the county.[31]

Hill had no intention of turning his prisoners over to the civil authorities. That procedure had failed before. He had requested martial law so that he might compel obnoxious persons to leave the district without regard to civil authority. Besides, referral would recognize the jurisdiction of civil officials and would subject the military to restraining orders from the local courts. He wanted no judicial interference in purging the county of these strikers, whom he believed must be removed for the "best interest of peace and harmony" in the district. Peabody could rest assured, Hill wrote, that he would deport only the "principal agitators and trouble makers" from the county. By February 2 he had banished eighty-three men.[32] Rutan gave strong support.

Meanwhile, Hill's subordinates registered and collected all firearms except those owned by "good law-abiding citizens," enforced the curfew as if critical conditions prevailed in the district, and censored all press reports except those sent out by mail. The major justified censorship as necessary to "correct false and misleading" statements about military activities in the county which might jeopardize his "plan of campaign."[33] Censorship continued throughout the period of military control, despite the quick reaction of newspapers like the *Rocky Mountain News* of January 5, which condemned the procedure and charged that Hill was attempting to prevent a public scrutiny of his actions in the mining camp. Hill ignored such criticism.

Nevertheless, the major's actions raised the possibility that the WFM would initiate litigation against officers of the guard as it had done at Cripple Creek and Colorado City. As a countermeasure, Hill sent agents to circulate among the deported strikers who had gathered at Montrose to obtain information which could be used if suits occurred. But as the campaign progressed, he stopped worrying about possible lawsuits. As early as January 8 he decided to ignore all court orders that might arise from banishing the striking miners, unless the governor instructed him to the contrary. Three days later Hill received instructions from Denver "to pay no attention to such orders, neither by permitting service or to obey the mandate of the court if such order

133

is issued."[34] Rather than jeopardize the military campaign then underway against the union, Peabody was now prepared to defy the courts, a fact which confirmed Hill's belief that unrestricted martial law prevailed in the county.

Both Peabody and Hill continued to search for new means to "pacify" San Miguel County. Because the major worried about the Italian aliens living in the district, the governor contacted the Italian Secret Service, obtained a list of fugitives, and passed it on to the major to check against the strikers still in Telluride. He also employed the Pinkerton Detective Agency to investigate several Italian aliens. And he sent Dr. Joseph Cuneo, Italian consul in Denver, a list of Italians banished from Telluride, asking for character assessments based on the Italian government's records. Hill was also anxious that the United States Secret Service expedite its investigation and arrest of any Italian criminals residing in his area of jurisdiction. He believed that this would "put a new terror into the rest of the foreigners living here now, and those deported."[35]

Officials of the TMA and the TCA also joined in the search for means to wreck the union. They had come to realize that the harassment of the strikers had increased the likelihood of retaliation once the troops withdrew. No one wanted to become another Arthur Collins. As early as December, therefore, they had become aware of the need for a force capable of controlling the county when Hill departed with his command. Following the lead of their counterparts in other mining camps who were experiencing labor troubles with the WFM, they concluded that a unit of the National Guard, permanently stationed in Telluride, would provide the protection they needed. Hill supported the idea. He said that a local unit would be "a great support to the law-abiding portion of the County" after his withdrawal. Moreover, a sufficient number of the "right" kind of people had indicated their willingness to join the cavalry troop which the mine owners and businessmen had proposed. Twenty men had agreed to serve without pay if the governor would consent to the plan. Peabody, who had withheld his consent because of the expense involved, finally endorsed the proposal. The governor gave consent for such a plan in a letter of December 30, 1903 to Bulkeley Wells, manager of the Smuggler-Union properties, who had submitted a petition from forty-six county residents asking for a troop of cavalry.[36]

After Peabody's proclamation of January 3, Hill rushed the creation of the local troop. He asked Wells to persuade the men who had endorsed the petition to enlist immediately for preliminary training, for, having promised the governor to make every effort to withdraw by January 18, he was anxious to get the new organization in shape. Mustering-in ceremonies for forty-one men were on January 11. This created Troop A, First Squadron Cavalry. The new troopers chose Wells as their captain.[37] Thus, a man who had led the employers' opposition to the local miners' union, who managed a major property in the district, who was a charter member of the San Juan Mine Operators' Association, who had been a leader in obtaining state intervention, and who had played a key role in forming Troop A became both an agent of the state and the local employers' associations within the guard. Hill's departure would leave Wells strategically positioned to act for the state and his associates in the TMA and the TCA.

After the formation of Troop A, which was filled with men whom Peabody believed had "entered the service with the determination to carry on the work successfully inaugurated and brought to almost a conclusion," Hill pressed for a withdrawal of all his forces by January 18. However, in discussing the matter with officials of the TMA, he found unexpected opposition. The mine owners were confident that they could control the district when Hill withdrew, but they feared the effects of his withdrawal upon their nonunion employees. Rumors had spread that the WFM would retaliate against the strikebreakers as soon as the soldiers left, and the mine owners feared that their men would quit if not protected. They asked that one troop of cavalry be retained on active duty for at least two more weeks, with or without the power to "enforce the edicts of martial law" then prevailing, to prevent the stampeding of their men. Hill agreed to delay his withdrawal until February 1, subject to the governor's approval. Peabody, who had received a similar request from Wheeler of the TCA, agreed to the delay.[38]

Meanwhile, the troops continued to send away various strikers. As the date for withdrawal approached, Hill, with the consent of the TCA and the TMA, began reducing his command, although he had second thoughts about the reduction. Much to his dismay there remained a "considerable lawless element not yet convinced that further disorder and violence was useless," despite all the effort made to convince them otherwise. Moreover, he had learned that the banished miners were gathering at Montrose, about seventy-five miles away on the Denver and Rio Grande railroad, and that they were planning to return to Telluride as soon as the troops had withdrawn. If that happened, the results of military intervention would be cancelled. The mine owners were also concerned, and they sent Wells to Denver to confer directly with Peabody. As an alternative to a total withdrawal of the troops, Wells recommended that Troop A, which he commanded, be activated for service upon Hill's departure and that it be supported by a detail of men selected by the major. He also advised that military rule continue. Wells convinced the governor that neither a total withdrawal nor a revocation of military rule on February 1 was advisable.[39]

Hill, officials of the TMA and TCA, and the civil authorities consulted intermittently on how to end military intervention and yet meet the alleged threat from the striking miners. On February 12 they reached an agreement based substantially upon Wells's recommendations to Peabody. Hill was to withdraw on February 21, and Troop A was to be activated. Martial law would prevail until February 23, when Wells's command would be placed under civil authority. The purpose of the two-day extension of military rule was to place the telegraph and telephone lines under Wells's control so that the withdrawal might be kept secret as long as possible. Hill fully expected his withdrawal, if publicized, to set off an armed invasion by the banished miners at Montrose. Peabody supported this arrangement and on February 18 ordered Troop A into active service. He was confident that Wells would use his command to prevent any disturbance that would hinder milling and mining in the district.[40]

On February 20 Wells assumed control of San Miguel County and thus ended the first phase of state intervention, which had involved 451 men. Although the mines and mills were operating, nothing else had been accomplished by three months of military occupation except the forced expulsion of dozens of strikers who now threatened to return at the first opportunity. The strike continued, and the fear which had brought the troops still prevailed, as Hill's resort to secrecy indicated. The major's withdrawal suggested an end to state intervention; however, Wells soon dispelled this illusion.

Contrary to the agreement of February 12, martial law did not end on February 23 but was further extended by the governor upon the request of the mine owners. Censorship continued. Wells examined, and in some instances wrote, news dispatches sent over the wires from the district, and his telephone censor monitored all incoming calls to union members. By this procedure he hoped to gain information for use against the striking miners. Wells also closed the potential meeting places of alleged "agitators," arranged for a Pinkerton agent to circulate among the strikers to gather "evidence," and supported Rutan's continued legal harassment of the miners' union. For example, on February 29, Wells's troopers aided the sheriff in arresting thirty-seven men on vagrancy charges. Through correspondence Wells remained in close touch with Zeph Hill, who referred the captain's letters to the governor.[41]

As February ended, Wells and his associates realized that military rule could not prevail indefinitely. They also discovered that formal responsibility for maintaining peace restricted rather than expanded their means for eradicating the influence of the WFM in the district. After a week of command, Wells concluded that everything the military could do to break the strike had been done. He now believed that a more "lasting" settlement could be "effected by the citizens of the district, through asserting and protecting themselves, without the assistance of troops or martial law." He found support for his position. On March 8, after a joint meeting of county officials and members of the executive committees of the TMA and the TCA, Wheeler, the chairman of the TCA, discussed with Peabody the sentiments of the district employers on the matter. Like Wells, they agreed that the time had come for the total withdrawal of the state. However, so that they might have several days for preparing to "take care of themselves," Wheeler asked that the revocation of martial law and the release of Troop A not occur until March 11.[42] The governor consented to this arrangement. The next day he issued an order, effective March 11 at eight p.m., suspending "qualified martial law" in San Miguel County and deactivating Troop A. For the first time since January 3, civil authorities would control the county.

What the employers feared now happened. As soon as military rule ceased, many of the banished strikers began to return from Ridgeway and Montrose. A group of fifty arrived in Telluride on March 14. Their arrival triggered what must have been a prearranged plan among the law and order element to remove not only the men who returned, but all known union sympathizers. Having failed to resolve the strike problem with legal harassment and military force, opponents of the union apparently decided to resort to extralegal means of proven success— the Idaho Springs solution—counting on the governor's support if matters escalated out of their control.

On the night of March 14 a large number of the mine owners, mine operators, bankers, merchants, and gamblers gathered in Red Men's Hall behind closed doors to discuss the return of the exiles. The meeting, from which newspaper reporters were barred unless sworn to secrecy, erupted into a stormy session. Should the returned strikers be permitted to remain or should they be driven out? Members of the TCA and the TMA, who favored immediate removal finally wrested control of the meeting. They convinced the throng that drastic action was imperative if the gains of the past four months were to last.

Members of the mob left the hall together and armed themselves mainly with the weapons furnished by the state to Troop A. They reassembled in front of the first National Bank. There Bulkeley Wells and John Herron, manager of the Tomboy properties, took charge. The two were strongly supported by other mine owners, prominent citizens, and gamblers. The mob began a systematic, early-morning roundup of all the returned strikers and their sympathizers, using force when necessary to enter private homes. Included among the seventy to eighty men caught up in the dragnet were officials of the union and the local Socialist party. Their captors rushed them to the depot where two special coaches waited to take them to Ridgeway. They were warned never to return.[43] Since the incident included the participation of prominent citizens and law enforcement officials, it was one of the most glaring examples of lawlessness during the Peabody administration.

The outbreak placed Peabody in an awkward position. Three times he had ordered out the National Guard when the law and order group had petitioned for aid to prevent an anticipated outbreak of massive violence by the WFM. Now for the first time large-scale violence perpetrated by Peabody's supporters had occurred in Telluride. An angry mob had threatened lives, destroyed property, and violated wholesale the civil rights of union members and their sympathizers. The instigators of this lawlessness were the very people whose interests Peabody had tried to protect. Recently honored by them as a "Law and Order Governor," he now had an opportunity to validate that title by protecting union men as he had protected the corporate representatives among his supporters. Nevertheless, he refused to act until the authorities in Telluride requested his intervention. Law enforcement officials there had not only sanctioned the action of the mob, however; some had participated in the criminal activities. Now that the town had again been purged, the police force strengthened, and members of the TCA engaged to patrol the streets armed with revolvers and Winchesters, the possibility that civil authorities would demand state intervention was indeed remote, unless the victims of the mob reacted more violently than anticipated.[44]

If Peabody hoped that he could avoid involvement, he soon learned otherwise. Bill Haywood, who had concluded that "ordinary channels of justice" were closed to members of the WFM in Colorado, announced that the deported men would return, by force if necessary. Unintentionally, the governor encouraged such a procedure. For three days John H. Murphy, an attorney for the WFM, and A. H. Floaten, Stewart Forbes, and Antone Matti, three victims of the mob, attempted to discuss the matter with him in Denver, but Peabody refused to meet with them.[45] Despite the growing public pressures to intervene, he steadfastly refused, until new developments forced him to reconsider his position.

Across the range in Ouray County, which lies adjacent to San Miguel, members of the WFM reacted strongly to the second banishment of their fellow unionists from Telluride.

Rumors reached Denver that the Ouray miners' union had chosen an armed band of fifty men to escort the exiles back into Telluride. The news disturbed Peabody, for, if it were true, industrial war was imminent. In an interview on March 21, he advised the deported strikers to use the courts for redressing their grievances, the same advice he had offered to the banished miners of Idaho Springs. Members of the WFM, he emphasized, would not be allowed to arm and march on Telluride or any other mining camp in Colorado. Meanwhile, Murphy, without waiting for Peabody's advice, had initiated proceedings for an injunction to restrain members of the TCA, the TMA, and others from blocking the peaceful return of the exiles. On March 22, Judge Theron Stevens of the District Court issued the order, and Murphy immediately announced that the men would return to Telluride.[46]

Members of the law and order group now questioned their ability to maintain control over the district. Rumors spread that the banished miners were preparing an armed invasion of the city. News also arrived of Murphy's move for an injunction. Because of Stevens's known sympathy for organized labor, it was assumed that he would act favorably upon Murphy's application. Once again the employers turned to Denver. On the day that Stevens issued his order, nine local officials and twenty-two members of the TMA and the TCA petitioned Peabody for help in blocking the rumored invasion which they believed would result in a "great loss of life and sacrifice of property" unless stopped. With a very few exceptions, the petitioners were the same individuals who had signed the request for troops in October.[47]

Upon receiving the petition from the "proper authorities," the governor felt free to act, although not to relieve the deported miners but to rescue the new order which he had helped to create. Moving swiftly, he referred the petition to Nathan Miller, who advised him that, if conditions were as represented, intervention was his duty and was necessary to preserve order. Whether intervening meant imposing martial law, however, was unclear. The attorney general pointedly advised the governor that if prisoners were taken, they must eventually be dealt with by the courts. But how long the prisoners remained under military jurisdiction before being remanded to the civil authorities was up to the governor. Backed by Miller's opinion, Peabody on March 23 again placed San Miguel County under military rule.⁴⁸ What effect this would have on Stevens's injunction was not immediately clear, but in honoring the petition of persons restrained by the order, the governor seemed ready to defy the court. Certainly he showed no inclination to enforce the judge's order.

Sherman Bell, whose exploits at Colorado City and Cripple Creek had already earned him national notoriety and the hatred of organized labor, further confused the status of Stevens's injunction. As soon as the governor had acted on March 23, Bell ordered Wells, who had been restrained by the court from preventing the return of the banished strikers, to activate Troop A and to recruit up to 100 men. Moreover, Bell commanded Wells to proclaim martial law and block any armed invasion by the exiles. Wells followed orders.⁴⁹ He and his enlarged troop, now under the direct command of Bell, once again controlled the county. Many of the men who rushed to join Troop A had engaged in the mob action which banished the strikers.

Furthermore, on March 24 Charles Moyer, president of the WFM, asked Peabody to protect the men who planned to return under Stevens's injunction. In his reply of March 25 the governor stated that he had "no disposition" to block the movement of lawful, unarmed citizens; however, he pointedly refrained from offering protection, and he emphasized that he would not permit any "armed bodies of men" to move within the state other than the guard. A followup telegram to Bell further revealed Peabody's intentions regarding the injunction. Although he ordered Bell to allow "unarmed, law-respecting citizens to return to Telluride unmolested," he also instructed him to arrest any returning man who engaged in inflammatory talk or armed himself.⁵⁰ Under the circumstances, the returning miners would have to travel through an armed camp where their safety depended upon the restraint of their enemies, many of whom wore the uniform of the guard.

Events of the next several weeks demonstrated that the actions of the military and civil authorities were determined more by the interests of the TCA and the TMA than by any consideration of law and order. A few of the exiles returned, but they stayed only if they remained quiet about their expulsion and refrained from criticizing the guard. Men who were thought to be "agitators," "trouble-makers," "generators of discontent," and leaders of the strike could not return. Under Wells's direction, Troop A scouted the district and watched the trains for returning strikers whom the local employers considered obnoxious. Although the court injunction required otherwise, such men were not permitted to reenter Telluride. On March 26, for example, Wells intercepted six undesirables and escorted them again from the county, warning them not to return.[51] Three days later military authorities arrested Moyer in Telluride on "charges of military necessity as well as military discretion" and detained him for more than two and one-half months, despite repeated court orders issued to release him.

On April 8, seven union leaders led approximately sixty of the deported miners back into Telluride to test the protective power of the injunction. If this group was successful, others planned to follow. But Bell, Wells, and Troop A, joined by an armed throng estimated at more than 100 which included individuals restrained by the order, met the men as their train arrived in the early evening and escorted them to Red Men's Hall, where they were searched for concealed weapons. After feeding their prisoners, Bell and his supporters marched all but the leaders back to the depot for deportation. Boarding a train, Bell, Wells and a detail of thirty soldiers took their captives to the county line where they were released and ordered never to return.[52] Their action dispelled any doubt that the governor's primary objective in placing San Miguel County under military rule again was to prevent the return of the banished miners. Under the facade of official duty, Bell and his mob effectively circumvented Stevens's order, and, in some instances, even violated it. In the process they upheld the mob action of March 15.

The members of the TCA and the TMA, encouraged by Peabody's stand, stepped up their campaign to eradicate the local miners' union. They promptly squelched a rumor published in the *Rocky Mountain News* of April 3 that negotiations were underway to end the strike on terms proposed by the WFM in August 1903. They declared in a published statement of April 5 that they had not and would not negotiate with the WFM, that they did not recognize its local union, and that there was no strike in progress at Telluride. Because their mines and mills had a full complement of employees with no grievances, they had nothing to negotiate. They had no business with a union which they did not recognize about a strike which they claimed did not exist. In their opinion, disgruntled "outsiders" were responsible for the troubles which plagued the district.[53]

On April 16, Bell transferred control of the county to Wells. During the next few weeks the latter's command diminished as men were released from active duty with Troop A. By April 30, only a token force remained, operating under rules less restrictive than martial law. Wells continued to banish returning strikers, whether they came singly or in groups. He also warned the fifty or more striking miners remaining in Telluride that they ought to leave, because his command was inadequate to guarantee their safety against the radical members of the TCA who clamored for still further action. Although Telluride remained outwardly calm, peace was precarious, as indicated by Wells' reaction to a visit by Judge Stevens and to the disaster at Independence depot on June 6.

On May 9, Stevens arrived in Telluride to hold the spring term of the district court. His coming had been announced by the *Journal*, which also informed its readers that he would be accompanied by ten or twelve "deported agitators." Acting in accordance with General Bell's instructions from Denver, Wells and Troop A and several hundred armed civilians met the judge's train and searched it for the "agitators." Stevens was alone. He descended from the train to walk between "files of soldiers and armed citizens," which he interpreted as an insult to the court. The next day Stevens refused to convene the court and instead delivered a scathing denunciation of the Peabody administration and local leaders. He continued all pending cases until the November term, refusing to conduct any business until the supremacy of the civil authorities in San Miguel County was acknowledged.[54] Moreover, after the Independence explosion, which killed thirteen nonunion miners and seriously injured six others, Wells rounded up fifty to sixty idle men for questioning about the tragedy. After the interrogation he released some of his prisoners, held others for deportation, and ordered the rest to leave town.[55] Under such conditions, peace was fragile.

Eventually, county residents became tired of military rule. Even Congressman Hogg, who had played a significant role in Peabody's decision to intervene on November 20, called for a return to civil control. On June 6 he wired Peabody: "I guess you had better call off this foolishness here." Peabody was under growing pressures from Telluride citizens and also from the issuing on June 15 of a writ of habeas corpus in behalf of Moyer by federal Judge Amos M. Thayer of the Eighth Circuit Court in St. Louis, which named Peabody, Bell, and Wells as respondents. He suspended military rule and released Moyer on June 15, thus permanently ending his intervention in the district.[56]

Nevertheless, there was no immediate improvement in the district. Throughout July and August the civil authorities continued to banish undesirables. And on July 1, Wells, once again a mine manager, closed the Smuggler-Union properties because he claimed that fear of the WFM made it impossible to find a sufficient number of competent nonunion miners. A number of Wells's associates followed his lead. By November, however, conditions had stabilized so that mining had resumed throughout the district. Following the example of the Smuggler-Union, which granted an eight-hour day with a $3 minimum to all its employees, effective December 1, the other companies conceded the eight-hour day to all their workers, including the millmen. The concession did not result from negotiations with the WFM but from TMA members' expectations that the next session of the legislature would enact an eight-hour law. The mine owners wanted their employees to feel that the shorter day had been freely given rather than forced by law. But whatever the reason for the change, it caused the San Juan District Union to call off its strike on November 29, 1904. The eight-hour day with a $3 minimum wage for the millmen fulfilled the union's demands made in August 1903.[57] The union's calling off of the strike did not alter the mine owners' determination never to employ a member of the WFM, however.

State intervention did little to settle the issues of the strike. Members of the TCA and the TMA remained hostile toward and fearful of the WFM, which had been the original cause of Peabody's intervention. An eight-hour day had been gained for the millmen, but to the unemployed member of the union the shorter day was meaningless. The more fundamental question of discrimination against members of the WFM remained, for the mine owners flatly refused to recognize the existence of the local union. Few, if any, known WFM members found employment in the district. From the standpoint of the TCA and the TMA the official ending of the strike was unimportant. They had a full force of nonunion labor, so their concern now centered on the body of idle union members whose presence made the working miners apprehensive. Peabody had not solved this problem; nor had the vigorous action of the TCA and the TMA.

Peabody's intervention had helped to reduce the power of the WFM in San Miguel and surrounding counties by destroying its ability to determine industrial conditions there. He defined the strike of 1903–1904 as a rebellion against the state, and he then vigorously suppressed the disorder in the name of law and order. To continue the resulting weakness of the union the mine owners, with Peabody's approval, imposed a card system similar to that in the Cripple Creek district. The technique successfully blocked a resurgence of the union's prestige and power.[58] For anti-union forces in Colorado, the mauling of the WFM in Telluride was an important, though costly, victory. Peabody's wrecking of Miners' Union 63 cost the state $200,292, exclusive of interest.[59] What the TCA and the TMA paid in the form of subsidies like food and quarters cannot be calculated. But to those individuals and groups who wanted the destruction of the WFM in Colorado, the expense to the taxpayers, the corporations, and individual businessmen was of little concern. Peabody's use of the state to realize the anti-union objective of the state's employers had their full support.

7

The "Law and Order" Governor

During the summer and fall of 1903 the number of alliance organizations increased substantially throughout Colorado. Alliance organizers James C. Craig and Herbert George, backed by the Denver alliance, vigorously preached a message of resistance to militant unionism among the employers of the mining and milling towns where strikes were either threatened or in progress. The employers responded readily, organizing themselves into alliances to combat militant unions more effectively. Moreover, Craig convinced his listeners that although the majority of union members in Colorado were neither socialists nor anarchists, labor organizations in the state were employing "socialistic and anarchistic" methods to obtain their objectives, and that union leaders, especially those of the WFM, had chosen Colorado for enacting such "socialistic" measures as an eight-hour law, employers' liability legislation, the initiative and referendum, the single-tax scheme, and similar measures. The state's employers, threatened by union militancy and convinced that socialism posed a genuine threat to the status quo, swiftly organized to preserve their interests and to thwart a "socialist" victory.[1] In doing so, they became a part of David Parry's national employers' movement, which had as its goal the bringing to heel of organized labor.

The new alliances forged by Craig and George were facsimiles of the Denver organization in structure, purpose, and function. Their constitutions were identical in substance, although minor variations did occur in membership requirements; for example, some associations permitted affiliation of union members. But most organizations flatly refused to admit anyone belonging to a *militant* labor union.[2] Regardless of minor differences, all shared the objective of resisting any labor organization that refused to accept the passive role assigned to it in the existing order. In realizing this objective they welcomed help from any source. Governor Peabody's intervention on behalf of corporate interests in the strikes of the WFM thus received the hearty approval of the newly organized alliances.

Peabody gradually became more deeply involved in the spreading alliance movement. After he intervened in the Cripple Creek district, his relationship to the movement became more deliberate and formal. This occurred partly because the alliances, joined by other employers' organizations, rallied to his support, while labor and its sympathizers strongly condemned his involvement in the strikes. Peabody responded warmly to congratulatory resolutions from the organized employers who were the principal beneficiaries of his labor policies. He believed that their support verified the rightness of his course.

In response to the Cripple Creek District Citizens' Alliance, which had sent resolutions praising his efforts to assist the "civil authorities in controlling the lawless classes," Peabody expressed his "sincere gratitude" and "appreciation of an occasional work of commendation from the people most interested in the success of [his] efforts in their behalf." He received other resolutions from newly organized alliances in Colorado Springs, Canon City, Telluride, and Goldfield—all praising him for his courageous stand for law and order. Organizations like the Colorado State Realty Association and the Cripple Creek Mine Owners' Association also forwarded their strong support of his intervention.[3] Their approval convinced Peabody that his action in

Cripple Creek had been completely justified, for he interpreted the support of the employers as a grassroots endorsement by the people. Convincing the governor of the correctness of his stand in the state's labor troubles was a major victory for the Colorado employers' movement.

An equally important effect of the resolutions was their influence on Peabody's conception of his role in the state's labor troubles. In answering his supporters he was forced to elaborate on the motives behind his intervention. He constructed a rationale which, although drawing heavily on the rhetoric of the resolutions, amounted to a reaffirmation of his own fixed beliefs regarding the existing social and industrial order. By early October he was explaining to the Colorado State Realty Association that his role in the Cripple Creek strike was one of establishing "law and order upon the principles of truly American doctrines" which made a retreat impossible. He wrote:

> The principle that any citizen of this country shall have the lawful right to labor in a lawful manner, under the protection of our law, must and shall be established once and for all time, else our industries which we have for thirty years been seeking to upbuild within this State must decay and cease to exist, and ourselves be at the mercy of an irresponsible and dictatorial class of people, who are not, in my opinion, working for the public good. It seems to me an outrage upon the public economies to solicit capital to come to Colorado and build up large industries . . . and then sit idly by and see any element within our midst crush it out of existence, and no honest man should lend his aid or influence to such a condition of affairs.[4]

The events of 1903 had obviously not diminished Peabody's determination to make Colorado an attractive place for investment. The resolutions usually spurred a restatement of his commitment to property interests which confirmed to his organized supporters that they had a reliable ally against militant labor.

Peabody increasingly focused upon union leaders, particularly those of the WFM, as the principal cause of the strikes erupting during his administration. Writing to the Canon City alliance, he charged that labor leaders too often demonstrated "an utter lack of knowledge of the true system of our splendid form of government or the rules of industrial economics, and consequently their advice is generally bad and their leadership infinitely worse." Moreover, he believed that they were

> narrow in their views regarding equal rights, or of any semblance of loyalty to constituted authority . . . [and are] unsafe leaders for either class of the laboring element, whether organized or unorganized. I therefore oppose such impudent pretenses as are put forward by these so-called leaders of labor unions, but who are never known to labor, because they have been proven in the past to be greater oppressors of the laboring man than the employer has ever been, and I fearlessly assert that many a man is a member of some labor organization, not from choice upon his part, but because he is forced to belong.[5]

In thanking the Telluride alliance for its support, he wrote that he was fighting "against the usurpation, through poor advice and ignorant leadership, assumed by those who have been chosen, or have usurped the prerogatives of controlling the intelligent laboring element of this State." Peabody wanted "freedom of action," like "freedom of speech," to prevail throughout Colorado and to be exercised in security under the law. He defined his policy as one of "liberty and law" in a letter to the Goldfield alliance. What he wanted the laboring man to thoroughly understand was that his salvation was in the "old-fashioned virtues of sobriety, frugality, industry and faithfulness"; that these alone promoted and maintained the "best interests" of labor. Strikes, boycotts, force, and intimidation led only to disaster.[6] In Peabody's opinion, ignorant labor leaders were responsible for the state's labor unrest. He insisted that his administration was not hostile to the laboring man.

As the strikes spread, Peabody increasingly dropped all pretenses of impartiality, throwing the powers of his office against any labor union which dared to threaten the industrial and political status quo. The formation of the State Citizens' Alliance of Colorado helped to expose his developing alliance with the organized employers.

As the labor crisis deepened, the necessity for a closer connection among the scattered local citizens' alliances had become apparent. A state federation, for example, would make possible a more efficient utilization of assets against unions like the WFM. At the suggestion of A. J. Woodruff, secretary of the Pueblo alliance, twenty-two delegates from twelve alliances assembled on October 25, 1903, in Pueblo to form a statewide organization and to select representatives to a national convention of employers scheduled to meet in Chicago four days later. The next day the delegates created the State Citizens' Alliance of Colorado (SCAC), the first of its kind in the nation and the only one represented at the Chicago meeting. The delegates elected James C. Craig president and filled the organization's executive board with anti-unionists like Herbert George.[7]

The published objectives of the SCAC reflected the goals of every alliance in the state and were entirely compatible with Peabody's position on the labor question. These were

> To promote the stability of business and the steady employment of labor; to encourage friendly relations between employers and employees; to discourage lockouts, strikes, boycotts and all kindred movements of oppression or persecution; to protect our members, communities and all persons who desire to work from unlawful interference [and to] declare anew the right to contract and freedom to perform the contract.[8]

Although the delegates publicly recognized labor's right to organize and to work for its improvement within the law, they insisted on the right of any employer to manage his affairs without interference. To guarantee the latter, they placed the SCAC strongly behind the enforcement of law. One of their first official acts was to pass resolutions endorsing Peabody's "efforts to preserve peace and order in this state." On the evening of October 26 at a smoker sponsored by the Pueblo alliance, additional resolutions praising the governor were passed. These came after speeches by Craig and Congressman H. M. Hogg, who was soon to influence Peabody's decision to order troops into Telluride. The governor responded: "Such words of commendation, coming from such a source, are the means of convincing one of the correctness and humanity of their [sic] actions, and strengthens ones [sic] efforts in continuing upon the course taken."[9]

After the Pueblo convention Craig and a strong delegation left for Chicago, where they helped to form the Citizens' Industrial Association of America (CIA), led by David Parry, president of the National Association of Manufacturers. The groundwork for the anti-union CIA had already been laid by Parry and other leaders of the national employers' movement at an organizational meeting in Chicago on September 29, 1903. That the CIA would aggravate labor relations became certain when delegates at the meeting castigated the moderate National Civic Federation as "antagonistic to the welfare of the business interests" and criticized its officials who represented both labor and capital and who stressed arbitration and conciliation as the ideal way of settling labor disputes.[10] The new organization was founded by delegates representing more than 500 employers' associations located in fifty-seven cities from coast to coast. Parry was the unanimous choice for president and Craig, president of Colorado's SCAC, was elected first vice-president, a fitting tribute to their leadership.

The objectives of the CIA as expressed in its constitution were moderate. These were to uphold constituted authority and the supremacy of the law, to resist violation of constitutional rights, to encourage harmonious industrial relations, and to influence public opinion in support of "individual enterprise and freedom of management of industry" by means of a Bureau of Organization and a Bureau of Education. But late in 1904, the CIA began publishing its official organ, *The Square Deal*, under the direction of Parry. The publication left no doubt regarding the group's anti-union bias. Printed in each issue were these "principles": opposition to closed shops, boycotts, sympathetic strikes, and the compulsory use of union labels; opposition to restrictions on the use of machinery, production, and the number of apprentices or helpers; and support of nonunion workers against unions. These principles more realistically portrayed the purpose of the CIA than the objectives found in its constitution. Behind a facade of deep concern for the rights and liberties of the workingman, the organization was really intended to disrupt and rout labor unions.[11] As J. T. Holle, third vice-president of the CIA, stated on November 7, the CIA had been "thoroughly Parryized."[12]

The methods used by the CIA proved to be as violent and as class-oriented as those of the most militant unions.

Within a year its affiliate organizations challenged the right of organized labor to exist. That right had already been challenged in Colorado as early as the spring of 1903. In their crusade against militant unions the employers' associations deftly used both the methods and the philosophy of class warfare. The WFM, clearly the most aggressive labor union in the West, immediately sensed the dangers of the CIA and prepared for the worst.[13]

Peabody almost certainly drew inspiration from the CIA and its Colorado affiliates. The presence of a strong state federation of employers linked with a national organization which advocated the principles he believed in and which opposed militant unions undoubtedly was a source of strength during the subsequent crises of his administration. The fact that Parry was president of both the CIA and the NAM added luster to the employers' movement. Parry and Marshall Cushing, secretary of the NAM, assiduously cultivated the governor. Cushing saw that he received free copies of *American Industries*, the organ of the NAM, which preached the "gospel of the employers" as an "authoritative exponent of the interests of the employers of America," and the proceedings of the NAM's annual convention. *American Industries* occasionally carried articles commending Peabody's methods of handling Colorado's labor troubles. Parry himself sent "splendid words of approval" of the governor's policies.[14] What really encouraged Peabody, however, was the strong support of the state's employers, who stood squarely behind his administration.

In the year after its formation the SCAC expanded to include approximately twenty-five local associations, eighteen of which were extremely active. Because membership in some of the organizations was kept secret, it is impossible to ascertain the SCAC's numerical strength, although in November 1904, Craig estimated the membership at nearly 30,000.[15] Since those who joined the alliances included the leading citizens of their localities, the SCAC's political and economic power was significant. Peabody early realized the importance of the alliances springing up over the state, and he relished their support when his opponents scathingly denounced his administration. The polarization of forces in the escalating labor crises, particularly after the military intervention in Telluride on November 20, 1903, further hastened the governor's open identification with the alliance movement.

The employers continued to encourage a greater commitment by Peabody. Whenever Peabody took a major action against labor they sent numerous resolutions of support, reminding Peabody that they heartily approved of his efforts in their behalf. In the governor's responses, he often expressed his approval of the alliances.[16] The cordial dialog reflected an awareness of common purpose in the attacks upon the WFM. However, it was an out-of-state alliance which first included Peabody in its membership.

Within a week of his December 4, 1903 declaration which placed Teller County under martial law, Peabody accepted election as a charter member in the San Francisco alliance. The group had been organized by Herbert George, a principal architect of the Colorado alliance movement. Peabody, believing that the alliance supported his principles, on December 10 acknowledged with "feelings of intense gratification" his acceptance of membership card "No. 103." After George had organized the Los Angeles alliance, the governor received "union card No. 98," making him an honorary member of that body. He regarded the gesture to be evidence of both "appreciation and endorsement" of his efforts to "preserve law and order and to protect every citizen in the lawful pursuit of a livelihood," and he gratefully accepted the membership on February 1, 1904.[17]

Nineteen days later Peabody officially became a member of the alliance movement in Colorado. Possibly at the suggestion of George, Craig forwarded the governor a membership card in the Denver association. Peabody's response clearly indicated his endorsement of the movement and the importance to his administration of alliance support. He wrote to Craig:

> I consider it a distinctive honor to accept from your organization membership card No. 1, for the year of 1904, and in this connection I wish to take occasion to thank you and the numerous members of the Citizens' Alliance for their support, encouragement and assistance in establishing within this Commonwealth a recognition of "personal liberty" and personal freedom under the law, granting and guaranteeing to every individual the right to labor when he will, where he will, and at what wage is satisfactory, in

153

a lawful manner, without intimidation, coercion or abuse. Without the assistance and support of your organization and its membership the victory which now belongs to the people of this State would have been longer deferred, if at all attainable, and I am proud to be a member of the Citizens' Alliance of Denver.[18]

The governor's membership formalized what had long existed— the linking of his administration with a strong statewide employers' movement.

Other considerations may have determined the timing of the governor's decision to ally himself openly with the alliances. For some time preparations had been underway for a great testimonial banquet to honor him for his stand on law and order. After several delays its sponsors finally scheduled the event for February 23, 1904. Although the banquet presumably was a nonpartisan tribute, Peabody used the occasion to announce his candidacy for renomination by the Republican party. His acceptance of membership in the alliance prior to the Law and Order Banquet suggests that he was seeking to exploit the potential power of the movement for his own purpose, knowing that he could not reasonably count on the support of union labor in an election.

No event of his administration more visibly associated Peabody with anti-union interests than the Law and Order Banquet. Sponsors of the testimonial exerted extraordinary efforts to make the event the most memorable in Colorado's history, and they succeeded. Business and industrial leaders flocked into Denver from all over the state to honor the governor. To assure the presence of the invited guests the railroads offered half-priced, round-trip tickets from any point in the state to Denver for those planning to attend.[19] Although Craig's state federation of alliances had no significant role in engineering the affair, those persons whose interests it served not only provided the leadership but underwrote the expenses. For example, Simon Guggenheim, local head of the American Smelting and Refining Company which had successfully resisted the demands of the Mill and Smeltermen's Union, No. 93, for an eight-hour day, guaranteed all expenses, estimated at $4,500 to $5,000; however, in return he demanded absolute control over the proceedings.[20]

Behind the scenes, E. B. Field, president and general manager of the Colorado Telephone Company, solicited funds from corporations to broaden the base of support for the banquet. Field previously had asked Peabody to work against the Rush Senate Bill No. 176, which provided for a greater municipal control over public utilities.[21] On February 24, Field forwarded to Peabody a list of donors who represented a formidable array of industrial and financial power within Colorado. Field requested that Peabody write each of the contributors, pointing out how much each had strengthened his "position in sustaining law and order" by letting him know that he had the backing of the "best element in the State."[22]

The banquet proceedings also suggested the extent of corporate influence. At a reception prior to the evening's festivities a number of prominent businessmen joined the governor in receiving the guests. At the elaborate banquet Peabody, as honored guest, was surrounded by his supporters and the direct beneficiaries of his labor policies (for example, Charles M. MacNeill). Guggenheim introduced D. C. Beaman, an attorney for the Colorado Fuel and Iron Company, who had been chosen to deliver the principal address. He was an excellent choice for the occasion.

Beaman leveled a blunt attack upon organized labor, charging that during the past decade Colorado had been "dosed with the experimental health food of legislative cranks and dreamers, who [had] undertaken to regulate nearly every phase of industry by so-called constitutional amendment and statutory laws." Their efforts had resulted in unstable industrial conditions, which Beaman blamed on labor leaders, a sensational press, and apathetic businessmen. He held union officials principally responsible for the existing widespread dissatisfaction with the status quo and for the legal and statutory confusion of the past decade. Beaman particularly condemned their resort to violence and their doctrine that a union member had a "vested right to his job equal to his right to life," either of which he could defend to the death. That such people might eventually control the machinery of government was appalling; however, the appearance of the citizens' alliances indicated that businessmen were finally alert to the danger.

Beaman ridiculed the eight-hour amendment of 1902, describing it as a "miserable subterfuge or botch legislation" and asking his listeners to work for its immediate repeal; he upheld the use of the injunction against striking workers, defended the beneficial character of trusts, denied that Colorado corporations wanted exclusively beneficial legislation, and claimed that their legislative activities were strictly defensive; he denied that the militia had been called out at the requests of capitalists to coerce labor, and he defended military intervention as necessary and constitutional. In a remarkably candid statement, Beaman declared that the prevailing strikes, which included that of the United Mine Workers against the CF&I, were equivalent to war, rebellion and insurrection against laws which assured the protection of liberty and property. In his opinion, had it not been for the "indulgent and merciful penalty" of deportation, riots and bloodshed would have occurred for which union officials and their sympathizers would have been severely punished. The deportation of striking workers by the state, therefore, was a humane policy.[23] So impressed were the members of the Denver alliance with Beaman's address that they later published it for widespread distribution.

After a toast to President Roosevelt by Chancellor Henry A. Buchtel of the University of Denver and a toast to the governor by Charles E. Gast, a former attorney for several Colorado railroads, Peabody addressed the crowd on his role in the strikes.[24] He defended military intervention in the name of "free" labor. It was to protect the right of the workingman to be free from dictatorial and unreliable leaders, free from coercion and abuse, and free to work whenever and wherever he wished in any lawful occupation that had compelled him to act against lawlessness and disorder. Industrial freedom and the right to work within a context of law and order were his objectives. As he put it:

> If I have . . . been instrumental in infusing new life into the laws of this state, which were found lying upon our statute books, unread, uncared for and unfulfilled, and . . . have applied them to conditions as they existed, I am glad indeed. If I have compelled a lawless element within our midst to be obedient to our laws and to observe a rea-

sonable recognition of constituted authority, I have but enforced laws which were made for the government and protection of all alike. If I have aided to some degree in establishing industrial peace and industrial prosperity; if I have assisted in restoring commercial activity within our state; if I have guaranteed to the honest laborer the protection of his life, his liberty and his property, I have done no more than my duty as a citizen and a public official. I grant the right of any person to stop work, either as individuals or as a union of organized labor, if such strike is not in violation of any existing contract, but the nonunion man has the same right to lawful employment in this state . . . as is possessed by the unionist, and while the union man has the right to refuse to work, he has no possible right to resort to brute force, nor to molest, threaten or coerce any other working man or to prevent him from working if he so desires.[25]

Confident that Coloradans supported his stand as being in the best interest of all and heartened by the demonstrated support of the "best element" of the state, Peabody concluded by announcing his candidacy for renomination by the Republican party.

The banquet, organized and financed by the corporations of Colorado, presided over by Guggenheim of the "smelter trust," exhorted by corporate attorneys Beaman and Gast, and sanctioned by some of the state's prominent religious and educational leaders, demonstrated corporate approval of the administration and Peabody's approval of the corporations.[26] The affair was essentially an anti-union rally managed by corporate officials.

Throughout the remainder of his time in office Peabody worked in harmony with the interests represented at the banquet, his cooperation ranging from legislative and propaganda efforts to the wholesale deportations at Telluride and Cripple Creek. After conferring with the governor on March 11, 1904, A. J. Woodruff, secretary of the Pueblo alliance, forwarded a copy of an Alabama boycott law and asked that Peabody support a similar but stiffer law for Colorado. In responding, Peabody promised that he would recommend the passage of such a law in his biennial message to the legislature. He kept his promise.[27]

Peabody did not restrict himself to cooperating with the Colorado alliance movement, for he maintained contact with Herbert George. In late October 1904 he sent George a copy of *Walter Wellman's Indictment of Moyer, Haywood and the Western Federation of Miners*, a reprint of Wellman's letter to the New York *Herald* of August 13, 1904. George was favorably impressed with the anti-WFM tract, and he requested that the governor relay George's order for 1,000 copies to the "proper source." He wanted to distribute them in California's mining districts where he and his associates were organizing a mine owners' association.[28]

The close cooperation between Peabody and the employers destroyed his freedom of action and made it impossible for him to administer the affairs of state impartially. Within a month after the banquet of February 23, alliance members in Telluride took extraordinary liberties with the law and violated the civil rights of union members. The governor's response was military intervention which effectively upheld the work of the alliance-directed mob. Within four months of the banquet angry mobs which formed after the Independence depot explosion and the Victor riots completely overthrew several local governments in Teller County and intimidated county officials into doing their will. Led by "law and order" advocates of the employers' associations, the mobs openly violated the rights of unionists. Peabody supported these violations. Peabody was assured by the Colorado Supreme Court's decision of June 6 in the Moyer case, which upheld his administration, and he allowed his subordinates to take command of the wholesale deportations which systematically broke the WFM in the district.

8

Peabody and the Courts

The most dramatic clashes between Peabody and the courts occurred in the Cripple Creek district where Adjutant General Sherman Bell, broadly interpreting the governor's executive order of September 4, 1903, ignored civil authorities and arbitrarily arrested anyone whose words, deeds, or sympathies for the WFM provoked his displeasure. Because Bell refused to file formal charges, his prisoners quickly applied to the district court for writs of habeas corpus. When Bell was unable to present sufficient evidence to justify their further detention, the court had no choice but to order their release from military custody. Peabody believed that the court was unduly influenced by the WFM, but he nevertheless reluctantly instructed his officers to obey its mandates. However, he immediately searched for legal ways to circumvent its jurisdiction. That way was found in *In re Boyle,* a decision of the Idaho Supreme Court rendered in 1899, which appeared to be a readymade solution to the problem of obstructive courts. Under this ruling, the court had acknowledged the right of Idaho's governor to suspend the writ of habeas

corpus, or to ignore it if issued, in cases of insurrection and rebellion. It had further held that the "facts" recited in the governor's proclamation of such cases were not subject to judicial review upon applications for the writ. Moreover, the court
ruled that wherever insurrection or rebellion had been declared,
"limited" martial law prevailed, a condition entirely compatible
with the state constitution because the court deemed it imperative that the governor have the means to preserve the state.[1]

Because the sections of the Colorado and Idaho
constitutions regarding the suspension of the writ of habeas
corpus were worded almost the same, Peabody believed that the
Idaho case provided an excellent precedent for his bypassing the
district court in Cripple Creek.[2] After his proclamation of December 4, 1903, which declared that Teller County was in a state
of insurrection and rebellion, he was confident that the Colorado Supreme Court would sustain his suspending the writ or
his ignoring it if it were issued by the lower courts.[3] A case had
already originated in the Cripple Creek district which set the
stage for having the state's highest court decide whether the
governor possessed such extraordinary power. On November 21
the military authorities arrested Victor Poole, a union member
suspected of being involved in the Vindicator explosion.

Four days later Poole applied to the district court
for a writ of habeas corpus, which was granted, returnable on
December 3, one day before the governor's proclamation. When
S. D. Crump, an attorney for the military and the administration,
was unable to file formal charges against Poole, the court ordered
his release. Nevertheless, officers of the guard, openly defying
the court, rearrested Poole as he left the courthouse and detained
him for three days before transferring custody to H. M. Robertson, sheriff of Teller County, with the stipulation that the prisoner
was subject to their orders. On December 7, Poole's attorneys
applied for a second writ, alleging that their client was illegally
imprisoned without due process of law. Granting the writ, the
court ordered guard officers Colonel Edward Verdeckberg, Major
H. A. Naylor, Major Tom E. McClelland, and Robertson, respondents, to produce Poole on December 11 and show cause
why he should be further detained.[4]

To prevent Poole's release Peabody intervened personally in the case. On December 9 he issued a special proclamation, stating: "In my judgment the public safety especially requires that the privilege of the writ of *habeas corpus* be suspended in his case, to-wit: In the case of Victor Poole aforesaid, and I further direct the said writ of Habeas Corpus be suspended in his case, until furthered ordered by me."[5] His suspension of the writ placed the governor and the court in open conflict. Despite his extraordinary act, the next day the attorneys for the respondents filed answers to the writ. They argued that the court had no jurisdiction in the case because Peabody's executive orders and proclamation were sufficient authority for holding Poole since his detention was a "military necessity." Moreover, they charged that Poole was a "dangerous character engaged in inciting other dangerous and lawless characters to violence and the commission of crimes" in the district. Their answer demanded the discharge of the writ. As for Robertson's separate return, it stated only that he held Poole at the request of military authorities.[6]

Nevertheless, on December 12 the court ordered Poole released from military custody. But when Coroner James Doran attempted to serve the order, Verdeckberg and McClelland refused to accept service and "forcibly pushed" Doran down a flight of stairs while ejecting him from their offices.[7] Fearing that an attempt would be made to release Poole from Robertson's custody, Verdeckberg ordered Poole moved from the county jail to the military guardhouse at Goldfield to guarantee his detention.

When they were unable to release Poole by proceedings in the district court, attorneys for the WFM on December 16 petitioned the Colorado Supreme Court for a writ of habeas corpus. In their petition they reviewed the events surrounding Poole's inability to obtain relief and charged that, in the absence of laws authorizing a suspension of the writ, Peabody had violated the state constitution because no insurrection or rebellion existed in Teller County. The courts were in session there, and their orders were obeyed by all except the military authorities. The civil officials were also performing their duties without interference, except from the military. They further alleged that Poole's detention violated the fourth, fifth, sixth, and fourteenth amendments of the U. S. Constitution. The lawyers described their client's imprisonment as an "arbitrary, wicked, unlawful and malicious act" in the absence of formal charges, and they asked the court to accept jurisdiction because Peabody had publicly stated that if it did, he would abide by its judgment.[8] The Supreme Court issued the writ.

On December 26, Nathan Miller, assisted by special counsel, filed a return to the writ along with motions to cancel the order and to strike portions of Poole's petition. Miller argued that the district court lacked authority to order Poole's release because of the governor's proclamations of December 4 and 9; he also denied the right of any court in the nation to review the "facts" cited in the returns of the respondents (Verdeckberg, Naylor, and McClelland) to the district court or the Supreme Court. He contended that the Supreme Court's authority in the case extended no further than quashing its writ and dismissing Poole's petition.[9] After attorneys for the WFM had answered Miller's return, the court was faced with deciding the governor's power to suspend the writ, either specifically or generally.

The ruling was never made. Peabody's supporters in Cripple Creek, apparently not confident that the court would sustain the suspension of the writ, took steps which prevented the Supreme Court from assuming further jurisdiction. On December 30, S. R. Leck filed a complaint with a local justice of the peace charging that on March 15, 1902, Poole had assaulted H. S. McCellecher with a deadly weapon with intent to kill. Consequently, a warrant was issued for Poole's arrest. Verdeckberg, surprisingly amenable to civil authority, transferred custody of Poole to Robertson on December 31. Two days later the attorney general filed an amended return with the Supreme Court in which he recited the new developments in the case. Since the guard had turned the petitioner over to the civil authorities, his clients no longer had him in custody.[10] Since custody had been surrendered and because a criminal charge had been filed, there was no basis on which the court could assume jurisdiction. It seems certain that the charge of assault was trumped up to allow a face-saving transfer of custody to prevent the court's ruling, for when Poole's trial on the assault charge began on January 9, 1904, Leck failed to appear. The lower court promptly discharged the defendant.[11]

The extraordinary role of the National Guard in the mining camps made it impossible for the courts to avoid further involvement in the labor unrest because harassed union miners fled to them for relief. Unfortunately, they often failed as sanctuaries. The case of Sherman Parker, secretary of the Free Coinage Union, No. 19, WFM, at Goldfield, illustrates the point.

On September 10, 1903, officers of the guard arrested and imprisoned Parker for fifteen days without bothering to file formal charges. Habeas corpus proceedings in the district court finally secured his release. Rearrested on November 21, Parker remained in military custody until, after habeas corpus proceedings, the court ordered a transfer of custody to Robertson, with instructions that Parker be held to answer charges of "train wrecking" that had been filed. Bond was set at $19,000. Parker, unable to provide bail quickly, remained in jail until January 14, 1904 when, upon being released, he was promptly rearrested by military officials who refused to file charges. Verdeckberg explained to Parker that Teller County was under martial law as a result of the governor's proclamation of December 4 and that Peabody had ordered his arrest and suspended the writ to assure his detention.

After they failed to obtain a Colorado Supreme Court ruling on the governor's unorthodox procedures, attorneys of the WFM on January 18 applied to the United States Circuit Court, Eighth Circuit, Colorado District, for a writ of habeas corpus in Parker's behalf. Alleging that insurrection and rebellion did not exist in Teller County because the courts were operative and unchallenged except by the military authorities and that the district attorney was ready to file complaints and to prosecute when furnished with the necessary evidence, the WFM lawyers contended that conditions in the district did not warrant a suspension of the writ. Even so, the legislature had not suspended the writ, and the governor lacked the authority to do so. They claimed that Parker was innocent of any crime which justified his detention and that as a civilian he was not subject to military authority. As in the previous case, they argued that his arrest and detention violated the fourth, fifth, sixth, and fourteenth amendments of the U. S. Constitution as well as federal law. Consequently, they asked the court to issue a writ ordering Verdeckberg to show cause why Parker should not be released from military custody.[12]

On January 20, Judge Moses Hallett rendered a decision on the petition which was a clear victory for the administration. It recognized the governor's authority to hold Parker without bail while determining whether or not he had violated a law. Hallett ruled that the governor possessed the authority and bore the responsibility to uphold law and thus might use the militia for such purposes. Regardless of the means employed to enforce the law, the national government could not "interfere with the State in the due administration of its laws." As for the jurisdiction of the federal courts in the Parker case, the judge held that they definitely lacked the authority to review the law-enforcement procedures of state officials and to "set them aside upon habeas corpus or any other process which may be invoked." Parker's detention was of no official concern to the Circuit Court. Hallett dismissed the petition because of lack of jurisdiction and congratulated the people of Colorado for having a governor "disposed to enforce the laws of the State."[13] His decision further convinced Peabody of the correctness of his course.

In a maneuver obviously designed to prevent Hallett from assuming jurisdiction had he been predisposed to do so, officers of the guard filed a complaint against Parker, charging him with harboring a criminal. Had it become necessary, custody could have been immediately transferred to civil authorities, as was done in the Poole case. On January 22, S. D. Crump, representing the Cripple Creek District Mine Owners' Association and Peabody, also filed an affidavit charging Parker with the felonious assault upon Thomas Stewart on September 1, 1903. At the hearing the court dismissed both complaints, for no one appeared to testify on either charge. Yet when Parker left the court, military authorities immediately apprehended him.[14] Even after his exoneration in the train-wrecking charges, he continued to be harassed.

On January 30, District Judge Theron Stevens rendered an opinion which sustained Peabody's anti-union campaign in San Miguel County. There civil and military authorities conspired to break the power of the WFM by relentless harassment. To end the arbitrary arrests and deportations of union miners, Guy Miller, president of Miners' Union No. 63, and others applied to the district court for an injunction to stop the unjustified harassment of the striking miners and to protect the men who were returning after being driven out of Telluride. In response to this action, Major Zeph Hill and Sheriff J. C. Rutan filed separate petitions for dismissal of the case.

Although the petition had stated that "irreparable injury would result to the plaintiffs" unless Rutan and Hill were restrained, Stevens ruled that the "property rights" of unionists were not involved but only their "civil rights . . . to go where they please." According to Stevens, attorneys for the plaintiffs had not shown that the deported miners would suffer "irreparable injury" to their civil rights. If Hill and Rutan had been guilty of violating the private rights of the striking miners, there was an adequate remedy in law. Refusing to interfere, Stevens denied the injunction.[15] This decision, which came from a man who had been looked upon as a strong friend of organized labor, was a significant victory for Peabody, for it clothed with legality the efforts of the local alliance, the mining association, and the administration to disrupt the local miners' union. Coming soon after Judge Hallett's decision in the Parker case, it strongly buttressed the governor's policy in San Miguel County. Peabody considered it a vindication.[16]

Members of the WFM may have concluded from Stevens's decision that relief from official harassment lay in civil suits charging false imprisonment and violations of civil rights. If so, they soon lost faith in this alternative. On February 11, District Judge Robert E. Lewis, a Republican friend of Peabody who believed the governor had brought "untold benefits to the business interests of Colorado," rendered a decision which apparently closed the door on corrective damage suits.[17] Sherman Parker and others who had been repeatedly subjected to military arrests had filed a suit for damages in the District Court of Teller County which charged that they had been falsely imprisoned by Adjutant General Bell, Brigadier General Chase, and Major McClelland.

The judge ruled that the central point in the case was whether a civil court might inquire into the action of military officers who, while on active duty, restrained the liberties of private citizens and, if so, whether the enquiry was the responsibility of the court or a jury. Lewis, anticipating the decision of the Colorado Supreme Court in *In Re Moyer* and relying heavily on *In re Boyle*, held that an enquiry into the "facts" recited in the governor's proclamations was unnecessary because they were conclusive. Insurrection existed; the governor's responsibility was to enforce the laws; the militia was an instrument of law enforcement; the court could not interfere. To do so would destroy the usefulness of the armed forces in upholding the laws. Under the circumstances, the "facts" did not indicate that the defendants had exceeded their discretionary powers in detaining the plaintiffs. The plaintiffs, therefore, had no case. In Lewis's opinion, appeals to the "sacredness of personal liberty" were inadequate in such cases because even "anarchists appeal to the bill of rights found in the national and state constitutions as the cornerstone of his [sic] doctrine to destroy." Liberty was not "unbridled license"; it did not endow one with the right to violate the rights of others, to incite riots, or to destroy property. In conclusion, he ordered the foreman of the jury to return a verdict of "not guilty."[18] This decision upheld the role of the National Guard in the Cripple Creek district and sustained the administration. But six weeks later a more serious challenge to Peabody's procedures materialized when civil authorities arrested Charles H. Moyer for a misdemeanor in Ouray County.

The case which most decisively vindicated Peabody began innocuously. Early in 1904 officials of the WFM published and distributed paper copies of the American flag with an inscription on each stripe sharply criticizing the role of the state in the strikes.[19] Anti-union factions clamored that Moyer and William Haywood, WFM secretary-treasurer, had violated a state law prohibiting the desecration of the flag.[20] On March 26, acting on a warrant alleging flag desecration, deputies arrested Moyer in Ouray where he was working among the miners who had been driven from Telluride earlier that month. Moyer was taken to Telluride and released on March 28 after posting bail of $500. But the next day Bell and Wells rearrested him on "charges of military necessity as well as military discretion."[21] Moyer's arrest climaxed the military harassment of union leadership and initiated litigation that eventually reached the United States Supreme Court.

On March 30, Moyer's attorneys petitioned Judge Stevens for a writ of habeas corpus, contending that the vague reason of "military necessity" was inadequate to legalize a detention when formal charges had not been filed. Stevens agreed, and the next day he issued the writ ordering Bell and Wells to produce Moyer on April 11 in chambers at Ouray and show cause why he should not be released. Neither obeyed the order. Instead, Deputy District Attorney E. C. Howe of San Miguel County, assisted by Attorney General Miller and Assistant Attorney General H. J. Hershey, attempted to file an answer in their behalf. Stevens rejected this procedure because they had failed to produce Moyer as ordered. Responding to their defiance, he ordered Moyer released from military custody, placed Bell and Wells in contempt of court, and ordered their arrest and confinement without trial until either or both had obeyed. He also levied fines of $500 on each, payable to Moyer, and assessed each one-half of the costs of court proceedings.[22]

When Ouray County Sheriff Maurice Corbett attempted to arrest the two officers on April 13, they successfully resisted and forced him to call on Rutan for assistance. However, claiming that they were "exempt and free from arrest" because they were military officers on active duty at the command of the governor, Bell and Wells again refused to be arrested. The sheriffs decided that they could not forcibly seize the men, and they made no further attempts to execute the orders of the court. Consequently, Moyer remained imprisoned, the military authorities were apparently victorious in the matter. On April 15, however, Moyer's attorneys turned to the Colorado Supreme Court for relief.

In a lengthy petition for a writ of habeas corpus the WFM attorneys reviewed the military's defiance of Stevens's court. The lawyers pointed out that Moyer had been arbitrarily arrested on the "grounds of pretended military necessity," and they contended that his continued confinement was the result of an "unlawful conspiracy, combination, confederation and agreement" of the Telluride alliance which had the support of Bell and his command. Bell's refusal to accept arrest and his public threats to kill anyone who attempted to seize him precluded relief for Moyer in the district court, because the civil authorities did not possess the power to counter superior military force. Furthermore, appeals to the governor were useless because, in sanctioning his officers' defiance of the courts, he, like them, was acting above the law. Moyer's attorneys charged that his arrest was calculated to destroy the WFM; that attempts had been made to provoke him into resistance to justify slaying him; and that Peabody had suspended the writ of habeas corpus in his case. Again emphasizing that the courts of San Miguel County were fully operative and obeyed by everyone except Bell and Wells, they denied the existence of insurrection, rebellion, or invasion which would have necessitated suspending the writ. They further charged that the only identifiable lawbreakers were members of the alliance who had the full backing of Peabody and Bell. As in the cases of Poole and Parker, they claimed that the detention of Moyer violated the fourth, fifth, sixth, and fourteenth amendments of the federal Constitution. If the Supreme Court failed to assume jurisdiction, they predicted that bloodshed would result, because to carry out the orders of the district court, the civil authorities of Ouray County would have to arm the citizens and take Moyer from the state militia. The Supreme Court immediately issued the writ, which ordered Bell and Wells to appear with Moyer on April 21 and show cause why he should be detained.[23]

In a maneuver apparently designed to evade the order, Bell on April 16 transferred command of San Miguel County to Wells with instructions to hold Moyer until either he or the governor ordered his release and to refuse the service of "any civil process or other papers issued from the civil courts of the State, of any character, kind or nature whatsoever" unless otherwise directed.[24] That same day when Rutan attempted to serve the writ, both officers refused to accept service, although on April 21 they appeared in Denver with Moyer as the Supreme Court had ordered.[25]

Nathan Miller now took personal charge of the defense. In his return he contended that the Supreme Court should dismiss the proceedings. Bell, who had been ordered to suppress the insurrection and rebellion in San Miguel County which Peabody had proclaimed on March 23, concluded that Moyer was an "active participant" whose confinement was "absolutely necessary" to carry out his instructions. The governor agreed. All parties to Moyer's arrest and imprisonment had acted in good faith and, when conditions permitted, they intended to release him. At that time, however, the "exigencies of the military situation" demanded that Moyer remain confined to prevent his "lending aid, comfort, direction, instructions and commands to . . . lawless persons" who were rebelling against constituted authority. An "uninterrupted" exercise of military authority was vital to restore the peace in San Miguel County. Consequently, Peabody had ordered Bell not to release Moyer "either upon writ of habeas corpus, or otherwise, until commanded by him." Miller attached statements from the governor, certifying that insurrection and rebellion prevailed in San Miguel County and that Moyer's detention was therefore necessary, and the petition of March 22 to the governor from members of the Telluride Mining Association, the Telluride Citizens' Alliance, and local officials, allegedly substantiating the governor's proclamation. In separate motions to quash and dismiss the writ, Miller denied the jurisdiction of the court, claiming that it lacked the lawful authority to intervene and release Moyer, whose detention was necessary to restore order. He also insisted that the presence of Bell and Wells with Moyer in the court did not constitute a recognition of its jurisdiction. They were there only to demonstrate the governor's respect for the court and to advise it of the circumstances behind the detention.[26]

Attorneys for the WFM responded that there was no lawful reason for imprisoning Moyer who, on the face of the attorney general's return, should be released immediately. Contrary to the "facts" recited in the governor's proclamation, the WFM lawyers argued that insurrection and rebellion did not exist in San Miguel County. Rather, members of the Telluride alliance had conspired with the governor to impose unlawful military rule to block the return of the miners who had been banished on March 15. This procedure was necessary if the alliance members were to retain control over the labor situation in the district. Whether or not insurrection and rebellion existed was irrelevant, because Peabody did not have the authority to suspend the writ and violate the rights of Moyer, which were protected by both the state and federal constitutions.[27] In short, the attorneys attempted to discredit the "facts" recited in Miller's return and to persuade the court of its power to order the release of Moyer.

In the absence of Associate Justice John Campbell, Chief Justice William H. Gabbert and Associate Robert Steele refused to rule on the matter of jurisdiction. When they agreed to consider Moyer's application for bail, Miller questioned their power to release Moyer on bail or by any other means while insurrection and rebellion existed in San Miguel County. Miller argued that it was improper for the court to release Moyer until its jurisdiction had been determined. He also contended that there was no imperative in the statutes or the common law requiring Moyer's temporary release. Convinced that the "facts" cited in Miller's return of April 21 were true, the court denied bail, ruling that to grant bail prior to a determination of its jurisdiction in the case would be an intrusion upon the governor's authority.[28] It also granted a writ of supersedeas to Bell and Wells, which placed in abeyance District Judge Stevens's order of April 11 for their arrest and confinement.

In his brief to the court on May 5, Miller elaborated extensively on the points which he had previously raised. He stated that only the executive had the responsibility for recognizing the existence of rebellion, and he insisted that after such a condition had been proclaimed, the governor was the supreme authority until he had officially declared the restoration of order. If the court intervened (for example, in cases like that of Moyer), it would hamper the governor's performance of a constitutional duty. Until the challenge to constituted authority had been suppressed, therefore, his military subordinates were under no obligations to the court except to show the "causes" and the authority for their actions. Having done this in the case of Moyer's detention, there was nothing else for the court to do except dismiss the writ because it had no legal authority to review the validity of the "facts" cited in the earlier return, the truth of which was a political rather than a legal question and outside the jurisdiction of the court. Whether or not the governor could legally suspend the writ of habeas corpus was thus an extraneous issue, because once insurrection had been proclaimed, his powers were virtually unlimited. Describing the alleged insurrection in San Miguel County as a "continuing crime" in which Moyer was both a "participant and the sole [*sic*] and inspiration of the lawlessness and disorder," Miller argued that it would be foolish to arrest and then release him on bail, for such a procedure would encourage the conditions which the governor was attempting to suppress. Moyer, as a participant in a "continuing crime," was not entitled to bail. Nor did his confinement violate his constitutional rights. Although the writ was designed to protect a person's rights, no one had the right to participate in insurrection. The detention of Moyer, therefore, was entirely compatible with both the state and federal constitutions. As for Bell and Wells, they had no choice but to obey the orders of the governor, a civil officer, and to disregard all threats of damage suits and possible enquiries into their activities. If ordered to arrest and detain an individual engaged in rebellion, they had to do so without question. Whether the governor allowed them to file formal charges and remand a prisoner like Moyer to the civil authorities was entirely at his discretion. With supreme power to enforce the laws, the governor might use "every available means to accomplish that end," including the suspension of the writ and the use of the militia, because preserving the state was of far greater importance than one man's temporary loss of liberty. Whether the governor had abused his powers while suppressing a proclaimed insurrection and rebellion was a question for the people to decide at the polls, not a responsibility of the court.[29]

Although neither the records of Miller nor of the Supreme Court contain the brief filed by Edmund Richardson, attorney for Moyer and the WFM, fragments of his oral arguments to the court appeared in the daily press. Richardson denied that Peabody had acquired unlimited power, particularly that of suspending the writ of habeas corpus, when he proclaimed the existence of insurrection and rebellion in San Miguel County. He argued that the constitutional and statutory provisions designed to protect the rights of the people could not be so easily swept aside, and he emphatically rejected Miller's contention that an

171

executive declaration made available implied powers which authorized the use of extraordinary means in suppressing an alleged
insurrection. He stated that implied powers, if they existed, were
necessarily subservient to expressed powers in the state constitution, and he noted that nowhere in that document had the governor been specifically authorized to suspend the writ of habeas
corpus or its privileges. Countering Miller's argument that the
executive should not be denied extraordinary power (for example, to suspend the writ of habeas corpus) in cases of insurrection
and rebellion because he might abuse it, Richardson insisted that
the improbability of the misuse of power was not an adequate
reason to justify its existence. He did not believe that a free people would voluntarily surrender to anyone the power to destroy
their liberties. If the people of Colorado had delegated such authority to their governor, they had established a potential tyranny.
Richardson warned that some future governor might declare an
insurrection to imprison bankers, just as Peabody had confined
Moyer, and he detailed the inherent dangers in granting the
governor the extraordinary powers which Miller claimed for him
as a result of an executive declaration. Insurrection and rebellion
were an open state of war and were not just declaratory conditions. Neither insurrection nor rebellion existed in San Miguel
County at a time when the courts were fully operative. Conditions there neither justified the imposition of military rule nor the
endowment of the governor with extraordinary powers. But even
had insurrection ended the exercise of civil authority in the
county, Richardson contended that Peabody's powers had definite constitutional limitations. No one was above the law.[30]

At the close of oral arguments on May 6 the Moyer
case dropped from public notice until the court rendered its decision, which came within hours after the disastrous explosion
at Independence depot on June 6. Campbell joined Chief Justice
Gabbert in the majority opinion. Steele dissented. Although Richardson had contended that Moyer should be released because
Peabody lacked the "power to suspend the privileges of the writ
of *habeas corpus* or declare martial law," the court bypassed these
issues and based its decision on Miller's arguments.[31]

The majority opinion concurred that the governor
had the authority under the state constitution and the statutes

to proclaim insurrection and rebellion and to call out the militia to suppress such conditions. The court rejected its power to intervene—even to review the fact of insurrection—as long as the governor acted within his legal authority. The crucial question was whether the detention of Moyer was legal under the "facts" cited in Miller's return of April 21, "facts" which the court had no authority to review. Under a "reasonable construction" of the constitution (that is, a construction essential for the preservation of the state), the governor possessed the power during insurrections to use all necessary means to restore order, unless the means were prohibited by law. Regarding this point, the court held:

> In suppressing an insurrection it has been many times determined that the military may resort to extreme force as against armed and riotous resistance, even to the extent of taking the life of the rioters. Without such authority the presence of the military in a district under the control of the insurrectionists would be a mere idle parade, unable to accomplish anything in the way of restoring order or suppressing riotous conduct. If, then, the military may resort to the extreme of taking human life in order to suppress insurrection, it is impossible to imagine upon what hypothesis it can be successfully claimed that the milder means of seizing the persons of those participating in the insurrection or aiding and abetting it may not be resorted to. This is but a lawful means to the end accomplished. The power and the authority of the militia in such circumstances are not unlike that of the police of a city or the sheriff of a county aided by his deputies or *posse comitatus*, in suppressing a riot. Certainly such officials would be justified in arresting the rioters and placing them in jail without warrant, and detaining them there until the riot was suppressed.[32]

Continuing, the court pointed out that chaos would result if military authorities followed regular judicial procedures when they arrested and detained insurrectionists like Moyer. Although irregular, their deviations from standard practices did not violate the constitutional rights of an insurrectionist because he was not

> tried by any military court or denied the right of trial by jury; neither [was] he punished for violation of law nor held without the process of law. His arrest and detention

in such circumstances [were] merely to prevent him from taking part or aiding in a continuation of the conditions which the governor . . . [was] endeavoring to suppress.[33]

Although Moyer was being held without benefit of formal charges, his confinement was authorized by law. Nor did his detention violate Section 22 of the Colorado Bill of Rights, which provided for the subordination of military to civil authority. In ordering Moyer's arrest Peabody had acted in a "civil capacity" through Bell and Wells to protect the people from the throes of insurrection.

In conclusion, the court ruled that Moyer was not "illegally restrained in his liberties." Although it acknowledged that the decision acquiesced in placing enormous power in the hands of the governor which he might unlawfully exercise, it noted that the authority to uphold the laws and protect the state had to be lodged somewhere. The possibility that the governor might misuse his power was not a sufficient reason to deny it. The court discounted the authorities cited by Richardson as irrelevant because they dealt with problems of martial law and the suspension of the writ of habeas corpus, and it dismissed its writ of April 15 and remanded Moyer to Bell and Wells.[34]

The Supreme Court had ruled that Peabody had extraordinary authority to suppress insurrection and rebellion. Officials in Denver quickly informed the governor, who was in St. Louis attending the Exposition of 1904. Realizing the breadth of the decision, Samuel Wood, Peabody's private secretary, wired that the court had recognized the power of the governor to determine the existence of insurrection, denied itself the power to intervene in its suppression, and acquiesced in all the means necessary to restore order, including his "power to kill and imprison." Bell also relayed the decision, noting that Miller was elated because the court had quoted his "arguments and propositions" in its decision.[35] The court opened the floodgates for radical attacks on the WFM in the Cripple Creek district, for its decision upheld the methods of harassment previously employed by the governor and his supporters.

Justice Steele, who had had ample opportunity to observe the results of the court's decision, rendered a dissenting opinion on June 30 which reflected on the tragic blows to demo-

cratic principles and procedures that anti-unionists, supported by
the governor, had employed in eradicating the WFM in the
Cripple Creek district. Point by point, Steele strongly contra-
dicted his colleagues. He refused to concede that the governor
constitutionally assumed extraordinary power, particularly that of
suspending the writ of habeas corpus, by a mere executive declaration, and he rejected the view that the Supreme Court could
not examine the "facts" behind such a declaration. Steele concluded that the "facts" cited in Miller's return of April 21 did not
justify Moyer's detention. Furthermore, he regarded the decision
of June 6 as a "fatal wound upon civil liberty," a decision filled
with malicious implications. His opinion had no effect upon Peabody and his supporters. It provoked only a defensive retort
from Chief Justice Gabbert, who observed that Steele's belated
opinion dealt with issues extraneous to the essence of the case.[36]

Moyer's attorneys filed a petition for a rehearing of
the case, contending that the court had violated rights of Moyer
which were guaranteed by the U. S. Constitution. But they had
second thoughts on this procedure and withdrew the petition and
turned to the federal courts. They petitioned Judge Amos M.
Thayer of the United States Circuit Court, Eighth Circuit, Missouri District, in St. Louis for a writ of habeas corpus and obtained the order, returnable on July 5, 1904.[37] On that day, however, Peabody ordered an end to military rule in San Miguel
County, effective at 9 p.m., and ordered that "all military prisoners, including Charles H. Moyer," be surrendered to Rutan at
8:59 p.m. During the day the governor learned that Moyer had
obtained a writ and, in a move similar to one in the Victor Poole
case, he took steps to release Moyer from military custody prior
to receiving service. Adjutant General Bell commanded Captain
Wells by telephone to release Moyer at 3:45 p.m. rather than
8:59 p.m.[38] Nothing but a determination to block further intervention of the federal courts can explain this hasty amendment
to the earlier order. In his return to the court Miller's principal
argument was that the respondents (Peabody, Bell, and Wells)
could not produce Moyer because he had not been in their custody since service of the writ.[39]

Despite the legal maneuvering, the case eventually
returned to the federal courts. On March 11, 1905, Moyer insti-

tuted a damage suit for $100,000 in the United States Circuit
Court in Denver against Peabody, Bell, and Wells, charging
them with false imprisonment and violations of his constitutional
rights.[40] The defendants were financially aided by the mine owners, and they successfully fought the suit through the circuit
court, which finally refused to accept jurisdiction.[41] Nevertheless,
the case went to the United States Supreme Court on a technicality, presenting that body with its first opportunity to rule on
a significant case involving martial law within the U. S. since
Ex parte Milligan (1866).

On January 18, 1909, Justice Oliver W. Holmes, Jr.,
handed down the decision of the court which followed closely
that of the Colorado Supreme Court. Holmes ruled that as long
as such arrests as Moyer's were made in good faith and in the
honest belief that they were needed to block insurrection, the
governor was the final judge and could not be subjected to an
action on the ground that he had no reasonable basis for his
belief. Holmes wrote:

> If we suppose a governor with a very long term of office,
> it may be that a case could be imagined in which the
> length of the imprisonment would raise a different ques-
> tion. But there is nothing in the duration of the plaintiff's
> detention or in the allegations of the complaint that would
> warrant submitting the judgment of the governor to re-
> vision by a jury. It is not alleged that his judgment was
> not honest, if that be material, or that the plaintiff was
> detained after fears of the insurrection were at an end.

Holmes continued that when it came to a decision
by the head of the state on a matter involving the survival of the
state, the ordinary rights of individuals must yield to what the
governor saw as the necessities of the moment.

> Public dangers warrant the substitution of executive proc-
> ess for judicial process. . . . This was admitted with re-
> gard to killing men in the actual clash of arms; and we
> think it obvious, although it was disputed, that the same
> is true of temporary detention to prevent apprehended
> harm. As no one would deny that there was immunity for
> ordering a company to fire upon a mob in insurrection, and
> that a State law authorizing the governor to deprive citi-
> zens of life under such circumstances was consistent with

the Fourteenth Amendment, we are of the opinion that the same is true of a law authorizing by implication what was done in this case. As we have said already, it is unnecessary to consider whether there are other reasons why the Circuit Court was right in its conclusion. It is enough that in our opinion the declaration does not disclose a "suit authorized by law to be brought to redress the deprivation of any right secured by the Constitution of the United States."[42]

For all practical purposes the Supreme Court's ruling upheld the extraordinary methods used against the WFM during its strikes of 1903–1904. The court assumed, as had the Colorado Supreme Court, that Peabody had acted in "good faith" in confining Moyer. Like the state court, it refused to examine alleged "facts" underlying Moyer's confinement. Although the greatest abuse to the personal liberties of Moyer and other union members always occurred after Peabody's declarations of rebellion, the court did not seriously entertain the possibility that such proclamations might serve as the instruments of oppression. Rather, it accepted the alleged "facts" contained in such edicts as "conclusive" and not subject to review. Peabody's authority, therefore, had been limited only by his "good faith."

Thus, the wholesale deportations of union men from the Cripple Creek district after the depot explosion at Independence were within the law. In attempting to uphold the state's power to preserve itself in times of crisis, the U. S. Supreme Court sanctioned the methods used by Peabody and his subordinates. By his ready military intervention in the strikes of the WFM against the mine and mill operators, the governor had converted the strikes into unacceptable challenges to state authority which legally justified extreme, repressive measures. Peabody had done well in his relations with the courts, for, despite his extraordinary tactics against the WFM, they ultimately provided his strongest vindication.

177

9

Peabody: Workingman's Friend or Corporate Tool?

Although his role in the strikes of the WFM against the mill and mine owners was very controversial, Peabody was convinced that the course he had taken was the only one open to him, a conviction undoubtedly influenced by his background in business, banking, and industry. From the beginning he readily acknowledged that his was a "business administration," and he gratefully accepted the support of business and industrial leaders of the state whose interests he felt obligated to protect. As one of them, he believed deeply in their values. When they urged that "freedom of contract" and the "right to work" were essential, for example, he understood them perfectly. The governor believed that his class was responsible for whatever progress the state had made and that it should rightly control the social and economic order. Consequently, Peabody was thoroughly in tune with the anti-union currents in the state and the nation at that time. There is no evidence that he tried to avoid involvement in the employers' movement to guarantee a more impartial administration.

In his interventions in the strikes Peabody was a strict legalist. He delayed ordering troops into Colorado City until his attorney general had advised that intervention was legal. On legal technicalities he refused to help the banished miners of Idaho Springs. He would not intervene in the Cripple Creek district until after the farcical "investigation" of Chase, McClelland, and Miller had taken place. He held off intervening in Telluride until the "evidence" had been assembled and Nathan Miller's go-ahead opinion was in hand. But later, when crises such as the Vindicator mine and Independence depot explosions seemed to justify action in behalf of conservative interests, he cast aside legal scruples and acted without obtaining evidence or supporting legal opinions. Legal opinions he used only to rationalize inaction when he was confronted with appeals for assistance from harassed union miners. Nevertheless, the nation's highest court tolerated the governor's actions by upholding his authority to determine the existence of insurrection and to use any method to suppress it.

Peabody often acted on the basis of his view of history, a conclusion supported by his correspondence, messages, and official explanations of his actions to the voters. In its first decade in Colorado the WFM earned a reputation for violence, although its enemies shared equal responsibility for provoking the destructive clashes which produced the reputation. Wherever the WFM had engaged in strikes, violence erupted. This fact deeply impressed the governor and colored his attitude toward the union. It entered into his every decision to send troops into the mining camps. In justifying his actions to the voters during the gubernatorial campaign of 1904, he wrote:

> I well knew the history and character of this organization. It is . . . a matter of common knowledge in Colorado that for ten years this Federation has stopped at nothing to accomplish its purpose—threats, intimidation, assaults, dynamite outrages, murders, have everywhere characterized its policy. It has been the occasion of more trouble and expense to the state than all other causes combined, including Indian raids. It has never had a strike that has not been bloody. The catalogue of its crimes affright humanity. In times of strike its action has amounted to open insurrection against the state. The leaders of this organization have

179

instilled into the minds of the membership the necessity of arming themselves for the purpose of resisting constituted authority.[1]

The increasing socialistic tendencies of the WFM's annual conventions also helped to determine Peabody's response to the strikes in the mining camps. The prevailing view among the state's business and industrial leaders was that socialists and anarchists within the WFM were conspiring to use it for seizing political control to pass allegedly socialistic measures like the eight-hour law. Peabody, too, saw union officials as demonic leaders who advocated un-American concepts and utilized reprehensible methods in realizing socialistic objectives. To him they were an infamous "inner circle" for whom the rank and file must be saved. He did not think that conservative workingmen of the state would accept the socialistic principles of men like Boyce, Moyer, and Haywood, whose actions had forced the state to spend more than $2,000,000 on its military forces during the past ten years. (Peabody himself spent $625,936.50 of that sum in responding to the alleged "socialistic, anarchistic objects and methods" of the WFM.)[2] But the resolutions which had emanated from the WFM's annual conventions, embellished with socialistic and revolutionary rhetoric, suggested that radicals like Haywood had acquired an influence over the membership beyond acceptable limits. Part of the governor's strategy, therefore, was to discredit union officials in the eyes of the working miners.

Peabody usually intervened in the strikes of the WFM after proclaiming insurrection and rebellion, a procedure which implied that wholesale lawlessness existed and that it required strong executive measures to restore order. However, during 1903 the only widespread lawlessness in the mining camps that possibly may have warranted military intervention to correct was the banishment of the union miners from Idaho Springs after the Sun and Moon mine explosion. The level of violence in the Cripple Creek mining district in September, for example, did not require nearly 1,000 soldiers to control. In his decision to intervene in Colorado City and the mining camps, Peabody's expectation of large-scale violence was more important than the actual existence of violence. He acted to prevent rather than to stop the destruction of lives and property, and this brought praise from some of his military subordinates.[3] He had concluded that an armed uprising was an inevitable part of any WFM strike, a reasonable conclusion in view of its history, and that under such circumstances local officials lacked the power to enforce the law, a judgment which the anti-unionist sheriffs of El Paso and San Miguel counties substantiated with affidavits.

Like many of his supporters, Peabody was convinced that one of the WFM's major objectives was to force the recognition of its right to participate in the "operation and management of the mines, mills and smelters" of the state and that this explained the "most senseless, causeless, unjustifiable and inexcusable 'strikes'" of his administration.[4] Such an objective was totally unacceptable to him and the numerous employers who flocked into the citizens' alliances. Peabody believed that the WFM was a criminal organization, and he easily interpreted its strikes as bona fide challenges to the authority of the state as well as to the industrial status quo. He believed that the WFM had no equal as a threat to the state, for "its official proclamations, full of defiance . . . have amounted . . . to a 'declaration of war against the state.'" He determined to end that threat, but, in doing so, he also eliminated the challenge to the industrial order which the WFM represented. In his 1904 campaign the governor declared:

> I have met the challenge with a policy none too vigorous for the outlawry I was called to oppose. But through it all I have had but one object, and that to show the people of Colorado that the laws will be upheld—that a criminal organization can not dictate the policy of this administration, and that everywhere within the borders of Colorado, property shall be secure and labor free.[5]

Peabody's commitment to law and order would have been more convincing had he impartially adhered to that principle. The year 1904 produced several massive outbreaks of lawlessness, not by the WFM but by the organizations which strongly supported the governor. His failure to uphold the law when mobs of businessmen and prominent mine owners drove scores of union miners from Telluride on March 15 shows his unequal application of principles. Although refusing on technicalities to intervene when requested to protect their return home, he immediately ordered out the troops when leaders of the mob asked that he intervene to protect them from their victims, who then threatened to return to Telluride, peacefully or otherwise. In this case, Peabody obviously acted to protect the perpetrators of violence from possible harm rather than to stop acts of insurrection by WFM members. He used the National Guard in Telluride to uphold the results of lawlessness by his supporters, for his decision, which came after Bell and Wells repeatedly had harassed union members, threw into doubt a protective injunction which the district court had issued in behalf of the banished miners and raised serious questions regarding the impartiality of his administration.

Even more damaging to Peabody's reputation as a law and order governor was his use of the guard to uphold local revolution in the Cripple Creek district. In the aftermath of the atrocity at Independence depot and the subsequent riots at Victor, the leaders of the citizens' alliances and the mine owners' association forced the resignation of dozens of duly elected officials. Peabody not only sanctioned this extraordinary procedure but took an active part in it when he permitted General Bell to use the guard to deport the ousted officials, thereby helping to guarantee the overthrow of local governments in the district. Moreover, when it came to breaking the WFM, the governor showed no reluctance in using force and violence, methods he professed to abhor when they were employed by organized labor. To guarantee a new order in the mining camps (that is, one dominated by his supporters and characterized by the absence of the WFM) Peabody used the power of the state, cautiously at first, to aid the mine owners and businessmen in ridding the camps of strong unionists. But when a crisis developed like the one resulting from the explosion at Independence depot, he acted decisively, successfully exploiting the public clamor to assure the wholesale banishment of the members of the WFM. Later he wrote:

> If these men were scattered, the avenues which ten years of organization and association had opened for crime in that district [Cripple Creek] would be closed. It would require much time in any other community before they could gather about them a new band of conspirators with

the inclination and daring to inaugurate in a new field
another condition of terrorism. These men . . . had determined never to yield the strike. The mine owners had resolved not to employ again the members of that organization. Therefore, the only employment which remained for
them was that of stirring up strife—committing depreda-
tions and intimidating by inhuman crimes the working
miners.

I resolved that they should be dispersed and I dispersed
them. This was done, however, only after careful investigation of each individual case.[6]

Except in Colorado City, Peabody managed to disperse the striking members of the WFM, by one means or another, wherever he
intervened.

Whether or not Peabody accepted violence depended upon who used it and for what purpose. The rampaging
mobs of August 1904, which destroyed union stores in the Cripple
Creek district, created conditions of lawlessness far surpassing
that which had brought troops into Colorado City, Cripple Creek,
and Telluride. Although Peabody offered to intervene if Sheriff
Edward Bell requested it, this did not eliminate the implications
his failure to intervene cast on his stand for law and order. His
intervention in Cripple Creek in September 1903 had not been
at the request of the county sheriff. After he had stretched the
state constitution to aid the mine owners, his refusal to act in
behalf of the miners on the technicality that he had received no
"official" request, the same excuse given for not intervening to
aid the banished miners of Telluride, was not convincing. He had
acted for the businessmen and mine owners when they presented
affidavits stating that they anticipated violence from members
of the WFM after so-called "investigations" by pro-business committees. But the union members who were actual victims of
mob violence were less successful in their appeals for protection,
and the governor simply advised them to seek relief in the courts.
However, when they turned to the courts, they found that Peabody was prepared to disobey or ignore mandates of the court
with which he disagreed. He imposed a double standard when
deciding how to use the power of the state in the strikes of 1903–
1904.

Peabody persistently claimed that he acted in behalf of all workingmen, whether or not they belonged to unions. In his biennial message of 1905 to the legislature, he said:

> The principles upon which I stand, and which caused me to take the action I have in maintaining law and order in this State, are that the rights of every citizen to enjoy life and liberty, and the right to acquire, possess, enjoy and protect his property, are inherent and indefensable. The right of the working man to sell his labor to any one wishing to purchase same for lawful purpose is equally his inherent right. Labor has undisputed right to organize and to cease work, either as individuals or as an organization, for such reasons as may seem themselves satisfactory.[7]

Unfortunately, he applied these principles unequally. The governor believed in freedom of contract, for example, but he helped to impose the card system of the mine owners which effectively prevented a member of the WFM from selling his labor without renouncing his union membership. Furthermore, the governor used his power to impose the system of discriminatory procedures in personnel on companies which had negotiated successful agreements with the WFM. Although he professed to believe in the "open shop," he did not hesitate to close the Portland mine, which had operated throughout the strike on the open shop principle, to strike at the WFM. Behind the facade of stamping out insurrection, he helped to establish the mine owners' brand of the closed shop, the card system. Principles were readily sacrificed to expediency when necessary to emasculate the union.

The governor's attitude toward boycotts also revealed his willingness to embrace expediency when profitable. Like the leaders of the employers' associations, he condemned boycotts as unethical when employed by labor unions. But the Citizens' Alliance of Denver, which Peabody joined in February 1904, used the boycott whenever it served an anti-union purpose. Most of the employers' organizations throughout the state supported boycotts of businesses which refused to enlist in the vendetta against the WFM. This discrepancy between rhetoric and action persisted throughout Peabody's term of office, although, ironically, he recommended a general anti-boycott law in his biennial message of 1905.

Although labor strongly condemned the method which Peabody used to finance the military ventures in the mining camps, the system was perfectly legal. Nevertheless, his insistence that the beneficiaries of the National Guard underwrite its expenses altered the character of this public force. It is unimportant that the state ultimately assumed the financial responsibility for paying the costs of intervention, for the system placed the guard under the control of private interests at crucial times. Basic decisions regarding the troops in the field (for example, the disposition of troops, the number of men required) were made as much by the mine owners as the governor. Although at times he expressed impatience at the owners' reluctance to allow troops reductions in the camps, Peabody invariably deferred to their wishes on such matters. He might not have done so had he financed troops in a different way. In effect, however, the governor placed the guard at the disposal of the mine owners and their supporters, converting the troops into low-paid guards to protect the mines.

The relationship between Peabody and corporations was unusually cordial, and the conclusion that he served corporate interests is well justified. Throughout his administration rumors circulated that the mine and mill operators had heavily subsidized his campaign of 1902 in return for his promise to use the National Guard in whipping the unions of the state, particularly the WFM, into line. As early as December 31, 1902, after the governor's election, the *Colorado Chronicle*, a strong pro-labor voice, reported that the mine owners were demanding that Peabody allow them to name the new adjutant general. They reportedly wanted a man with sufficient "nerve" to stand up to the WFM. According to the report, they intended to provoke trouble with the union and then "demand that the full power of the state" be thrown against it. The *Chronicle* (Feb. 25, 1903) subsequently charged collusion between Peabody and the mine owners in the appointment of Sherman M. Bell as adjutant general. *Polly Pry* (Oct. 3, 1903), the most outspoken supporter of the governor's policies, revealed that the charge had substance and it editorialized: "At the time Peabody was nominated it was well understood among all the party leaders that if elected he would call on the armed forces of the state to stamp out assassination, dynamiting and other forms of violence wherever it existed." To the editor, Mrs. Leonel Ross Anthony, herself a near victim of an assassination attempt, this meant that Peabody had committed his administration to ending the problem of the WFM by standing firm behind the corporations.

Stronger evidence of corporate support emerged after Peabody's reelection attempt in 1904. He was extremely anxious to be vindicated at the polls because in the Moyer decision the Colorado Supreme Court had ruled that the people should decide the wisdom of his actions in the strikes. A Republican victory was also vital to the corporate interests which had benefitted from the governor's policies. Not only did they need an anti-unionist governor, but they also needed a friendly legislature to guarantee the repayment of their heavy investment in the certificates of indebtedness.

With "Peabodyism" as the principal issue, the gubernatorial campaign of 1904 between Peabody and Alva Adams, the Democratic candidate, was bitterly fought. Although hampered by a division within the Republican party caused partly by his labor policies, Peabody waged a vigorous campaign in which he defended his action in the mining camps as necessary to protect the best interests of the state. The beneficiaries of his policies, particularly the mining companies, rallied firmly behind him. Organized labor worked diligently to defeat Peabody. At the request of the Republicans, the Colorado Supreme Court, which had refused to review the facts behind Peabody's decision to order out the troops, assumed virtual control over the election. So significant was the gubernatorial contest that special interests in both parties resorted to fraud to assure victory. In the Democratic stronghold of Denver "repeaters," protected by election officials and the police, moved from poll to poll casting ballots for Adams, while in the mining camps where the guard had intervened, the mine and mill owners, supported by local officials, engaged in widespread intimidation of the miners to assure a majority of the votes for Peabody. When the final returns were tabulated, Adams had received 123,092 votes to Peabody's 113,754, a plurality for Adams of nearly 10,000 votes. Peabody had apparently been repudiated.

Peabody was unwilling to accept this result and filed a formal protest which charged that the Democratic majorities in the Denver precincts had resulted from fraud. He asked that the votes there be thrown out. Peabody's decision to contest the election results further exacerbated political conditions in the state.

Charges and countercharges of corruption and intrigue forced the legislature to form a special joint-commission of twenty-seven legislators to investigate the contested returns. After hearing hundreds of witnesses, whose testimony filled thousands of pages, the committee reported that it could not determine who was elected.[8] Consequently, the legislature devised a plan whereby Peabody would replace Adams as governor but only after Peabody had signed a prior agreement to resign within twenty-four hours, thus paving the way for the swearing in of Jesse McDonald, the lieutenant governor, also a Republican. Colorado, therefore, had three governors within twenty-four hours.[9]

U. S. Senator T. M. Patterson, whose newspapers were highly critical of the campaign to oust Adams, later charged that the utility companies of Denver, the coal corporations, the corporate members of the Mine Owners' Association, the "smelter trust," and various railroads had conspired with Peabody to effect his reelection. According to the allegations, the corporations had spent nearly $40,000 to assure Peabody's renomination and more than $200,000 to assure his reelection. In return Peabody had promised to allow them to select two of the four new members of the supreme court. The additions had been authorized by a constitutional amendment of 1904. After Adams's victory, the corporations offered to underwrite the expenses of a contest if Peabody would submit the names of their judicial candidates for confirmation prior to Adams's inauguration. Peabody agreed. Subsequently, he plotted to remove from office various Democratic members of the legislature to assure his success in the contested election and the confirmation of his nominees to the court. The conspiracy was aborted, however, when a number of Republican legislators balked at the scheme. Patterson charged that before Peabody was sworn in, he had agreed to resign immediately in

favor of McDonald and that he had actually written his resignation prior to the vote of the legislature. But he did so only after
material promises had been followed by threats. Although Peabody's correspondence contains nothing to substantiate these
charges, Patterson apparently did not make them carelessly.
When Patterson was threatened with contempt proceedings by
the court, itself the subject of his allegations, he was not allowed
to present the proof of his charges, although he claimed to
have it.[10]

Peabody constantly held that the eight-hour ques-
tion was not a factor in causing the strikes and that the issue had
been raised by the WFM to cloak its socialistic objectives. His
position was only partially correct. But had an eight-hour law
been enacted or had he actively worked to secure such legislation and failed, the results would have been a defusing of Colorado's labor troubles during 1903–1904. The eight-hour question
did not cause the Colorado City and the Cripple Creek district
strikes. However, it was a central issue in the strikes of the Denver smeltermen, of the Idaho Springs miners, and of the millmen
of Telluride. The issue that precipitated the strike against the mill
owners of Colorado City was more crucial than the eight-hour
question; it was the right of the millmen to organize and to
affiliate with the WFM. This soon became a vital issue in all the
union's strikes. Although Peabody frequently reiterated his belief in the right of workingmen to organize, he did not recognize
their right to belong to unions like the militant WFM, which he
believed was under the control of criminals.

During the military occupation of the mining camps
the union members often reacted to extreme provocation in an
admirable way. Certainly they posed little danger to the troops
in the field, a fact which the governor recognized.[11] The expectation of anti-unionists that the military control of a district would
result in the discovery of evidence necessary to convict WFM
members of the unsolved crimes of the past decade was never
realized. Although in complete control of the Cripple Creek district after the Independence depot explosion, for example, the
National Guard, citizens' alliances, and mine owners could not
uncover sufficient evidence to convict any member of the WFM
of any crime. Nevertheless, officials of these organizations re-

peatedly blamed the union for the atrocity at the depot and
the riots at Victor and claimed that they had the evidence to imprison as many as forty of its members for the crimes. In reporting to the miners' annual convention in 1905 regarding the pending litigation in the Cripple Creek district, Frank Hangs, an attorney for the WFM, concluded:

> With thirty cases filed in the District Court against them,
> and charging over one hundred men with having com-
> mitted felonies, not one has been convicted. Not a single
> member of the organization is now charged with crime. In
> view of the fact that on September 4, 1903, about one
> thousand militia were brought into this district, and since
> that time the mine owners have completely dominated the
> county, this record is indeed remarkable. Every effort that
> human ingenuity could devise was made to railroad Fed-
> eration men into the penitentiary. More than $30,000 was
> spent in attorneys' fees to convict Federation men. Per-
> jured testimony was procured. Detectives joined the unions
> and endeavored to incite lawlessness. Failing this, they put
> up "jobs" and charged them against the Federation. Many
> former union men became spies and traitors. . . . Had the
> union men stooped to crime it would have been impossible
> to escape detection. The men in this district suffered and
> endured things that cause the blush of shame to mantle
> the cheek of every loyal American citizen.[12]

The failure to convict members of the WFM of crimes under the
most favorable circumstances seriously undermined the mine
owners' charge that the WFM was responsible for the entire criminal history of the Cripple Creek district in the decade preceding
Peabody's inauguration.[13] The failure also threw into serious
doubt Peabody's charges in the fall of 1903 that only the WFM's
control of the courts and the law enforcement offices of the district prevented the conviction of criminals within the union. Furthermore, in the other camps where enemies of the WFM controlled the local governments, the record of conviction of union
members for crimes was no better. There was obviously a wide
divergence between the violent rhetoric of some union leaders
and the deeds of the rank-and-file. At no time did the WFM en-
gage in armed resistance against the constituted authorities, even
when their extreme harassment and provocation might have justified it.

Although the causes of the labor troubles in 1903–1904 are complex, certain factors stand out as most significant. Of singular importance was the intransigence of employers like Charles M. MacNeill of the United States Reduction and Refining Company. They openly discriminated against members of the WFM. Such employers met the campaigns to organize the miners and the millmen with intense hostility, and when they failed to block the organization of their workers, they refused to recognize the union. When walkouts resulted, they refused to negotiate or to arbitrate if doing so meant concessions of any type. No other individual was more responsible for the disastrous strikes at Colorado City and Cripple Creek than MacNeill, whose stubbornness was only increased by Peabody's ready response to appeals for military intervention. Had the governor flatly rejected aid until corporate officials had made an honest attempt to reach a quick, peaceful settlement with union leaders, the escalation of the labor unrest might have been averted. When agreements resulted, they usually were beneficial to all parties when the mine and mill operators met the WFM halfway. The agreement of August 1903 between the union and James Burns of the Portland mine is an example.

The absence of machinery for compulsory arbitration undoubtedly intensified the labor unrest by forcing Peabody to play an active role in disputes. If there had been means to compel negotiations, the obstinacy of some employers might have been overcome. To the governor's credit, he proposed in his biennial message of 1905 a constitutional amendment providing for compulsory arbitration in those labor disputes which seemed capable of disrupting the economy of the state. His position had substantially changed from that of 1903 when he had recommended abolition of the State Board of Arbitration rather than endowment of it with sufficient powers to function effectively by constitutional amendment.

The officials of the WFM were not blameless in the labor troubles, for they frequently were antagonizing in pressing their demands upon the mine and mill operators. The demands, embellished by revolutionary rhetoric, were often equivalent to ultimatums, embodying implied or open threats of violence if they were not granted. This increased resistance rather than facilitated negotiated settlements. Employers of the state, already rallying to counter the ominous socialistic rumblings from the miners' annual conventions which had fallen increasingly under the control of radicals like Haywood, reacted in a manner destructive to the union's interests. Their response partly determined Peabody's labor policies. When confronted with a choice between a MacNeill and a Haywood, the governor chose the former without hesitation. The industrial character of the WFM, its radical leadership, its tendency toward socialism, and its power frightened him as much as it did the employers. The abrasive actions and language of WFM leaders, therefore, were an important factor in explaining the determined stand of the antiunionists who broke the power of the WFM in Colorado.

The debacle in Colorado did not diminish the commitment of Moyer, Haywood, and other WFM leaders to militancy, industrial unionism, and political action. On the contrary, they capitalized on the bitterness of the rank and file and in 1906 led the WFM into the radical Industrial Workers of the World (IWW), a link-up that was beset at the start by factional disputes which ultimately divided the WFM's leadership and its members. Nevertheless, in the years immediately after the strikes of 1903–1904 the WFM aggressively expanded into other metal mining states, such as Missouri, and attempted to bring the nation's coal miners within its jurisdiction. Consequently, although its power declined in Colorado, the WFM's membership temporarily soared until internal dissension over the WFM's relationship with the IWW and related issues proved detrimental to the union's growth and effectiveness.[14]

The WFM never regained the commanding position in the Cripple Creek and Telluride districts which it held prior to the strikes of 1903–1904. Because it wisely ended its strike in Telluride in December 1904 after the mine owners granted the eight-hour day, the miners' union survived there. Anti-union forces retained control but they grudgingly tolerated the existence of the organization they had tried to destroy. In the more important Cripple Creek district the WFM foolishly refused to accept defeat and prolonged the strike for several years. Once-powerful unions like the Victor Miners' Union No. 32, unable to work out an accommodation because of the hostility of anti-unionists groups and the WFM's strike policy, disappeared from the WFM's roster. In both districts local unions were forced to turn over valuable properties to the parent organization to be held in trust until better days. For example, the Cripple Creek miners' union hall, the union hospital at Telluride, and 27,000 shares of stock in the Victor Miners' Union Building Association became the administrative and financial responsibility of the WFM. Despite these salvage efforts, the local unions which had been involved in the strikes never regained their prestrike power in the affairs of their district.

Peabody, a highly successful businessman and local politician, assumed office determined to maintain order and to make Colorado safe for investment capital. Too quickly, however, he found his administration engulfed in labor problems which he persisted in making more complex. Relying upon inexperienced advisers and partisan businessmen, he early committed his administration to an anti-labor posture. His administration was joined so firmly to corporate interests that the two acted as one against the WFM. Yet Peabody was no ordinary businessman-governor whose values and way of life was threatened by a militant labor union. He was not just a "man of his times," clinging ferverishly to old, cherished values. He was more than this. As governor, he headed the state whose powers should have been used to protect the interests of all its people. Instead, he used that power to war against a labor union which dared to challenge the supremacy of the class and the values he represented. Under the pretense of preserving the state, he attempted to break a militant union which threatened to disrupt the prevailing social order. In many ways he was like Haywood and other labor leaders whom he despised. He was forceful, stubborn, aggressive, courageous, and determined to the point of losing his better judgment. But he was also easily swayed, compromised, and flattered by those who wished to use the powers of his office for their own purposes. Peabody left office still asserting his belief in law and order, freedom of contract, and the right of labor to work unmolested.[15] He undoubtedly believed in these principles, although not enough to apply them impartially to all citizens.

notes

CHAPTER ONE

1. See Western Federation of Miners, *Constitution* (1903), Art. 4, sec. 10 in U. S., Congress, Senate, Commissioner of Labor, *A Report on Labor Disturbances in the State of Colorado from 1880 to 1904, Inclusive, with Correspondence Relating Thereto,* 58th Cong., 3d Sess., 1905, Doc. 122, pp. 36-38. Hereafter cited as *Labor Disturbances.* See also Western Federation of Miners, *Proceedings, Eleventh Annual Convention* (Denver: Western Newspaper Union, 1903), p. 89. Hereafter cited as WFM, *Proc., 11th Ann. Conv.*

2. Colorado, Bureau of Labor Statistics, *Eighth Biennial Report, 1901–1902,* p. 341. Hereafter cited as BLS, *Eighth Biennial Report.*

3. Colorado, Bureau of Labor Statistics, *[Fifth] Biennial Report, 1895–1896,* p. 9. Hereafter cited as BLS, *Fifth Biennial Report.*

4. Colorado, Bureau of Labor Statistics, *Seventh Biennial Report, 1898–1900,* pp. 44–45. Hereafter cited as BLS, *Seventh Biennial Report.*

5. BLS, *Eighth Biennial Report,* pp. 72–73, 342.

6. WFM, *Proc., 11th Ann. Conv.,* pp. 86–89.

7. Haywood's statistics are not above challenge, however. Because he changed his method of computing the enrollment for 1903, basing it on quarterly and annual reports rather than on receipts from a per capita tax levied on members as in the past, union membership for 1903 showed an extraordinary increase over 1902, rising from 19,633 to 27,154. Even so, it never approached the Bureau's estimate of 48,000 active members for 1902. Western Federation of Miners, *Proceedings, Tenth Annual Convention* (Denver: Chronicle Press, 1902), p. 59. Hereafter cited as WFM, *Proc., 10th Ann. Conv.*

8. This account of the strike is based upon data found in *Labor Disturbances*, pp. 75-85.

9. Ibid., p. 83.

10. In retaliation for Tarsney's pro-labor role, both in the strike and the litigation which followed, a masked mob of fifteen abducted the general from a Colorado Springs hotel near midnight on June 23, hauled him to an isolated area east of the city, stripped him and covered him with tar and feathers. His assailants then abandoned him. Ibid., p. 85.

11. BLS, *Fifth Biennial Report*, pp. 61–89 and *Labor Disturbances*, pp. 86–101.

12. In 1899 a violent strike occurred in the Coeur D'Alene district which further convinced the employers of Colorado that the WFM was a cancerous growth on the labor movement. For accounts of this strike, see U. S., Congress, House, *Coeur D'Alene Labor Troubles*, 56th Cong., 1st Sess., 1900, Rept. 1999; Senate, *Coeur D'Alene Mining Troubles*, 56th Cong., 1st Sess., 1900, Doc. 142; Senate, *Coeur D'Alene Mining Troubles*, 56th Cong., 1st Sess., 1899, Doc. 25; Senate, *Labor Troubles in Idaho*, 56th Cong., 1st Sess., 1899, Doc. 42; Senate, *Coeur D'Alene Mining Troubles*, 56th Cong., 1st Sess., 1899, Doc. 24.

13. BLS, *Seventh Biennial Report*, pp. 164–65 and *Labor Disturbances*, pp. 102–105.

14. In describing the fathom system, the bureau reported that a "fathom as applied to mining, means 6 feet high, 6 feet long and as wide as the vein, whatever it may be. If a miner happened to get into a wide vein of ore, he might work an entire month without earning much more than the value of the powder, fuse and candles used. The work was not even let by contract that the workmen helped to make. The management simply fixed a given price per fathom, and the miners could accept it or go without work." BLS, *Eighth Biennial Report*, p. 166.

15. *Labor Disturbances*, p. 106.

16. Ibid., p. 107.

17. The commission included Lieutenant Governor D. C. Coates, who had held a number of offices in the Colorado State Federation of Labor; John H. Murphy, an attorney for the WFM; and District Judge Theron Stevens, who sympathized with the striking miners. BLS, *Eighth Biennial Report*, pp. 169–70.

18. *Labor Disturbances*, pp. 109–10.

19. Ibid., p. 111.

20. See WFM, *Constitution* (1903), Preamble, in ibid., pp. 36–38.

21. Selig Perlman and Philip Taft, *Labor Movements* (New York: MacMillan Company, 1935), p. 173.

22. Boyce to Gompers, March 16, 1897, quoted in *Labor Troubles in Idaho*, p. 8.

23. Gompers to Boyce, March 26, 1897, quoted in ibid., p. 10.

24. Quoted in Colorado Mine Operators' Association, *Criminal Record of the Western Federation of Miners from Coeur D'Alene to Cripple Creek, 1894–1904* (Colorado Springs: Colorado Mine Operators' Association, 1904), p. 7.

25. William D. Haywood, *Bill Haywood's Book* (New York: International Publishers, 1929), p. 79.

26. Western Federation of Miners, *Proceedings, Ninth Annual Convention* (Pueblo, Colo.: Pueblo Courier Print, 1901), pp. 10–11. Hereafter cited as WFM, *Proc., 9th Ann. Conv.*

27. Ibid., pp. 89, 90–92, 106.

28. WFM, *Proc., 10th Ann. Conv.*, pp. 10–13 [Italics added].

29. Ibid., pp. 83, 94, 96.

30. Ibid., pp. 131, 177.

31. WFM, *Proc., 11th Ann. Conv.*, pp. 20–21, 175–76, 252–53.

CHAPTER TWO

1. This biographical sketch of Peabody is based on the following sources: M. W. Grand Lodge of A. F. and A. M. of Colorado, *Proceedings, 41st Annual Communication* (Denver: The W. F. Robinson Printing Co., 1901), n.p.; M. W. Grand Lodge of A. F. and A. M. of Colorado, *Proceedings, 58th Annual Communication* (Denver: The W. F. Robinson Printing Co., 1918), pp. 97–102; *Canon City Record*, July 17, 1902.

2. See Colorado, Canon City, City Council, Minutes, 7 (1900–1902), 161, 210–11, 216, 239, 277, 351, 380, 385 and 8 (1902–1903), 28, 50, 68, 78, and 108–109.

3. Canon City Minutes, 7, 349.

4. Canon City Minutes, 8, 139, 152.

5. For example, see the editorials of the *Denver Republican*, Aug. 21 and Sept. 3, 1902.

6. Although beyond the scope of this study, Peabody's Masonic activities should be noted for their possible influence upon his business and political career. Peabody devoted twenty-four years of serv-

ice to his local lodge, Mt. Moriah, No. 15, mostly in leadership roles. For twenty-seven years he served in various positions in Chapter No. 3 (Pueblo), Royal Arch Masons. He devoted twenty-two years of active service to Commandery No. 3, K. T. (Pueblo). In 1884 he was elected Grand Master of M. W. Grand Lodge, A. F. and A. M. of Colorado. He became Grand Commander, Knights Templar of Colorado in 1888. He was elected Most Excellent Grand High Priest of the Grand Royal Arch Chapter in 1896 and was elected an Honorary Inspector General of Thirty-third Degree in 1899. M. W. Grand Lodge, *Proceedings, 58th Annual Communication*, pp. 100–101.

7. Suggestive of the significance which Republicans placed on the election of 1902 is the series of editorials appearing in the *Denver Republican*, a leading party organ, on Sept. 13, 23, and 29, 1902; Oct. 2 and 12, 1902; and Nov. 2, 1902.

8. Campaign quote of Peabody in E. M. Sobin to Peabody, Jan. 28, 1903, Colorado, State Archives and Records Service, Records of the Office of the Governor: James H. Peabody, 1903–1905, Correspondence: Document Box—Applications for State Office, II, 1902. Hereafter cited as DB: Applications, Peabody Papers. This study draws heavily upon the Peabody Papers, located in the Colorado State Archives, Denver. Hereafter, citations from this material will specify only the location of individual items within the collection.

9. *Denver Post*, Oct. 29, 1902.

10. *Cripple Creek Times*, Oct. 15, 1902.

11. See party platform in *Denver Republican*, Sept. 13, 1902.

12. *Victor Daily Record*, Nov. 1, 1902.

13. Colorado, House, *House Journal*, Fourteenth General Assembly (1903), p. 96. Hereafter cited as *House Jour.*, 14th Gen. Ass'y.

14. Ibid., pp. 115-16.

15. Ibid., p. 99.

16. Ibid., pp. 110-11.

17. Ibid., p. 117.

18. Ibid., pp. 105–107.

CHAPTER THREE

1. For statistical information relating to the United States Reduction and Refining Company, see *Rocky Mountain News*, Feb. 17, 1903.

2. *Labor Disturbances*, p. 112.

3. Charles M. MacNeill to Peabody, Mar. 8, 1903, DB: Correspondence and Investigation of Strikes, Peabody Papers. Hereafter cited as DB: Investigation of Strikes.

4. Enc., William D. Haywood to Peabody, Mar. 8, 1903, ibid.

5. *Labor Disturbances*, p. 113.

6. For Peck's and Fullerton's views of their meeting with the committee, see Peck to Peabody, Mar. 8, 1903, and Fullerton to Peabody, Mar. 9, 1903, DB: Investigation of Strikes, Peabody Papers.

7. Testimony of MacNeill to Peabody's Advisory Board, Mar. 28, 1903, *Proceedings of Advisory Board Appointed by Governor James H. Peabody to Investigate and Report upon Labor Difficulties Existing in the State of Colorado and More Particularly at Colorado City* (microfilm), William E. Borah Papers, Idaho Historical Society, Boise, Idaho. Hereafter cited as *Report of Advisory Board*.

8. MacNeill to Gilbert, Mar. 3, 1903, DB: Investigation of Strikes, Peabody Papers.

9. Peck to Gilbert, Mar. 2, 1903, and Gilbert to Peabody, Mar. 3, 1903, ibid.

10. Gilbert to Peabody, Mar. 3, 1903, ibid.

11. Testimony of Gilbert to Advisory Board, Apr. 1, 1903, *Report of Advisory Board*.

12. Miller to Peabody, Mar. 3, 1903, DB: Investigation of Strikes, Peabody Papers. Miller based his opinion on Art. 4, sec. 5 of the Colorado Constitution (1903) and Art. 7, sec. 3 of the National Guard Act (1897).

13. Colorado, Office of the Adjutant General, *Biennial Report to the Governor, 1903–1904*, p. 11. Hereafter cited as Adj. Gen., *Biennial Report, 1903–1904*.

14. MacNeill to Gilbert, Mar. 3, 1903, DB: Investigation of Strikes, Peabody Papers.

15. *Rocky Mountain News*, Mar. 4, 1903.

16. Petition from citizens of Colorado City to Peabody, Mar. 3, 1903, DB: Investigation of Strikes, Peabody Papers.

17. *Rocky Mountain News*, Mar. 4, 1903; *Colorado Chronicle*, Mar. 4, 1903.

18. Peabody to Kebler, Mar. 4, 1903, and Peabody to Thatcher, July 24, 1903, Letterpress Books 37 and 39, respectively, Peabody Papers. Hereafter the Letterpress Books will be designated LB.

19. Colorado, General Assembly, *Session Laws* (1897), pp. 22-27.

20. See editorials for Mar. 6 and 7, 1903.

21. Colorodo, Bureau of Labor Statistics, *Ninth Biennial Report, 1903–1904*, p. 56. Hereafter cited as BLS, *Ninth Biennial Report*.

22. Telegram, Peabody to MacNeill, Mar. 7, 1903, LB 37, Peabody Papers.

23. MacNeill to Peabody, Mar. 8, 1903, DB: Investigation of Strikes, ibid.

24. Peck to Peabody, Mar. 8, 1903, ibid.

25. Fullerton to Peabody, Mar. 9, 1903, ibid.

26. Haywood to Peabody, Mar. 8, 1903, ibid.

27. Peabody to MacNeill, Peck, and Fullerton, Mar. 9, 1903, LB 37, ibid.

28. *House Jour.*, 14th Gen. Ass'y, p. 785.

29. BLS, *Ninth Biennial Report*, p. 56.

30. Report on Governor Peabody's interviews with workers at the Standard mill, Mar. 11, 1903, DB: Investigation of Strikes, Peabody Papers; statement of Portland mill employees, Mar. 12, 1903, ibid; undated statement of the striking Telluride mill employees, ibid.

31. *Rocky Mountain News*, Mar. 13, 1903.

32. *House Jour.*, 14th Gen. Ass'y, pp. 846–47.

33. Peabody to MacNeill, Peck, Fullerton, and Moyer, Mar. 12, 1903, LB 37, Peabody Papers.

34. Miller to Peabody, Mar. 13, 1903, DB: Investigation of Strikes, ibid.

35. Telegram, Peabody to Root, Mar. 13, 1903, LB 37, ibid.

36. BLS, *Ninth Biennial Report*, p. 58.

37. *Labor Disturbances*, p. 119.

38. BLS, *Ninth Biennial Report*, pp. 58–59; *Colorado Chronicle*, Mar. 18, 1903.

39. *Labor Disturbances*, p. 120.

40. Ibid., pp. 120–21.

41. Ibid., p. 129.

42. Peabody to the Public, Mar. 19, 1903, Executive Record Book XV, 179, Peabody Papers.

43. See Peabody to MacNeill, Mar. 19, 1903, LB 37, ibid. The other letters were identical to this one.

44. Moyer to Advisory Board, Mar. 21, 1903, *Report of Advisory Board*.

45. Moyer to Advisory Board, Mar. 23, 1903, ibid.

46. Babbitt to Advisory Board, Mar. 23, 1903, ibid.

47. Hawkins to Advisory Board, Mar. 24, 1903, ibid.

48. MacNeill to Advisory Board, Mar. 24, 1903, ibid.

49. MacNeill to Advisory Board, Mar. 28, 1903, ibid.

50. Ibid.

51. *Labor Disturbances*, p. 127.

52. Franklin to Advisory Board, Mar. 31, 1903, *Report of Advisory Board*.

53. Moyer to Advisory Board, Mar. 31, 1903, ibid.

54. Murphy to Advisory Board, May 23, 1903, Second Report and Proceedings of Governor Peabody's Advisory Board, in DB: Correspondence, Peabody Papers.

55. Babbitt to Advisory Board, May 23, 1903, ibid.

56. Exhibit 1 (USRRC), Hawkins to Hayt, May 23, 1903, ibid.

57. Exhibit 2 (WFM), Burr to Advisory Board, May 23, 1903, ibid.

58. Murphy to Advisory Board, May 23, 1903, ibid.

59. Report of Advisory Board to Peabody, May 31, 1903, ibid.

CHAPTER FOUR

1. Perlman and Taft, *Labor Movements*, pp. 129–33.

2. *The New York Times*, Apr. 15, 1903.

3. Ibid., Apr. 16, 1903.

4. Throughout the spring and summer of 1903, Parry was busy rallying the nation's employers to his anti-union standard. Hostility and vindictiveness against organized labor characterized his public addresses. For example, see *The New York Times*, July 28 and Aug. 14, 1903.

5. Impressed by the fight of the Colorado alliances against the WFM, the businessmen of San Francisco employed George during the winter of 1903–1904 at a "substantial salary" to organize alliances in their region. (Robert E. L. Knight, *Industrial Relations in the San Francisco Bay Area, 1900–1918* [Berkeley and Los Angeles: University of California Press, 1960], p. 141; also, Perlman and Taft, pp. 134–35.) In a letter of introduction to H. C. Huntington, vice-president of the Southern Pacific Railroad, Peabody paved the way for George, de-

scribing him as an "esteemed" and "prominent gentleman" who was "deeply interested in the bringing about of industrial peace throughout the country." Peabody to Huntington, Jan. 19, 1904, LB 42, Peabody Papers.

6. James C. Craig, *The History of the Strike that Brought the Citizens' Alliance of Denver, Colorado into Existence* (n.p.: n.d.), p. 4. Reprinted from *George's Weekly* (Denver), July 4, 1903.

7. *Denver Republican*, Apr. 28 and 29, 1903; *Colorado Chronicle*, Apr. 29 and May 6, 1903.

8. Denver Alliance, *Constitution and By-Laws* (1903), Art. III, sec. 1.

9. Craig, p. 7.

10. Denver Alliance, *Constitution*, Art. III, sec. 1. Later revisions of the constitution specifically banned union members. See Constitution (1903), Art. III, sec. 1 and Art. IX, sec. 1 in *Labor Disturbances*, pp. 46–47, and *Colorado Chronicle*, Apr. 29, 1903.

11. This account of the strike, except where indicated, is taken from the exchange of correspondence between Craig, D. C. Coates, chairman of the labor committee, Frank Adams, president of the Denver Fire and Police Board, and John F. Harley, head of the State Board of Arbitration, which is reprinted in Craig.

12. *Polly Pry* (Denver), Jan. 23, 1904, p. 5.

13. This account of the strike, except where indicated, is based on data found in *Labor Disturbances*, pp. 132–46.

14. *Denver Republican*, July 5, 1903.

15. Ibid., July 6, 1903.

16. *Denver Post*, July 7, 1903.

17. *Denver Republican*, July 9, 1903.

18. For example, see Peabody to John Brisbane Walker, Apr. 22, 1904 and Peabody to G. R. S. McInturff, May 11, 1904, LB 43, Peabody Papers. A recent study of the eight-hour question in Colorado is David L. Lonsdale, "The Fight for An Eight-Hour Day," *The Colorado Magazine*, *43* (Fall 1966), 339–53.

19. July 16, 1903, LB 39, Peabody Papers. Later, in a letter of Jan. 25, 1904 to Harrison Gray Otis, president of the Times-Mirror Company (Los Angeles), Peabody claimed that he had opposed eight-hour legislation in the interests of the workingman, who ought to have the right to sell his labor as he pleased. LB 42, ibid.

20. Colorado, General Assembly, *House and Senate Journal*, Extraordinary Session (1903), pp. 26–27, 84.

21. LB 39, Peabody Papers.

22. *Denver Republican,* July 30, 1903.

23. *Rocky Mountain News,* July 30, 1903.

24. *Denver Post,* July 31, 1903.

25. See editorials in the *Denver Post,* Aug. 4 and 5, 1903; the *Rocky Mountain News,* Aug. 4, 1903; the *Denver Republican,* July 31, 1903.

26. *Colorado Springs Gazette,* July 31, 1903.

27. *Denver Republican,* Aug. 4, 1903.

28. Thomas Walsh, et al., to Peabody, July 31, 1903, DB: Reports, Resolutions, Petitions, Peabody Papers.

29. *Rocky Mountain News,* Aug. 1, 1903.

30. N.d. (c. Aug. 1, 1903), DB: C-G, 1903–1904, Peabody Papers.

31. *Denver Republican,* Aug. 2, 1903.

32. Peabody to Walsh, Aug. 3, 1903, LB 39, Peabody Papers.

33. On Aug. 15 the *Rocky Mountain News* quoted Peabody as saying that the miners had to learn that they could not violate the law, assassinate men, or destroy property, "not even if they do have the protection of District Judge Owers." Owers responded with an open letter to Peabody characterized by caustic and eloquent criticism. Among other things Owers stated: "I regret, that, lacking the advantages of blood, breeding and education which are yours in so eminent a degree, I am not gifted with that delicate sense of discrimination which enables you to distinguish so nicely between a mob led by a banker and a dance hall proprietor, and one led by a miner, and which makes it possible for you to regard an actual trespass upon human rights with equanimity, while you look upon even a threatened invasion of property rights as, by comparison, an unpardonable sin." (Owers to Peabody, DB: I-L; Mc-P: 1903–1904, Peabody Papers.) Haywood later wrote that Owers had consulted him about this letter to the governor prior to its publication. Haywood, *Bill Haywood's Book,* pp. 122–23.

34. *Labor Disturbances,* p. 158.

35. Craig to Peabody, Sept. 24, 1903, DB: C-G, Peabody Papers.

36. Craig went to Chicago to assist Parry and others in laying the groundwork for a national organization to "fight union labor and to promote the interests of employers and independent workmen by all legitimate means." *The New York Times,* Sept. 30, 1903; Craig to Peabody, Sept. 24, 1903, DB: C-G, Peabody Papers.

37. *Canon City Record,* Nov. 26, 1903.

38. *House Jour.,* 14th Gen. Ass'y, p. 117.

39. See DB: Applications, Peabody Papers.

40. *Rocky Mountain News*, Feb. 21, 1903 and S. B. Strong to Peabody, Nov. 5, 1903, DB: P-R; S, Peabody Papers.

41. *Rocky Mountain News*, Feb. 21, 1903.

42. In an editorial of Mar. 12, 1903, the *Rocky Mountain News* raised serious questions regarding Bell's fitness for office and the propriety of the appointment.

43. Examples of this practice are abundant. See MacDonald to Peabody, Feb. 21, Mar. 12, Apr. 7 and 22, June 1, Aug. 28, Sept. 3, 1904, DB: I-L, Peabody Papers.

44. See Executive Order, May 5, 1903, LB Miscellaneous; Executive Order, July 27, 1903, Executive Record Book XV, ibid; Adj. Gen., *Biennial Report, 1903–1904*, p. 24.

45. Peabody to MacNeill, Apr. 18, 1904, LB 43, Peabody Papers.

CHAPTER FIVE

1. Benjamin M. Rastall, *The Labor History of the Cripple Creek District* (Madison: University of Wisconsin Press, 1908), p. 88.

2. WFM, *Proc., 11th Ann. Conv.*, p. 208; *Labor Disturbances*, p. 39.

3. See *Labor Disturbances*, pp. 161–62; for estimate and statements of delegates from the Cripple Creek mining district to the Eleventh Annual Convention about anti-strike sentiments of the miners, see WFM, *Proc., 11th Ann. Conv.*, pp. 169–70.

4. *Labor Disturbances*, pp. 147–50.

5. Some mine owners were under heavy bond, as much as $100,000, to continue shipments. *Polly Pry* (Denver), Feb. 13, 1904, p. 8.

6. *Cripple Creek Times*, Aug. 15, 1903.

7. *Labor Disturbances*, p. 162.

8. Ibid., p. 164.

9. *Cripple Creek Times*, Aug. 25, 1903.

10. *Denver Republican*, Aug. 16, 1903.

11. *Cripple Creek Times*, Aug. 29 and Sept. 3, 1903.

12. *Labor Disturbances*, pp. 170–71.

13. See telegrams in DB: Investigation of Strikes, Peabody Papers.

14. Ibid.

15. Report of Cripple Creek Investigation Committee, n.d., ibid.

16. Ibid.

17. *Denver Post*, Sept. 6, 1903.

18. Carlton to Peabody, Mar. 12, 1904, DB: Correspondence and Adjutant General Office, *In Re* Law and Order Banquet, Peabody Papers.

19. See "Military Rule in Colorado," *Army and Navy Journal, 41*, No. 7 (Oct. 17, 1903), 166–67.

20. See opinion in Colorado, Office of the Attorney General, *Report, 1903–1904*, pp. 68–70. Hereafter cited as AG, *Report, 1903–1904.*

21. Adj. Gen., *Biennial Report, 1903–1904*, pp. 111, 130.

22. Peabody to George E. Randolph, Sept. 5, 1903; Peabody to Jethro Sanford, Sept. 21, 1903; Peabody to James A. McCandless, Sept. 24, 1903; Peabody to W. G. White, Sept. 27, 1903; Peabody to Herbert W. Burdette, Sept. 27 and Oct. 5, 1903; Peabody to Lyman Robinson, Oct. 5, 1903; Peabody to Albert W. McIntire, Oct. 12, 1903, LB 40; also Peabody to J. M. Douglas, Nov. 11, 1903; Peabody to A. S. Barnes, Nov. 16, 1903; Peabody to David Moffat, Nov. 25, 1903, LB 41, Peabody Papers.

23. Colorado, Teller County, County Commissioners' Record, III, 72–73. Hereafter cited as Teller County Record.

24. *Labor Disturbances*, pp. 178–79; also, "Governor Peabody Loyal to the Corporations," *Miners Magazine, 5* (Sept. 10, 1903), 6.

25. *Cripple Creek Times*, Sept. 5, 1903.

26. Resolutions from Citizens of Towns in the Cripple Creek District to Peabody, Sept. 5, 1903, DB: Reports, Resolutions, Petitions, Peabody Papers.

27. BLS, *Ninth Biennial Report*, pp. 86–88; *Denver Post*, Sept. 5, 1903.

28. *Cripple Creek Times*, Sept. 8, 1903.

29. Quoted in Ray Stannard Baker, "The Reign of Lawlessness: Anarchy and Despotism in Colorado," *McClure's Magazine, 23* (May 1904), 48.

30. *Cripple Creek Times*, Sept. 15, 1903.

31. *Victor Daily Record*, Oct. 2, 1903.

32. According to Bell, "military necessity recognizes no laws, either civil or social." Adj. Gen., *Biennial Report, 1903–1904*, p. 20.

33. Cole to Peabody, Sept. 14, 1903, DB: "A-B"; "B"; 1903–1904, Peabody Papers.

34. Cole to Peabody, Sept. 20, 1903, ibid.

35. Teller County Record, III, 85.

36. Quoted in *Cripple Creek Times*, Sept. 24, 1903.

37. *Labor Disturbances*, pp. 185–86.

38. Art. II, sec. 21 stated: "That the privilege of the writ of *habeas corpus* shall never be suspended, unless when in case of rebellion or invasion, the public safety may require it."

39. Art. II, sec. 22 stated: "That the military shall always be in strict subordination to the civil power; that no soldier shall, in time of peace, be quartered in any house without the consent of the owner, nor in time of war, except in the manner prescribed by law."

40. *Victor Daily Record*, Sept. 17, 1903.

41. Peabody to Bell, Sept. 22 and 24, 1903, LB 40, Peabody Papers.

42. *Colorado Springs Gazette*, Oct. 6, 1903; *Cripple Creek Times*, Oct. 17, 1903.

43. *Cripple Creek Times*, Oct. 31, 1903.

44. *Victor Daily Record*, Sept. 26, 1903.

45. Peabody to Bell, Oct. 3, 1903, LB 40, Peabody Papers.

46. Stenographic transcript of *The People of Colorado v. Sherman Parker, Thomas Foster and W. F. Davis*, No. 752 (microfilm), William E. Borah Papers.

47. Beaman to Peabody, Jan. 2, 1904, DB: "A-B"; "B"; 1903–1904, and Peabody to Beaman, Jan. 4, 1904, LB 41, Peabody Papers.

48. *Labor Disturbances*, pp. 192–93. The CCMOA offered a $5,000 reward for evidence leading to the arrest and conviction of the guilty party or parties (Rastall, p. 108); the CCDCA offered $1,000 (*Denver Post*, Dec. 1, 1903); and the Board of County Commissioners offered another $1,000 on Dec. 3 (Teller County Record, III, 162). Years later Harry Orchard, who confessed to numerous crimes in the district, revealed that he and an associate were responsible for the deaths at the Vindicator. According to Orchard, he had set a device in the mine after officials of the WFM had promised him $500 to "fix something . . . to kill some of them [strikebreakers] so as to scare the rest and make them quit, and keep our men from going back to work, and scare outside men from coming there to work" in the mines. (Harry Orchard, "The Confession and Autobiography of Harry Orchard," *McClure's Magazine*, 29 [Aug. 1907], 377.) It should be noted that there was never any legal substantiation of Orchard's confession to this and other gruesome crimes in the district.

49. *Denver Post*, Nov. 24 and 25, Dec. 2, 1903.

50. *Victor Daily Record*, Nov. 24, 1903.

51. Ibid., Dec. 4, 1903; Dec. 5, 1903.

52. Adj. Gen., *Biennial Report, 1903–1904*, pp. 113–14.

53. *Labor Disturbances*, pp. 209, 211–12.

54. *Rocky Mountain News*, Dec. 5 and 7, 1903.

55. Adj. Gen., *Biennial Report, 1903–1904*, pp. 114–15.

56. *Victor Daily Record*, Dec. 5, 1903.

57. Adj. Gen., *Biennial Report, 1903–1904*, pp. 116–17.

58. *Labor Disturbances*, pp. 216–17.

59. As defined by the proclamation, a vagrant was: "Any person able to work and support himself in some honest and respectable calling, who shall be found loitering or strolling about, frequenting public places or where liquor is sold, begging or leading an idle or immoral or profligate course of life, or not having visible means of support, shall be deemed a vagrant." Adj. Gen., *Biennial Report, 1903–1904*, p. 116.

60. *Labor Disturbances*, p. 218.

61. Peabody to Finley M. Newlon, Dec. 16, 1903; Peabody to S. B. Dick, Dec. 18, 1903; Peabody to M. T. Richardson, Dec. 18, 1903; Peabody to Guy Hardy, Dec. 21, 1903, LB 41, and Peabody to E. R. Hanley, Jan. 19, 1904, LB 42, Peabody Papers.

62. *Victor Daily Record*, Dec. 16 and 17, 1903.

63. *Labor Disturbances*, pp. 224–27.

64. Ibid., p. 219; U. S. Senate, Clarence Hamlin, *Review of the Labor Troubles in the Metalliferous Mines of the Rocky Mountain Region*, 58th Cong., 2d Sess., 1904, Doc. 86; Charles H. Moyer and William D. Haywood, *Statement of the Western Federation of Miners*, 58th Cong., 2d Sess., 1904, Doc. 163.

65. Adj. Gen., *Biennial Report, 1903–1904*, p. 168, and Peabody to Verdeckberg, Jan. 6, 1904, LB 42, Peabody Papers.

66. The management of the Independence mine would not allow union members on the property. On January 26 as the night shift came from the mine, the machinery hoisting a cage loaded with sixteen men ran amuck and rammed the sheve wheel at the top of the main shaft, throwing one man from the cage. The others plummeted 1,500 feet to their death. A coroner's jury blamed the management, which it charged with negligence in not providing the "usual necessary precautions," for example, a "safety device" to prevent overwinding of the cage cable. (*Labor Disturbances*, p. 220) The WFM supported the charge, but the operators claimed that the hoisting machinery had been sabotaged. Commissioner of Mines E. L. White appointed a board of inquiry on January 31, 1904, to make recommendations. Upon receipt of the report (Colo., Bureau of Mines,

Report, 1903–1904, p. 4), Peabody referred it to Miller, who advised that existing laws were adequate to enforce the recommendations included in the report. (AG, *Report, 1903–1904*, pp. 145–50) Peabody then advised White to implement the recommendations. The lack of hysteria accompanying the deaths of fifteen men charged to corporate negligence should be contrasted below to the convulsive violence produced by the dynamite deaths of thirteen men on June 6 at the Independence depot, deaths blamed on the WFM by a similar jury.

67. Adj. Gen., *Biennial Report, 1903–1904*, p. 121.

68. Carlton to Peabody, Mar. 12, 1904, DB: Correspondence and Adjutant General Office, *In Re* Law and Order Banquet, and Peabody to Carlton, Mar. 15, 1904, LB 43, Peabody Papers.

69. Peabody to Frank Essham, Mar. 18, 1904; Peabody to R. J. McInturff, May 11, 1904; Samuel H. Wood to Z. W. Cannon, Apr. 20, 1904, LB 43, ibid; also, Peabody to NAM convention, telegram, *The New York Times*, May 21, 1904.

70. The leading opponents of the strike, mostly mine owners and members of the alliance, had organized a unit of the guard to aid them in controlling the district. On Dec. 9, 1903, Peabody had obligingly ordered Company L, Second Regiment of Victor, mustered into active service. The men, all members of the alliance, chose as their captain H. G. Moore, president of the Victor Citizens' Alliance. *Cripple Creek Times*, Dec. 10, 1903.

71. Adj. Gen., *Biennial Report, 1903–1904*, pp. 222–24; Teller County Record, III, 282–83. On July 1, 1904, Robertson informed the commissioners by letter that his resignation had been signed under "compulsion and duress" and demanded reinstatement. They refused, incredibly claiming that they had no knowledge that coercion had been used to force Robertson's resignation and that they had acted in good faith. Teller County Record, III, 311–12.

72. *Cripple Creek Times*, June 10, 1904; *Labor Disturbances*, pp. 251–52; editorial, *The New York Times*, June 8, 1904.

73. *Cripple Creek Times*, June 7, 1904. Because the CCDCA and the CCMOA had seized control of the district, the official blame for the deaths at Independence depot and at Victor fell upon the WFM. Guided by E. C. Newcomb, a cashier in Carlton's First National Bank of Cripple Creek who was prominent in alliance affairs, a coroner's jury ruled that the explosion at the depot was premeditated, that it was similar to other crimes used to intimidate nonunion men, and that it was the "result of a conspiracy entered into by certain members of the Western Federation of Miners and known, incited and furthered by certain officers of that organization." (*Labor Disturbances*, p. 254) Another jury rendered a decision on July 1 which blamed the

riots and deaths in Victor on the executive officers of the WFM and Michael O'Connell. (Ibid, p. 258) The membership of the juries suggests that the oft-repeated charge in the past that the WFM had unduly influenced official decisions was now applicable to the CCDCA and the CCMOA.

Despite these findings, the WFM's responsibility has never been conclusively proved. Harry Orchard later confessed that, in addition to the dynamite murder of ex-Governor Frank Steunenberg of Idaho on Dec. 30, 1905, he and a friend had dynamited Independence depot at the request of WFM officials. His confession implicated Moyer, Haywood, and George A. Pettibone, who, with the connivance of Peabody's successor, Jesse McDonald, were kidnapped in Denver on Feb. 17, 1906 and whisked off to Idaho by special train. There they were charged with complicity in the murder of Steunenberg. After a long imprisonment and a sensational trial in which the prosecution failed to corroborate Orchard's testimony, Haywood was acquitted on July 28, 1907. Shortly thereafter Moyer and Pettibone were also released. A recent study of the Haywood case concludes that, although possibly a "murderer went free," the "verdict was a good one" because the prosecution failed to prove Haywood's complicity in the Steunenberg murder and, by implication, in the others to which Orchard had confessed. The matter remains unresolved. Joseph R. Conlin, "The Haywood Case: An Enduring Riddle," *Pacific Northwest Quarterly*, 59 (Jan. 1968), 31; see also, Emma F. Langdon, *The Cripple Creek Strike* (Denver: Great Western Publishing Co., 1904–1905), pp. 467–555; Stewart H. Holbrook, *The Rocky Mountain Revolution* (New York: Henry Holt & Co., 1956), pp. 227–73; *Idaho v. William Dudley Haywood*, transcript of testimony (microfilm), Idaho Historical Society, Boise.

The WFM blamed the atrocity upon the CCMOA. Union sympathizers charged that the mine owners wanted the state to help in driving the WFM from the district, but such help could not be obtained unless there was a serious "incident," which the enemies of the union conspired to produce. Unfortunately, the "incident" turned into a disaster when the agents of the CCMOA mistimed the explosion. This explanation of the Independence horror has never been substantiated, but for an elaboration upon this alleged conspiracy, see Walter Hurt, *The Scarlet Shadow: A Story of the Great Colorado Conspiracy* (Girard, Kansas: The Appeal to Reason, 1907).

74. Rastall, p. 125.

75. Ibid., p. 126; *Labor Disturbances*, pp. 260, 275. See complete List of Parties Deported and Recommended for Deportation or to Leave District, July 26, 1904 (microfilm), William E. Borah Papers.

76. *In Re Moyer*. 35 Colo. 154 (1904); Adj. Gen., *Biennial Report, 1903–1904*, p. 226.

77. *Cripple Creek Times,* July 27, 1904; *Labor Disturbances,* p. 295.

78. *Labor Disturbances,* p. 275.

79. *The New York Times,* June 14, 1904; *Denver Republican,* June 13, 1904.

80. *Labor Disturbances,* p. 285; Adj. Gen., *Biennial Report, 1903–1904,* p. 228.

81. Adj. Gen., *Biennial Report, 1903–1904,* p. 232; *Denver Republican,* June 17, 1904.

82. Tom E. McClelland to Peabody, Aug. 22, 1904, DB: "I-L"; "Mc-P"; 1903–1904, and Peabody to McClelland, Aug. 24, 1904, LB 44, Peabody Papers; also, *Labor Disturbances,* p. 263.

83. Teller County Record, III, 295–97, 501.

84. *Labor Disturbances,* p. 277; *Denver Republican,* June 15, 1904.

85. For editorials supporting the extraordinary tactics used against the WFM, see the *Cripple Creek Times,* June 12 and 25, July 1, 1904, and the *Denver Republican,* June 8, 9, 10, and 13, 1904; for editorials opposed, see the *Rocky Mountain News,* June 10, 11, 13, 14, and 17, 1904; for out-of-state editorial interest, see, for example, *The New York Times,* June 10, 12, and 23, 1904.

86. *Labor Disturbances,* p. 294.

87. Ibid., pp. 277, 308–10, and *Victor Daily Record,* Aug. 10, 1904. Deputy District Attorney Charles Butler, who had tried unsuccessfully to dissuade the mobs, filed charges against prominent members of the CCMOA and the CCDCA for their role in the destruction of the store. (For a complete list of the men charged, see *People* v. *Nelson Franklin, et al.,* Nos. 840–50, District Court, Teller County.) The charges were later dismissed by Clarence C. Hamlin, the district attorney elected in the November elections.

88. Peabody to Bell, Aug. 27, 1904, LB 44, and Bell to Peabody, Aug. 30, 1904, DB: "A-B"; "B"; 1903–1904, Peabody Papers.

89. Colorado, Office of the Auditor, *Biennial Report, 1903–1904,* p. 111. Hereafter cited as OA, *Biennial Report, 1903–1904.*

90. Peabody to *The New York Times,* June 12, 1904, LB Messages, Peabody Papers.

91. James Warford, a former deputy employed by the CCMOA, murdered two men at a polling station on election day. Clarence Hamlin, secretary of the CCMOA who was elected district attorney, later dismissed the case against Warford, claiming that it was impossible to convict him and that the costs to the county for extended prosecution was prohibitive. See *People* v. *James Warford* and *Thomas Brown,* Nos. 872–73, District Court, Teller County. For an example of how

successful the CCMOA and the CCDCA were in obtaining county offices, see Rastall, p. 137.

CHAPTER SIX

1. Langdon, *The Cripple Creek Strike*, p. 205; *Denver Republican*, Aug. 30, 1903, *Labor Disturbances*, p. 168.

2. *Labor Disturbances*, pp. 168–69.

3. Langdon, *The Cripple Creek Strike*, pp. 206, 208.

4. Ibid., pp. 208–209; Haywood, *Bill Haywood's Book*, pp. 103–104. The delegates to the Denver conference were Haywood, John H. Murphy, an attorney for the WFM, Guy Miller, Chase, Bulkeley Wells, manager, Smuggler-Union and Contention Gold Mining Company, and John Herron, manager, Tomboy Gold Mining Company.

5. *Pueblo Chieftain*, Oct. 28, 1903.

6. W. E. Wheeler to I. B. Melville, Nov. 12, 1903, DB: Reports, Resolutions, Petitions, 1903–1904, Peabody Papers.

7. Telegram, Peabody to Wheeler, Oct. 24, 1903, LB Messages; Hagar to Peabody, Oct. 27, 1903 and Randolph to Peabody, Oct. 27, 1903, DB: Reports, Resolutions, Petitions, Peabody Papers.

8. Peabody to Wheeler, Oct. 28, 1903, LB 41; Wheeler to Peabody, Nov. 2, 1903 and Hogg to Peabody, Nov. 4, 1903, DB: Reports, Resolutions, Petitions, ibid.

9. Telegram, Wheeler to Peabody, Nov. 7, 1903, DB: Reports, Resolutions, Petitions; and telegram, Peabody to Wheeler, Nov. 7, 1903, LB Messages, ibid.

10. Wheeler to Melville, Nov. 12, 1903, Charles G. Sumner, et al., to Melville, Nov. 14, 1903, Crump to Peabody, Nov. 13, 1903, and Chase to Peabody, Nov. 13, 1903, DB: Reports, Resolutions, Petitions, ibid.

11. Rutan to Peabody, Nov. 13, 1903, DB: Reports, Resolutions, Petitions, ibid.

12. For the correspondence between Denver and Washington, see *Labor Disturbances*, pp. 9–11. Peabody's request for federal troops followed General Bell's ludicrous telegram of Nov. 9 to Roosevelt: "Commending your action in the Panama question, and having in mind the possibility of military service, I desire to tender to you the service of the National Guard of Colorado, two thousand strong, now fully armed and equipped and organized under the provisions of the Dick Bill, who can be ready on twenty-four hour notice." LB Messages, Peabody Papers.

13. Bates to Lt. Gen. S. B. M. Young, Nov. 29, 1903, in *Labor Disturbances*, pp. 14–15, and Peabody to Franklin E. Brooks, Nov. 21, 1903, LB 41, Peabody Papers.

14. *Labor Disturbances*, p. 194; telegram, Bulkeley Wells to C. F. Painter, Nov. 18, 1903 and telegram, Alliance Executive Committee to Peabody, Nov. 19, 1903, DB: Reports, Resolutions, Petitions, Peabody Papers.

15. Miller to Peabody, Nov. 18, 1903, DB: Reports, Resolutions, Petitions, Peabody Papers; Adj. Gen., *Biennial Report, 1903–1904*, p. 12; Gen. Order No. 4, Nov. 24, 1903, Colorado, National Guard, Office of the Adjutant General: Sherman M. Bell, 1903–1905, Report of the Telluride Campaign. Hereafter cited as Telluride Campaign.

16. Langdon, p. 285; "Military Rule in Colorado," *Army and Navy Journal, 41*, No. 7 (Oct. 17, 1903), 166–67.

17. Hill to Peabody, Nov. 26, 1903, DB: C-D, U, V, W, X, Y, Z; Telluride Strike, Peabody Papers. Hereafter cited as Telluride Strike.

18. The individual agreements which Randolph negotiated with the companies between Nov. 27 and Dec. 1, 1903, can be found in ibid.

19. Peabody to Hill, Nov. 23, 1903, LB 41, Peabody Papers.

20. Rutan to Peabody, Nov. 13, 1903 and Hill to Peabody, Nov. 27, 1903, DB: Telluride Strike, ibid.

21. Moyer and Haywood, *Statement of the Western Federation of Miners*, p. 33; BLS, *Ninth Biennial Report*, pp. 159–61; U. S., *Congressional Record*, 58th Cong., 2d Sess., 1903, XXXVIII, Part I, 113.

22. *Labor Disturbances*, p. 197; Hill to Peabody, Dec. 4, 1903, DB: Telluride Strike, and Peabody to Hill, Dec. 7, 1903, LB 41, Peabody Papers.

23. Hill to Peabody, Dec. 2 and 10, 1903, DB: Telluride Strike, and Peabody to Hill, Dec. 12, 1903, LB 41, Peabody Papers. See Miller's formal opinion in AG, *Report, 1903–1904*, pp. 183–84.

24. Hill to Peabody, Dec. 10 and 14, 1903, DB: Telluride Strike, and Peabody to Hill, Dec. 12, 1903, LB 41, Peabody Papers.

25. Peabody to Hill, Dec. 18, 1903, LB 41, ibid.

26. Hill to Peabody, Dec. 20, 1903, DB: Telluride Strike, ibid.

27. Hill to Peabody, Dec. 23 and 27, 1903, ibid.

28. Hill to Peabody and Rutan to Peabody, Dec. 28, 1903, ibid; Colorado, Office of the Adjutant General, *Biennial Report, 1905–1907*, p. 46.

29. Ibid., pp. 14–15; Hill to Peabody, Jan. 3, 1904, Telluride Campaign.

30. Hill to Peabody, Jan. 3, 1904, DB: Telluride Strike, Peabody Papers; Special Orders No. 7, Telluride Campaign.

31. Miller to Peabody, Jan. 4, 1904, DB: Correspondence "I-L": "Mc-P"; 1903–1904, and Peabody to Hill, Jan. 4, 1904, LB 41, Peabody Papers.

32. Hill to Peabody, Jan. 5, 1904, DB: Telluride Strike, ibid; *Labor Disturbances*, p. 199.

33. Hill to Peabody, Jan. 5, 1904, DB: Telluride Strike, Peabody Papers.

34. Hill to Peabody, Jan. 6 and 8, 1904, Telluride Campaign, and Peabody to Hill, Jan. 11, 1904, LB 42, Peabody Papers.

35. Peabody to Hill, Jan. 14, 1904, LB 42; James McParland to Peabody, Jan. 16, 1904, DB: Corr. "P-R"; "S; 1903–1904"; Peabody to Cuneo, Jan. 18, 1904, LB 42, Peabody Papers; also Hill to Peabody, Feb. 15, 1904, Telluride Campaign.

36. Hill to Peabody, Dec. 11, 18, and 21, 1903, DB: Telluride Strike, and Peabody to Wells, Dec. 30, 1903, LB 41, Peabody Papers.

37. Hill to Peabody, Jan. 3 and 11, 1904, DB: Telluride Strike, ibid.

38. Peabody to Hill, Jan. 11, 1904, LB 42; Hill to Peabody, Jan. 13, 1904, DB: Telluride Strike; Peabody to Hill, Jan. 14, 1904, LB 42, ibid.

39. Adj. Gen., *Biennial Report, 1905–1907*, p. 47; Peabody to Hill, Feb. 4, 1904, LB 42, Peabody Papers; *Labor Disturbances*, pp. 199–200.

40. Hill to Peabody, Feb. 12 and 15, 1904, DB: Telluride Strike; Peabody to Hill, Feb. 15, 1904, and Peabody to Benjamin Lawrence, Mar. 4, 1904, LB 42, Peabody Papers.

41. Wells to Hill, Feb. 21, 24, 27, and Mar. 2, 1904, DB: Telluride Strike, ibid.

42. Wells to Hill, Feb. 28 and Mar. 8, 1904, and Howe to Peabody, Mar. 8, 1904, ibid.

43. Langdon, pp. 280–84; *Pueblo Chieftain*, Mar. 16, 1904; *Cripple Creek Times*, Mar. 16, 1904.

44. *Rocky Mountain News*, Mar. 18, 1904.

45. Ibid., Mar. 20, 1904.

46. Ibid., Mar. 21–22, 1904.

47. *Labor Disturbances*, p. 202.

48. Ibid., pp. 202–203.

49. *Rocky Mountain News*, Mar. 26, 1904.

50. Telegram, Moyer to Peabody, Mar. 24, 1904, DB: Telluride

Strike; telegrams, Peabody to Moyer, Mar. 25, 1904, and Peabody to Bell, Mar. 25, 1904, LB Messages, Peabody Papers.

51. *Labor Disturbances*, p. 204.

52. *Rocky Mountain News*, Apr. 9, 1904.

53. *Labor Disturbances*, p. 205.

54. *Rocky Mountain News*, May 11, 1904.

55. *Denver Republican*, June 8, 1904.

56. Telegram, Hogg to Peabody, June 6, 1904, DB: Correspondence H, 1903–1904, Peabody Papers; Petition (verified copy) and writ of habeas corpus (attested true copy), Colorado, State Archives and Records Service, Denver, Records of the Office of the Attorney General: Nathan C. Miller, 1903–1905, Cases: DB 6. Subsequent citations from the Miller Papers will specify only the location of individual items within the collection.

57. *Labor Disturbances*, pp. 288–92.

58. For a description of the way the card system worked in Telluride, see Edward L. Cokes to Hugo Selig, Nov. 22, 1905, DB 58, Miller Papers.

59. OA, *Biennial Report, 1903–1904*, p. 111.

CHAPTER SEVEN

1. *Labor Disturbances*, pp. 47–49.

2. Ibid.

3. L. F. Parsons to Peabody, Sept. 12, 1903, Walter C. Frost to Peabody, Sept. 15, 1903, F. E. Curry to Peabody, Oct. 19, 1903, Paul M. North to Peabody, Oct. 21, 1903, Thomas Parker to Peabody, Oct. 1, 1903, and Sherwood Aldrich to Peabody, Oct. 10, 1903, in DB: Reports, Resolutions, Petitions; Peabody to L. F. Parsons, Sept. 14, 1903, Peabody to Walter C. Frost, Sept. 18, 1903, and Peabody to James Turnbull, Oct. 19, 1903, in LB 40, Peabody Papers.

4. Peabody to Thomas Parker, Oct. 3, 1903, LB 40, Peabody Papers.

5. Peabody to James Turnbull, Oct. 14, 1903, ibid.

6. Peabody to F. E. Curry, Oct. 22, 1903, Peabody to Paul M. North, Oct. 24, 1903, and Peabody to James Turnbull, Oct. 19, 1903, ibid.

7. *Pueblo Chieftain*, Oct. 26 and 27, 1903.

8. Quoted in ibid., Oct. 27, 1903.

9. A. J. Woodruff to Peabody, Oct. 26, 1903, DB: Reports, Resolu-

tions, Petitions, and Peabody to Woodruff, Oct. 28, LB 41, Peabody Papers.

10. *The New York Times*, Sept. 30, 1903, and Marguerite Green, "The National Civic Federation and the Citizens' Industrial Association, 1900–1910," unpublished Master's thesis, Catholic University of America, 1953, pp. 47–48.

11. The constitution of the CIA and the "principles" printed in *The Square Deal* are quoted in Green, pp. 69, 93.

12. *The New York Times*, Nov. 8, 1903.

13. For an excellent contrast between the tactics of the moderate NCF and the militant CIA, see Green, pp. 55–83; for a comparison of the methods employed by organized labor and the employers' associations, see Ray Stannard Baker, "Organized Capital Challenges Organized Labor: The New Employers' Association Movement," *McClure's Magazine*, 23 (July 1904), 279–92; for the response of the WFM to the CIA, see "The Citizens' Industrial Association," *Miners' Magazine*, 5 (Nov. 19, 1903), 6.

14. Peabody to Cushing, Feb. 8, 1904, LB 42, Peabody to Cushing, July 29, 1904, LB 44, telegram, Peabody to Parry, May 19, 1904, LB Messages; Cushing to Peabody, July 27, 1904, DB: C-G, 1903–1904, Peabody Papers; also, see Clarence E. Bonnett, *Employers' Associations in the United States: A Study of Typical Associations* (New York: Macmillan Company, 1922), p. 338, and A Leading Mining Man of Denver, "Colorado's Problem: The Doom of the Western Federation of Miners," *American Industries* (Feb. 1, 1904), n.p., in Governor James H. Peabody's Scrapbooks, 1 (Western Historical Collection, University of Colorado), 332–33.

15. *Labor Disturbances*, pp. 47–48.

16. For an example of this tendency, see the resolutions from the Pueblo, Durango, San Miguel County, Idaho Springs, and Paonia alliances and Peabody's response following his declaration of Jan. 3, 1904, which placed San Miguel County under military rule. A. J. Woodruff to Peabody, Jan. 13, 1904, R. E. Sloan to Peabody, Jan. 12, 1904, W. H. Nicodemus to Peabody, Jan. 15, 1904, E. M. Moscript to Peabody, Jan. 18, 1904, C. C. Hawkins to Peabody, Jan. 18, 1904, in DB: Reports, Resolutions, Petitions; Peabody to A. J. Woodruff, Jan. 14, 1904, Peabody to Sloan, Jan. 16, 1904, Peabody to Sidney Moritz, Jan. 21, 1904, Peabody to Hawkins, Jan. 21, 1904, and Peabody to W. H. Nicodemus, Jan. 18, 1904, in LB 42, Peabody Papers.

17. Peabody to Andrew Carrigan, Dec. 10, 1903, LB 41, and Peabody to F. J. Zeehandelaar, Feb. 1, 1904, LB 42, in ibid.

18. Peabody to Craig, Feb. 20, 1904, ibid.

19. Form letter of Dennis Sheedy to prospective guests, n.d., DB:

Correspondence and Adjutant General Office, *In Re* Law and Order Banquet, ibid.

20. *Denver Post*, Feb. 22, 1904.

21. The Rush Bill would have required every city in Colorado granting a franchise on gas, water, telephones, electric lights, etc., to include a clause in the franchise guaranteeing the city's right to acquire the property of the grantee. Furthermore, each city council would be required to review biennially any franchise granted and to regulate the rates of the companies obtaining a franchise. See Field to Peabody, Feb. 18, 1904, DB: C-G, Peabody Papers.

22. The verbatim list follows:

Simon Guggenheim [American Smelting and Refining Company]
American Smelting and Refining Company, D. S.
The Western Mining Company, Leadville (Mr. Rodman)
E. B. Field [The Colorado Telephone Company]
The Daniels and Fisher Stores Co. (Mr. C. McA. Willcox)
A. V. Hunter (Leadville) [Carbonate National Bank]
C. M. MacNeill (Colo. Springs) [United States Reduction and Refining Company]
W. S. Cheesman [The Denver Union Water Company]
W. G. Evans [The Denver City Tramway Company]
First National Bank (Mr. Keely) [Denver]
Colorado and Southern Railway (Mr. Trumbull)
Continental Oil Co. (Mr. U. S. Hollister)
M. D. Thatcher (Pueblo) [First National Bank of Pueblo]
Denver and Rio Grande Railroad (Mr. J. B. Andrews)
Denver National Bank (Mr. J. A. Thatcher)
Colorado National Bank (Mr. Berger)
Colorado Fuel and Iron Company (Mr. Welborn)
Boston and Colorado Smelting Co. (Mr. Crawford Hill)
Denver Dry Goods Co. (Mr. Austin)
Messrs. Taylor and Brunton [Taylor and Brunton Sampling Company]
Messrs. Campbell and Wood [Vindicator Consolidated Gold Company]
The Chamberlain-Dillingham Ore Co. [W. J. Chamberlain]
Messrs. Rogers, Cuthbert and Ellis (Mr. Henry T. Rogers)
Dr. D. H. Dougan [National Bank of Commerce]
N. Maxcy Tabor [Brown Palace Hotel]
J. C. Osgood (by Geo. W. Bowen) [Colorado Fuel and Iron Company]
Victor Fuel Company (Mr. D. A. Chappell)
American National Bank, Leadville (Mr. C. T. Limberg)
Colorado Springs (First National Bank, Mr. Howbert)
Clearing House (El Paso National Bank, Mr. Homming)

Association (Exchange National Bank, Mr. Sharp) (Colorado Title and Trust Co.) [J. A. Connell] Field to Peabody with enclosure, Feb. 24, 1904, DB: Correspondence & Adjutant General Office, *In Re* Law and Order Banquet, ibid.

23. D. C. Beaman, *Address at the Testimonial Banquet to Governor James H. Peabody at Denver, Colorado, February 23, 1904* (Denver: Citizens' Alliance of Denver, n.d.), pp. 1–7.

24. Buchtel consistently supported the administration. On Dec. 21, 1904, he wrote Attorney General Miller requesting a Christmas check to help the University of Denver stay out of debt. As an afterthought he added: "When anarchy and socialism threaten civilization we always need an independent University that dares to speak out. In our recent fight you know that this University did speak out. No one at Boulder [University of Colorado] dared say a word for fear of what might happen in the legislature. In our next fight with socialism we will again speak out and no other University will dare do so. Surely we deserve to be sustained." See DB: 58, Miller Papers.

25. Quoted in the *Denver Republican*, Feb. 24, 1904.

26. For example, the Reverend Thomas Malone, a writer of antisocialist tracts, attended. Peabody approved of Malone's work. Bishop Nicholas C. Matz, head of the Roman Catholic Denver Diocese, also endorsed the governor's stand. (See Peabody to Malone, Dec. 30, 1903, LB 41, Peabody Papers, and George G. Suggs, Jr., "Religion and Labor in the Rocky Mountain West: Bishop Nicholas C. Matz and the Western Federation of Miners," *Labor History*, 11 [Spring, 1970] 190–206.) In addition to Buchtel of Denver University, William F. Slocum, president of Colorado College, supported the governor. Slocum did not attend the banquet but in declining an invitation sent a glowing endorsement of the administration's policies. See Slocum to Dennis Sheedy, Feb. 18, 1904, DB: Correspondence & Adjutant General Office, *In Re* Law and Order Banquet, Peabody Papers.

27. Woodruff to Peabody, Mar. 12, 1904, ibid., and Peabody to Woodruff, Mar. 14, 1904, LB 43, Peabody Papers; also, see *House Jour.*, 15th Gen. Ass'y, p. 29. Responding to Peabody's recommendation, the assembly enacted a boycott law. See *Sess. Laws*, 15th Gen. Ass'y, pp. 160–61.

28. George to Peabody, Sept. 2, 1904, DB: C-G, Peabody Papers.

CHAPTER EIGHT

1. *In Re Boyle*, 57 Pac. (Idaho), 706.

2. Art. II, sec. 21; Art. I, sec. 5, respectively (1904).

3. *Labor Disturbances,* p. 208; *Rocky Mountain News,* Dec. 7, 1903.

4. *Victor Poole* v. *Col. Edward Verdeckberg, et al.* (certified copy), DB: 6, Miller Papers.

5. Executive Record Book, XVI, 8, Peabody Papers.

6. *Victor Poole* v. *Col. Edward Verdeckberg, et al.* (certified copy), DB: 6, Miller Papers.

7. Return of James Doran (certified copy), ibid.

8. Colorado, Supreme Court, *In Re Victor Poole,* No. 4756 (microfilm), State Archives and Records Service, Records of the Supreme Court. Hereafter cited as *In Re Victor Poole.*

9. Motion to Quash (true copy), Motion to Strike (office copy), and Return to Writ (office copy), No. 4756, DB: 6, Miller Papers.

10. *In re Victor Poole.*

11. *Rocky Mountain News,* Jan. 10, 1904.

12. Petition (verified copy), DB: 6, Miller Papers.

13. Decision (revised copy), ibid.

14. *Cripple Creek Times,* Jan. 23 and 26, 1904.

15. Decision (copy), DB: Investigation of Strikes, Peabody Papers.

16. *Rocky Mountain News,* Feb. 3, 1904.

17. For Lewis's praise, see Lewis to Peabody, Nov. 6, 1903, DB: I-L, Peabody Papers.

18. *Cripple Creek Times,* Feb. 12, 1904.

19. The inscriptions read:

> Martial Law Declared in Colorado!
> Habeas Corpus Suspended in Colorado!
> Free Press Throttled in Colorado!
> Bull Pens for Union Men in Colorado!
> Free Speech Denied in Colorado!
> Soldiers Defy the Courts in Colorado!
> Wholesale Arrests Without Warrant in Colorado!
> Union Men Exiled from Homes and Families in Colorado!
> Constitutional Right to Bear Arms Questioned in Colorado!
> Corporations Corrupt and Control Administration in Colorado!
> Right of Fair, Impartial, and Speedy Trial Abolished in Colorado!
> Citizens' Alliance Resorts to Mob Law and Violence in Colorado!
> Militia Hired to Corporations to Break the Strike in Colorado!

Labor Disturbances, p. 229. For a large copy of the flag bearing the inscriptions, see the John R. Lawton Papers, Western History Department, Denver Public Library.

20. *Sess. Laws*, 13th Gen. Ass'y, pp. 182–83.

21. Bell to Peabody, Mar. 30, 1904, DB: Correspondence and Adjutant General's Office; *In Re* Law and Order Banquet, Peabody Papers. Rumors circulated that Peabody had ordered Moyer's arrest on the flag desecration charge to force him into the Telluride Military District, created by a proclamation of insurrection and rebellion of Jan. 3, 1904, where he would then be subject to military seizure. Moyer believed that his arrest was contrived by the citizens' alliance at Telluride. (Petition for Original Writ of Habeas Corpus [Supreme Court Original], *In Re Moyer*, No. 4828, DB: 6, Miller Papers.) Rutan also tried to arrest Haywood in Denver on the same charge. To avoid arrest, Haywood had a friend swear out a warrant for his arrest on a flag desecration charge. Although bail was set at only $300, Haywood refused to be bonded, preferring to remain in jail in Denver where he had unusual freedom as a prisoner. See *Bill Haywood's Book*, pp. 162–63.

22. Petition, writ, and order (verified copies), DB: 6, Miller Papers. Howe contended in his rejected return that Bell and Wells were military officers who had been ordered by Peabody to suppress rebellion in San Miguel County. Confining Moyer was "necessary" to accomplish that objective because he had helped to create the conditions said to exist in the county. If released, he allegedly would continue to incite lawlessness; therefore, his detention was essential to prevent a further "inciting" of insurrection. Howe charged that Moyer was guilty of creating disturbances in the mining camps of the county and that his presence in nearby Ouray had encouraged a continuation of lawlessness in the camps. When conditions warranted, Howe stated that his clients would transfer custody of Moyer to civil authorities. Howe contended that the "urgency" of their duties prevented Bell and Wells from "attending upon courts," and he asked that they be excused from producing Moyer. In any case, Peabody had ordered Bell to disobey the writ. Verified copy, ibid.

23. Petition (Supreme Court original) and writ (copy), ibid.

24. Adj. Gen., *Biennial Report, 1903–1904*, pp. 216–17.

25. Affidavit, Sheriff Rutan, *In Re Moyer*, No. 4828 (microfilm), Colorado, State Archives and Records Service, Records of the Supreme Court. Hereafter cited as *In Re Moyer*.

26. Return (copy), DB: 6, Miller Papers.

27. Return (copy), ibid.

28. Memorandum of Points and Authorities, *In Re Moyer*; also, *In Re Moyer*, 35 Colo. 154–59 (1904).

29. See Colorado, Supreme Court, *In Re Moyer*, No. 4828, *Brief and*

Oral Argument of Attorney General and Opinion of the Court, passim, but especially, pp. 2, 19–21, 23–25, 30, 32, 43, 73–79, and 81–94.

30. *Rocky Mountain News, Denver Post,* and *Denver Republican,* May 6 and 7, 1904.

31. *In Re Moyer,* 35 Colo. 163–64 (1904).

32. Ibid., pp. 166–67.

33. Ibid., pp. 167–68.

34. Ibid., p. 69.

35. Wood to Peabody, June 6, 1904, and telegram, Bell to Peabody, June 6, 1904, DB: Correspondence and Adjutant General's Office; *In Re* Law and Order Banquet, Peabody Papers.

36. *In Re Moyer,* 35 Colo. 170–225 (1904); Observation of C. J. Gabbert upon the Dissenting Opinion *In Re Charles H. Moyer,* No. 4828, DB: 6, Miller Papers.

37. Petition (verified copy) and writ of habeas corpus (attested true copy), DB: 6, Miller Papers.

38. Adj. Gen., *Biennial Report, 1903–1904,* p. 217. Shortly before Moyer's release, Sheriff Bell of Teller County requested that Rutan hold him on charges originating there. K. C. Stirling, a detective for the mine owners' association, had filed a complaint charging Moyer, et al., with the murder of Melvin Beck and Charles McCormick in the Vindicator mine explosion of Nov. 21, 1903. Officials of Teller County issued a formal warrant for Moyer's arrest on July 17. Exhibits "C" and "D," Answer and Return to the Original Writ of *Habeas Corpus* (copy), U. S. Circuit Court, Eighth Circuit, DB: 6, Miller Papers.

39. DB: 6, Miller Papers.

40. *Charles H. Moyer* v. *James H. Peabody, et al.,* No. 4704, complaint (true copy), ibid.

41. For evidence of the mine owners' support, see telegram, Peabody to Miller, Nov. 14, 1905, ibid; *Moyer* v. *Peabody,* et al., 148 Fed. Rep. 870 (1906).

42. *Moyer* v. *Peabody,* 212 U. S. 78 (1909).

CHAPTER NINE

1. James H. Peabody, *Gov. Peabody to the Voters: The Colorado Situation Discussed and Misstatements Refuted* (n.p.; n.d.), pp. 3–5; also, see Peabody to N. O. Davis, Jan. 4, 1904, LB 41, Peabody Papers.

2. Peabody, *Gov. Peabody to the Voters*, p. 6, OA, *Biennial Reports, 1903–1904*, p. 111.

3. Adj. Gen., *Biennial Report, 1903–1904*, p. 123.

4. *House Jour.*, 15th Gen. Ass'y, p. 29.

5. Peabody, *Gov. Peabody to the Voters*, p. 7.

6. Ibid., pp. 5–7.

7. *House Jour.*, 15th Gen. Ass'y, pp. 29–30.

8. See Colorado, General Assembly, Joint Convention Contest Committee, *Notice of Contest, Oral Testimony, Exhibits and Deposition in Behalf of Contestor, James H. Peabody v. Alva Adams*, 5 vols.; *Answer: Oral Testimony, Exhibits and Depositions on Behalf of Contestee, James H. Peabody v. Alva Adams*, 5 vols.; *Contestor's Rebuttal: Transcript and Deposition, James H. Peabody v. Alva Adams*; also, Colorado, House and Senate, Joint Session, *House Jour.*, 15th Gen. Ass'y, 1905.

9. For the most recent discussion of the Peabody-Adams contest, see Marjorie Hornbein, "Three Governors in a Day," *The Colorado Magazine*, 45 (Summer 1968), 243–60.

10. *People* v. *News-Times Publishing Company*, 35 Colo. 285–332.

11. Peabody to Charles T. Anderson, Oct. 3, 1903, LB 40, Peabody Papers.

12. Western Federation of Miners, *Proceedings, Thirteenth Annual Convention* (Denver: Reed Publishing Co., 1905), p. 274.

13. See the Colorado Mine Operators' Association, *Criminal Record of the Western Federation of Miners from Coeur d'Alene to Cripple Creek, 1894–1904* (Colorado Springs: Colorado Mine Operators' Association, 1904), and the union's rebuttal, Western Federation of Miners, *Category of Crime of the Operators' Association: A Partial List, Showing 851 Murdered in Less than Four Years* (Denver: The Miners' Magazine Print, 1904).

14. The best account of the post-strike development of the WFM is Jensen's *Heritage of Conflict*.

15. Resignation, Peabody to James Cowie, Mar. 17, 1905, Colorado, State Archives and Record Service, Records of the Office of the Secretary of State; James Cowie, 1903–1905, Removals and Resignations, 1883–1907, DB: 24.

essay on sources

$\mathbf{B}$asic to any serious study of the turbulent years of Colorado labor history covered by this book are the papers of contemporary public officials located in the State Archives and Records Service of Colorado in Denver. Of these the most significant collection is the records of Governor James H. Peabody. Peabody corresponded extensively with persons directly involved in the labor troubles of his administration, as well as other influential persons throughout the nation who approved of his course of action. Consequently, his papers are unusually revealing and indispensable to a study of the labor unrest of 1903–1904. The bulk of this material is in excellent condition. (The author was unable to locate any additional papers of the governor which might be held by relatives or other persons.)

Especially useful in studying the legal problems generated by the strikes are the papers of Attorney General Nathan C. Miller, who maintained a complete file of certified or attested duplicate copies of motions, briefs, and other documents submitted in important cases like *In re Moyer*. Many of his advisory opinions, moreover, are found in the Peabody collection. Less important are the items found in the records of James Cowie, secretary of state; however, among his papers is Peabody's controversial letter of resignation, which is of interest to students of Colorado's disputed gubernatorial election of 1904.

Valuable records of other agencies within the state government, which were used in the preparation of this book, are also available through the archives, for example, materials from the Colorado Supreme Court, the Colorado National Guard, and the General Assembly. These resources are available to qualified researchers.

The Western Historical Collection (WHC) in Norlin Library at the University of Colorado (Boulder campus) contains the extant records of the Western Federation of Miners and a number of its local unions. Unfortunately, the records of the WFM are scanty for the early years (for example, there is no correspondence of Charles H. Moyer or William D. Haywood), and there is little regarding the strikes other than that which can be found in the *Miners' Magazine*, the official organ of the WFM, or the Denver daily newspapers. The records of the local unions are still being processed. The WHC also contains the papers of various mining entrepreneurs, mining companies, and political leaders (for example, the John F. Campion Papers, the James A. Ownbey Papers, and part of the Henry M. Teller Papers) which offer insight into the complexities of Colorado's mining industry and the times. Of greater value are the WHC's Peabody Scrap books, compiled by a contemporary professional clipping service, which presents a variety of newspaper commentary regarding the governor's labor policies.

There are scattered collections containing information pertinent to the labor troubles of the Peabody years. The William E. Borah Collection in the Idaho Historical Society (IHS), Boise, holds the important stenographic report of Peabody's Advisory Board concerning the Colorado City strike (the followup report is in the governor's files in the Colorado Archives), various Pinkerton reports, and what remains of the transcript of the Haywood trial. Among the James Hawley Papers (IHS) are letters from various Colorado officials who were involved in the strikes (for example, Bulkeley Wells, who succeeded Sherman Bell as adjutant general) and who were determined to convict Haywood, Moyer, and Pettibone for the dynamite murder of ex-Governor Frank Steunenberg. Some of this material is now available on microfilm. The papers of Warren A.

Haggott, lieutenant governor under Peabody, and the larger portion of the Henry M. Teller Papers, located in the State Historical Society of Colorado, contain only a little that is useful to the study of Colorado's labor unrest in 1903–1904.

Another invaluable source of primary source material is the municipal records of Canon City, Colorado Springs, Colorado City, Cripple Creek, Victor, and Telluride. The city council minutes, ordinance books, and other records reveal much about the local response to the strikes of the WFM. Despite the passage of time, these records generally remain intact, in good condition, and accessible. However, a number of towns in the Cripple Creek district, such as Goldfield, have ceased to exist, and their records have been lost or destroyed. Equally significant in showing the reaction of local government to the labor unrest are the minutes of the boards of county commissioners for the counties in which the strikes occurred, including Teller and San Miguel. The records for Teller County are especially useful. Instructive also are the files of cases located in the state district courts for these counties which catalog the litigation between the parties involved in the strikes, including, in some instances, state officials. Today researchers may find many of these local records in the Colorado Archives, where a project of microfilming municipal records has been underway for several years.

Numerous state publications are essential to a study of the Peabody years. The published records of the General Assembly—the *Session Laws* (Denver, 1889–1905), the House and Senate *Journals* (Denver, 1903–1904), and the multi-volume legislative report on the disputed gubernatorial contest between Peabody and Adams in 1905—are very helpful in understanding the legislative role in the industrial unrest, as well as the state of Colorado politics at the time of the strikes. Most helpful in setting forth Miller's legal arguments in the Moyer case are *In Re Moyer: Brief and Argument for Respondents* (Denver: Smith-Brooks Printing Co. 1904) and *In Re Moyer: Brief and Oral Argument of Attorney-General and the Opinion of the Court* (Denver: Smith-Brooks Printing Co., 1904). The Colorado Supreme Court relied heavily upon Miller's arguments in reaching its decision in *In re Moyer* (35 Colo. 154 [1904]). Instructive, too, is the case

223

of People v. News-Times Publishing Company (35 Colo. 253 [1905]), which suggests the close ties of Peabody to the Denver utilities, the coal and gold mining companies, the railroads, and business in general.

An examination of the published records of the adjutant general's office is essential to understanding the historic role played by Colorado's National Guard in the state's industrial unrest, especially in the mining camps. The *Biennial Report*[s] (Denver: Smith-Brooks Printing Co., 1893–1907) provide useful summaries, from the viewpoints of the various adjutant generals and their staffs, of the guard's intervention in labor disputes. The *Biennial Report, 1903–1904* and the *Biennial Report, 1905–1907* are particularly valuable, containing such information as Peabody's proclamations, summaries of the guard's activities in the mining camps, and statistical data of guard organizations. Equally useful are the *Report*[s] (Denver: Smith-Brooks Printing Co., 1904–1906) prepared by the attorney general's office which contain several advisory opinions concerning various legal problems created by the strikes, for example, the legality of the certificates of indebtedness issued to finance Peabody's intervention in the gold camps. Of great importance in determining the financial costs of Peabody's labor policies is the state auditor's *Biennial Report, 1903–1904* (Denver: Smith-Brooks Printing Co., 1904). Statistical and other data relating to the growth and development of organized labor in Colorado can be found in the *Biennial Report*[s] (Denver: Smith-Brooks Printing Co., 1894–1908) of the state's Bureau of Labor Statistics.

Several federal documents are invaluable to the study of Peabody's campaign against the WFM. Foremost among these is U. S. Senate, Document 122, Commissioner of Labor, *A Report on Labor Disturbances in the State of Colorado, from 1880 to 1904, Inclusive, with Correspondence Relating Thereto,* 58th Cong., 3d Sess., 1905. This document contains short summaries of Colorado's problems with the WFM in the decade prior to the strikes of 1903–1904, a more detailed account of events during the Peabody years, and the exchange of correspondence between Peabody and members of the Theodore Roosevelt administration about federal intervention in the mining camps. An important statement of the position of the Colorado Mine Owners' Association concerning the strikes and the WFM is the testimony of Clarence Hamlin located in U. S., Senate, Document 86, *Review of the Labor Troubles in the Metalliferous Mines of the Rocky Mountain Region,* 58th Cong., 2d Sess., 1904. Charles H. Moyer and William D. Haywood's *Statement of the Western Federation of Miners* (U.S., Senate, Document 163, 58th Cong., 2d Sess., 1904) provides a sharp rebuttal to the charges of criminality leveled against the WFM in Hamlin's testimony and counters with similar charges against the MOA. Moyer v. Peabody, et al. (148 Fed. Rep. 870 [1906]) and Moyer v. Peabody (212 U.S. 78 [1909]) show the response of the federal judiciary to the extraordinary happenings in Colorado, although the Supreme Court's decision in Moyer's case came some years after the strikes. Other publications helpful in revealing the turbulent early history of the WFM are: U.S., House, Committee on Military Affairs, Report 1999, *Coeur D'Alene Labor Troubles,* 56 Cong., 1st Sess., 1900; U.S., Senate, Documents 24 and 25, *Coeur D'Alene Mining Troubles* 56th Cong., 1st Sess., 1899; Senate Document 142, *Coeur D'Alene Mining Troubles* 56th Cong., 1st Sess., 1900; and Senate, Document 42, *Labor Troubles in Idaho,* 56th Cong., 1st Sess., 1900. These documents are useful in explaining the origins of the WFM's reputation for violence which helped to shape the contours of Peabody's labor policies.

When tracing the evolution of the WFM's policies, the official *Proceedings* (Pueblo and Denver, 1901–1907) of the union's annual conventions offset the meagerness of the early records which are found in the University of Colorado's WHC, the official repository of the WFM's records. The presidential addresses of Boyce and Moyer, plus the reports of other officers such as Haywood, are extremely instructive about the intent of the WFM's leadership on such matters as political activism and socialism; however, these reports should be balanced against the debates and resolutions of convention delegates, who more accurately reflected the feelings and attitudes of the rank and file on the issues before the conventions. Because Peabody was very active in Masonic affairs, serving in most major state Masonic offices prior to his election in 1902, the *Proceedings* (Denver,

1884, 1901–1907, 1918) of the annual communications of the
M. W. Grand Lodge of A. F. & A. M. of Colorado aid greatly in
providing biographical and background information on Peabody's
career before he became governor.

There have been few histories specifically directed
to the events of Peabody's administration. To place the Peabody
years in the general sweep of Colorado's history one should consult the standard histories of the state. Especially useful are
James H. Baker and LeRoy Hafen's *History of Colorado* (Denver:
Linderman Co., 1927) 5 vols.; LeRoy Hafen, ed., *Colorado and
Its People* (New York: Lewis Historical Publishing Co., 1948),
4 vols.; Wilbur F. Stone, ed., *History of Colorado* (Chicago:
S. J. Clarke Publishing Co., 1918–1919), 4 vols.; and Jerome C.
Smiley, *Semi-Centennial History of the State of Colorado* (Chi-
cago: Lewis Publishing Co., 1913), 2 vols. Useful to a lesser de-
gree are Percy S. Fritz, *Colorado: The Centennial State* (New
York: Prentice-Hall, 1941) and Carl Ubbelohde, *Colorado History* (Boulder: Pruett Press, 1965).

Of direct value are the writings of several participants in the labor unrest. William D. Haywood's autobiography,
*Bill Haywood's Book: The Autobiography of William D. Hay-
wood* (New York: International Publishers, 1929), is an essential
book, although it must be used with caution because when it
was written, Haywood was in exile in the Soviet Union, was sick,
and was assisted by ghostwriters. An equally strong pro-labor
version of events during the strikes is Emma F. Langdon's *The
Cripple Creek Strike: A History of Industrial Wars in Colorado,
1903–4–5* (Denver: Western Publishing Co., 1904–1905), which
contains sections by major participants such as Guy E. Miller,
president of the miners' union at Telluride. Langdon was on the
staff of the pro-WFM *Victor Daily Record* and, consequently, her
account is unusually significant. It became the WFM's official
history of the strikes and the state's intervention. Vital to any
study of the labor wars is Harry Orchard's, *The Confession and
Autobiography of Harry Orchard* (New York: The McClure
Company, 1907), which blames an "inner circle" of the WFM for
the Independence depot murders and implicates the WFM in
other crimes in Colorado. The work of a confessed murderer, it
should be used with reservations.

Other contemporary works that are helpful in understanding the legal aspects of the strikes are J. Warner Mills, ed., *Mills' Annotated Statutes of the State of Colorado* (Denver: The Mills' Publishing Co., 1891–1897) 3 vols., a reference work which Miller and Peabody relied on when formulating policy, and Walter L. Wilder, *Robert Wilbur Steele: Defender of Liberty* (Denver: Carson-Harper Co., 1913), which is an excellent biography of the only dissenting member of the Colorado Supreme Court in *In Re Moyer.*

There has been little historical treatment of the strikes. Despite his failure to utilize the Peabody papers, possibly because they were unavailable to him, Benjamin M. Rastall's *The Labor History of the Cripple Creek District: A Study in Industrial Evolution* (Madison: University of Wisconsin Press, 1908) remains the best single account of the Cripple Creek strike. Rastall provides useful insights into the forces contending for supremacy in the Cripple Creek mining district. Since Rastall's book was published, there have been a number of general labor histories which have touched upon the Colorado labor unrest, but they, too, have concentrated upon the Cripple Creek strike and failed to make use of the papers of Peabody and other public officials. Among these are Selig Perlman and Philip Taft, *Labor Movements* (New York: The Macmillan Company, 1935) and Philip Foner, *History of the Labor Movement in the United States* (New York: International Publishers, 1964), vol. 3. Vernon H. Jensen's *Heritage of Conflict* (Ithaca: Cornell University Press, 1950), which relies heavily on the *Miners' Magazine* and Rastall's earlier work for treatment of the Colorado strikes, has made the events in Colorado part of a larger theme, the history of the WFM. Moreover, like the general histories above, Jensen does not consult the available archival materials of the public officials involved. A popular account of the Cripple Creek strike is Stewart Holbrook, *The Rocky Mountain Revolution* (New York: Henry Holt and Co., 1956), which relies principally upon Orchard's *Confession*, a questionable source.

Among other works helpful to this study are Clarence E. Bonnett, *Employers' Associations in the United States: A Study of Typical Associations* (New York: The Macmillan Company, 1922), which throws light upon the significance of the alliance movement in Colorado; the early studies on American labor radicalism, such as Paul F. Brissenden, *The I. W. W.: A Study of American Syndicalism*, 2 ed. (New York: Russell and Russell, 1957), John G. Brooks, *American Syndicalism: The I.W.W.* (New York: The Macmillan Company, 1913), and John S. Gambs, *The Decline of the I. W. W.* (New York: Columbia University Press, 1932); Marguerite Green, *The National Civic Federation and the American Labor Movement* (Washington: The Catholic University of America, 1956), which contains an excellent account of the formation of the Citizens' Industrial Association; and Walter Hurt, *The Scarlet Shadow: A Story of the Great Colorado Conspiracy* (Girard, Ks.: The Appeal to Reason, 1907), a novel which presents the view held by many contemporary labor leaders that the events in Colorado during the Peabody years were the results of a conspiracy among the mine owners and state officials to destroy organized labor, especially the WFM.

A number of articles treat aspects of the subject of this book. An excellent analysis of the background of the strikes, the role of the corporations in Colorado, and the eight-hour question is J. Warner Mills, "The Economic Struggle in Colorado," *Arena*, 34 (July 1905), 1-10; 35 (Feb. 1906), 150–58; and 36 (Oct. 1906), 375–90. In his "The Preliminaries to the Labor War in Colorado," *Political Science Quarterly*, 23 (Mar. 1908), 1–17, C. E. Strangeland explains the WFM's strikes in terms of Turner's frontier thesis and the rejection of eight-hour legislation, and the conservative response in terms of the WFM's socialist leadership, power, and acceptance of industrial unionism. Two articles by Ray Stannard Baker, "The Reign of Lawlessness: Anarchy and Despotism in Colorado," *McClure's Magazine*, 23 (May 1904), 43–47 and "Organized Capital Challenges Organized Labor: The New Employers' Association Movement," *McClure's Magazine*, 23 (July 1904), 279–92, outline the apparent lawlessness of all parties to the strikes and link the citizens' alliances with that part of the national employers' movement designed to wage war upon unions. After a review of the origins of the WFM, its early strikes in Colorado, and its struggle in Cripple Creek, T. H. Watkins's "Requiem for the Federation," *The American West*, 3 (Winter

1966), 4–12, 91–95, concludes that the WFM was a failure, that its struggle with anti-union forces was inevitable, and that it died principally by "its own hand." A good study of the eight-hour question in Colorado is David L. Lonsdale's "The Fight for an Eight-Hour Day," *The Colorado Magazine, 43* (Fall 1966), 339–53. In "The Origins of Western Working Class Radicalism, 1890–1905," *Labor History, 7* (Spring 1966), 131–55, Melvyn Dubofsky examines the factors that apparently caused the metal miners of the American West to adopt socialism and syndicalism as an acceptable alternative to the capitalistic system. He blames the introduction of industrial capitalism into the gold camps for separating the organized miners from the farmers, merchants, and so on, and driving the WFM into political action and socialism. A recent study which reexamines the Haywood case and throws light on the events in Colorado is Joseph R. Conlin's "The Haywood Case: An Enduring Riddle," *Pacific Northwest Quarterly, 59* (Jan. 1968), 23–32. For the story of the response of the Roman Catholic Church to the strikes of the WFM, see George G. Suggs, Jr.'s, "Religion and Labor in the Rocky Mountain West: Bishop Nicholas C. Matz and the Western Federation of Miners," *Labor History, 11* (Spring 1970), 190–206.

To appreciate the public uproar produced by the strikes of the WFM and Peabody's militaristic labor policies, one should consult the contemporary newspapers, journals, and magazines of Colorado. Several publications were outspokenly pro-labor. Foremost among these was the superbly edited *Miners' Magazine*, the official organ of the WFM, which is a reservoir of source material ranging from position statements of union leaders to narratives of the strikes. The *Colorado Chronicle* (Denver) was another pro-labor and socialist organ which supported the strikers until it ceased publication. In the Cripple Creek district the *Victor Daily Record*, the voice of the WFM locals, strongly supported the striking miners until the conversion of its editor to an anti-labor stance after the riots in Victor and destruction of the newspaper's equipment in June 1904. U. S. Senator T. M. Patterson's *Rocky Mountain News* (Denver) provided an in-depth coverage of the labor unrest and backed the striking miners with scathing editorials against the Peabody administration, editorials motivated as much by partisan factors as by any other. In contrast, the *Denver Post* was an objective observer and reporter of the events associated with the labor troubles, its editorials being directed at various times against the WFM, Peabody, and his subordinates.

The *Denver Republican*, an influential pro-administration organ, extended consistent editorial backing for the alliance movement and Peabody's labor policies and provided an effective counterpart to Patterson's *Rocky Mountain News*. However, several smaller publications in Denver provided a more passionate support for the administration, at times going so far as to criticize Peabody for not taking stronger measures against the WFM. *George's Weekly* (Denver), the official organ of the state's alliances, backed the pro-business forces down the line. But outstanding for its inflammatory rhetoric in support of the governor's policies was *Polly Pry* (Denver), a small weekly journal whose only criticism of Peabody was that he was too soft on the WFM and its suporters. In the mining camps and mill towns outside Denver there were pro-business organs that stood firmly behind Peabody's policies. Among the most important of these newspapers were the (Telluride) *Daily Journal,* the *Cripple Creek Times*, the *Colorado Springs Gazette*, and the *Pueblo Chieftain*.

Other newpapers are helpful to a study of the Peabody era. The *Canon City Record* provides useful data on Peabody's early career in Canon City. The *Denver Catholic Register* contains a series of anti-WFM sermons of Bishop Matz, which reveals the position of the church toward the WFM and militant unionism. Typical of the interest displayed by important out-of-state newspapers was *The New York Times's* significant editorial comments on aspects of the Colorado situation, as well as good coverage of the NAM annual convention of 1903 that spawned the employers' movement headed by David M. Parry. Very useful in noting the diversity of newspaper reaction are the governor's Scrapbooks found in the University of Colorado's WHC.

The labor wars in Colorado provoked a series of pamphlets and reprints that reveal the intensity of the struggle between the pro-business forces supporting Peabody and the pro-labor forces supporting the WFM. In its *Criminal Record of the Western Federation of Miners from Coeur d'Alene to Cripple Creek* (Colorado Springs, 1904), the Colorado Mine Operators' Association blamed the WFM for every crime committed in the gold camps of Colorado for the entire decade preceding the strikes of 1903–1904. A more sophisticated condemnation of the WFM and its leadership came in a reprint of Walter Wellman's report of Aug. 13, 1904 to the New York *Herald* entitled *Walter Wellman's Indictment of Moyer, Haywood and the Western Federation of Miners* (n.p., 1904), which was distributed as Republican campaign literature in the gubernatorial election of 1904. The right of Peabody to deport the miners from the mining camps was upheld by E. E. Rittenhouse in his *Deportations by Alva Adams' Brother Frank: Why Deportations are Sometimes Necessary* (Denver: Smith-Brooks Printing Co., 1904). No stronger statement of support for Peabody's policies can be found than D. C. Beaman's *Address at the Testimonial Banquet to Governor James H. Peabody at Denver, Colorado, February 23, 1904* (Denver: Citizens' Alliance of Denver, 1904). Blatantly anti-labor, this pamphlet was distributed by the Denver Alliance and expressed the sentiments of the leadership of the entire alliance movement. Peabody's contribution to his campaign for reelection in 1904, *Gov. Peabody to the Voters: The Colorado Situation Discussed and Misstatements Refuted* (Denver: n.p., 1904), explains his positions on the tumultuous events of his administration. Important as the official explanation of the origin of the Denver Citizens' Alliance, the parent of all the alliances in Colorado, is James C. Craig, *The History of the Strike that Brought the Citizens Alliance of Denver, Colo., into Existence* (Denver: n.p., 1903).

To counter the charges of the Colorado mine owners that the WFM was a criminal organization guilty of many heinous crimes, the WFM issued its *Category of Crimes of the Operators' Association: A Partial List, Showing 851 Murdered in Less than Four Years* (Denver: The Miners' Magazine Print, 1904). This pamphlet blamed all the deaths resulting from mining accidents in the gold camps upon the negligence of the mine owners. The WFM received support from a number of sources, a support often determined as much by hostility to the extraordinary methods employed by Peabody as by any sympathy for labor. Examples are the anonymously edited and written *Comments of the Greatest Papers of the Country—Republican, Democratic, and Independent—on the Defiance of Law and the Constitution by the Governor* [Peabody] *of Colorado* (n.p., 1904) and *$842,096.78. Cost of the Military in the Field, at Home, and at the Brown Palace Hotel in Denver during the Administration of Gov. James H. Peabody. $842,096.78.* H. E. Bartholomew, *Anarchy in Colorado: Who Is to Blame?* (Denver: Bartholomew Publishing Co., 1905), and James H. and Charlotte Teller, *The Colorado Labor War* (Denver: The Western Federation of Miners, 1904), and George H. Shoof, *Who Blew up the Independence Depot?* (Girard, Ks.: The Appeal to Reason, 1906)—all interpret the events of the strikes from a strongly pro-WFM point of view.

Several theses and dissertations treat various aspects of the labor unrest that swept Colorado in 1903–1904. Mildred Hornbein, "Industrial Struggle in El Paso and Teller Counties, Colorado," unpublished Ph.D. dissertation, University of Denver, 1914, is an early study of the Colorado City and Cripple Creek strikes which relies heavily upon several Denver newspapers and *Labor Disturbances* and adds little to Rastall's *Labor History of the Cripple Creek District*. The first study to exploit the Peabody papers is J. Paul Mitchell, "An Investigation of Governor James H. Peabody's Role in the Strike at Cripple Creek, Colorado, 1903–1904," unpublished M.A. thesis, University of Denver, 1960, which portrays Peabody's activist role in the largest of the strikes and concludes that in taking a strong anti-WFM stand, Peabody was a "man of his times." Marguerite Green, "The National Civic Federation and the Citizens' Industrial Association, 1900–1910," unpublished M.A. thesis, Catholic University of America, 1953, is an excellent study which exposes the anti-union character and objectives of the Citizens' Industrial Association with which the State Citizens' Alliance of Colorado affiliated in 1903. Useful in showing the role of the newspaper in one area of the strikes is Edith S. Jackson's, "The History of Journalism at Victor, Colorado, in the Cripple Creek Gold Mining District," unpublished M.A. thesis, Ohio State University, 1958. In tracing the growth of domestic corporations in his "Colorado Domestic Business Corporations, 1859–1900," unpublished Ph.D. dissertation, University of Illinois, 1966, Paul S. Barnett shows the proliferation of mining corporations in the 1890s and their pervasive influence upon the political life of the state.

index

George G. Suggs, Jr., is professor of history at Southeast Missouri State University in Cape Girardeau. He received his B.A. (1955), M.A. (1957), and Ph.D. degrees (1964) from the University of Colorado and has written numerous journal articles on the labor history of the West.

The manuscript was edited by Linda Grant. The book was designed by Don Ross. The typeface for the text is Caledonia, designed by W. A. Dwiggins about 1938, and the display face is Cooper Black, designed by Oswald Cooper in 1921.

The text is printed on EB Neutratext paper and the book is bound in Columbia Mills' Riverside Chambray cloth over binders' boards. Manufactured in the United States of America.